The Murder of Mr Moonlight

CATHERINE FEGAN

PENGUIN BOOKS

PENGUIN BOOKS

UK | USA | Canada | Ireland | Australia
India | New Zealand | South Africa

Penguin Books is part of the Penguin Random House group of companies
whose addresses can be found at global.penguinrandomhouse.com.

First published by Penguin Ireland 2019
Published in Penguin Books 2020
001

Printed and bound in Great Britain by Clays Ltd, Elcograf S.p.A.

A CIP catalogue record for this book is available from the British Library

ISBN: 978–0–241–98849–7

Contents

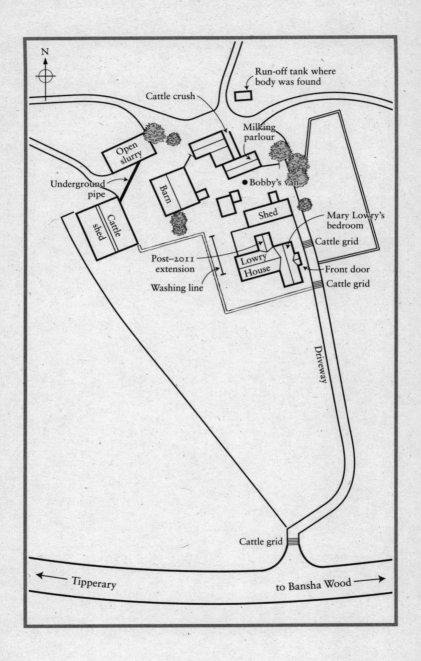

The Gardaí at Tipperary Town Garda Station are investigating the disappearance of local man Bobby Ryan, who was reported missing on Friday, the 3rd June 2011.

Bobby Ryan is 52 years of age. He is described as 14st, 5'2", bald with hazel eyes. When last seen he was wearing a navy polo T-shirt, navy tracksuit bottoms, navy jumper and white runners. He was well known in the area, he drove a truck for a local quarry and worked as a DJ in the area, known as Mr Moonlight.

Bobby Ryan's family are very concerned for his safety as he has not contacted family or friends since Friday morning, the 3rd June 2011.

From www.garda.ie, Missing Persons section

Prologue
August 2010: The ballroom of romance

Mary Lowry was sitting on one of the high stools dotted along the bar inside the Times Hotel ballroom. It was Sunday night, the most popular night of the week in the Tipperary town venue, and the crowds had been spilling on to the maple-sprung dancefloor since eight o'clock. As Mary sipped a glass of white wine, giggling and chatting to her friend Eileen, the music from the live band on the stage boomed loudly in the background. The two women had picked a quiet spot at the bar, where they could relax in their own company, but, even though they had tried to avoid attracting attention, Mary caught the eye of a nearby stranger.

Bobby Ryan had spotted her from his regular seat, the one he always occupied at the edge of the dancefloor beside his friend Dave. As Bobby stood up and made his way towards the striking, slender woman with the brunette hair, his trademark smile instantly lit up the room.

'Will you dance with me?' he asked.

'I will,' said Mary, smiling back at him and jumping excitedly from her seat.

She glanced at Eileen, her friend of more than twenty years, who could sense the instant chemistry between the two. Eileen smiled back at her, giving Mary a knowing glance as she headed towards the dancefloor, arm in arm with Bobby Ryan.

Eileen remained at the bar, listening to the music and minding the drinks, and she watched as Bobby led Mary around the floor, happy to see her friend having a good time.

She and Mary had been for a Chinese meal in the Crystal Palace restaurant earlier and Mary, who was mad into music and dancing, had wanted to come to the Times Hotel, a local spot renowned for having good live bands.

Eileen was on a mission to make sure her friend had a good time that evening. It was long overdue. Mary's husband had died almost three years before, leaving her widowed at forty-one and raising three young children alone. She had been left devastated by his loss and hadn't been the same since. The two women had a shared history. Like Mary's late husband, Martin, Eileen's husband, Arthur, was a dairy farmer. Martin and Arthur had grown up together, each taking on the family farm from his father and trying to make a living out of the land for their own families. The two men were great friends and, as a consequence, so were their wives.

Eileen had supported Mary through the darkest time in her life after Martin died and could see that her friend needed a boost.

So, on that balmy August night, the two women had put on their glad rags, dusted off their dancing shoes, and made their way to the Times Hotel to enjoy themselves. And as Bobby and Mary laughed and danced, Eileen could see something she hadn't seen in a long time. Mary Lowry, a grief-struck woman who had been numb and lost since the death of her husband, had come alive again in the arms of this stranger.

'They seemed to have really connected,' Eileen said about that night. 'They were very, very happy and seemed buzzing after the dancing together.'

When Mary returned to the bar with Bobby and introduced him, Eileen watched as her friend and her new admirer chatted passionately about their shared love of music. They liked the same bands, enjoyed dancing at the same venues and had the same favourite dance, the jive. It was clear they had much in common.

For all the joy of seeing Mary so happy, Eileen was wary. She didn't know anything about Bobby Ryan, what kind of man he was or how he might treat her friend. While all three of them talked at the bar, Eileen quietly told Bobby that after what Mary had been through these past three years, she wanted to make sure her friend was in safe hands. She asked him if his intentions were good and if he would look after Mary because she needed a refuge and minding, not some-one who would crush her heart and up and leave when it suited him. Mary, who could hear what Eileen was saying, laughed off her friend's protective words of advice for Bobby.

As it turned out, Eileen had no need to worry about Bobby Ryan. He was as kind-natured as they come, a gentleman who had never intentionally hurt anyone in his life. Although none of them could have known it then, if any warning needed to be given, it should have been for him to be careful about what he was getting himself into.

But that night, as he swept around the room with Mary in his arms, Bobby was blissfully unaware of all that was to come. They were locked in a close embrace, himself and Mary, feet and hearts leaping as they followed the rhythm of the music, his hand firm on the small of her back, her face glowing with the dance and the sense of anticipation.

It was a warm summer's night in 2010, a night when two people from two very different worlds fatefully collided: the night Mary Lowry met Mr Moonlight.

1. Keeping it in the family

The Lowry family farm sits perched on top of a lush green hill on the outskirts of Tipperary town, with panoramic views over the wooded ridge of Slievenamuck, a landscape of rolling pasture encircled by the stark beauty of the Galtee Mountains. The farm at Fawnagowan (*Fán an Ghabhann* in Irish, roughly translated as 'wandering blacksmith') came down through the Lowry family to John Lowry. His father, Martin, had farmed the land before him and the Lowry name was among the founding members of the Tipperary Co-Operative Creamery in 1908. After Martin passed, John took on the holding of about fifty acres and worked hard to turn it into a sustainable family business.

Dairy farming was the traditional livelihood for the family, but it was also part of their identity, a family dynasty that had been in existence for generations. John and his wife, Rita, farmed the land while raising eight children: Martin, Jimmy, Johnny, Denis (who died as a baby), Mary, Ann, Catherine and Imelda. They were a tightknit family, hardworking, respectable and devoted to their children. The brothers and sisters looked out for each other, with Martin, the eldest boy, taking particular care of Imelda, the youngest girl and baby of the house. She in turn looked up to him, particularly in later years when he began to excel in GAA circles.

It was Martin who inherited the farm and, with it, his father's lifestyle. He added a further thirteen acres to the holding by acquiring land in nearby Bansha to expand the operation. Rita could rest assured that the family legacy was in safe hands. Martin was a natural farmer, with a passion and vision for what the farm could be. Like his father before him, he made a good match, bringing home Mary Quigley and introducing her to his life at Fawnagowan. The farmland there is rich and fertile, an enviable bit of land that returns a good living to those who farm it well. Of course, good land like that can be a blessing and a curse in rural areas, where ties to the land can sow the seeds of quiet, bitter jealousies and life-long resentments. As Martin and his new wife settled into their stewardship of the farm, Rita no doubt hoped it would be a blessing for them, as it had been for her and John. With God's will, it would prove a blessing for the new Mrs Lowry.

Mary Quigley was born on 25 May 1966. Her father, Michael, had a very small fifteen-acre farm in Inchadrinagh, Newport, County Tipperary, and he also worked as a builder's labourer. Her mother, Annie, a proud housewife, also came from a farming background. The couple had four children: two boys, Pat and Eddie; and two girls, Margaret and Mary.

Mary was the third-born, and after attending secondary school in Newport, she got a job doing reception duties and some bookkeeping with a meat company on the Ballysimon Road in Limerick. It was a family-run business, employing about fifty people and Mary worked there for about fourteen years. She had also had other jobs, working in a co-op and with another large meat processor, and eventually she took a job as a teller in the credit union in Tipperary town.

Mary, or Giddy Mary as she came to be known because of her flighty and impulsive personality, loved dancing. She was in her early twenties when she met her future husband in the Golden Thatch disco in Emly, County Tipperary. She was introduced to Martin Lowry, a young farmer from just outside Tipperary town, by a woman she worked with, and a courtship ensued. After that meeting in the Golden Thatch, which took place around 1986/87, they began to see each other regularly and quickly became, and stayed, best friends.

Martin, according to those who knew him, was 'absolutely smitten' with Mary. They were opposites in many ways: he was shy and quiet, while Mary was a 'live wire' who was full of energy. Although she was outgoing and vivacious, she led a fairly sheltered life in Newport and never ventured far from home. She had a typical rural upbringing, playing camogie from a young age and going to Mass every week. Mary's family were very religious, and she too had great faith. Described by those who knew her as having 'a heart of gold', she became the kind of person people confided in.

'She was a confidante to many over the years,' said one friend. 'You could go to Mary with your problems and trust that she would never break a confidence. She was always very giving with her time.'

She was also the kind of person who people tended to 'attach themselves to'. When Mary was in the room, others wanted to be in her company.

'She wouldn't be a private person,' said the friend. 'She would put herself out there and get involved in whatever was happening, whether it was something in the community or a bit of craic at the bar. She has a very big personality.'

For Martin, his was a life of farming and football. From an early age he was passionately involved in Gaelic games. While hurling was his preferred sport, an eye injury sustained when he was young forced him to concentrate his efforts on Gaelic football. He won West and County minor football medals with his local Arravale Rovers Club and was described as an 'outstanding player' in his day. In the club's centenary year, 1985, he played left cornerback on the Arravale Rovers team that won the West Senior football final and was on the panel when the club won the County Senior Football title.

Mary's older brother Eddie, to whom she is very close, met Martin at GAA matches before he was finally invited to pay a visit to the Quigley family home. Martin was soon part of the family, and Eddie became very fond of the man in Mary's life. The way was clear for the young couple, who were mad about each other. Three or four years later, Mary and Martin decided to get engaged and she started to put money away in the credit union. Choosing to get married was not a big romantic gesture, Martin did not get down on one knee, and there was no grand announcement. But that was Martin, pragmatic, low-key and down to earth.

For Mary and Martin, their life together was to be one of rural idyll, albeit rising to the challenges of running a profitable farm. Martin had inherited the farm prior to his father's passing in December 1993, and before he and Mary got married they decided to build an extension on to the existing Lowry family home. Mary got a loan from the credit union and they built on a kitchen, sitting room and bedroom, leaving the original part of the house for Martin's mother, Rita, to continue living in. The young couple took one bedroom from her side of the house, with her permission.

In 1995, they married in Mary's home parish in Newport and held their wedding reception in the nearby Dundrum House Hotel. They moved on to the farm at Fawnagowan, where they took another room and bedroom from the original house. Although Rita was effectively living in a separate part of the house, Mary found herself living under the close scrutiny of her mother-in-law in those early years of marriage. As she had always done, Rita served up Martin's dinner every night, now adding his new bride to the table. As Martin and Mary's children were born, she was on hand to help Mary out as much as she could.

Their eldest child, Tommy, was born in September 1997, the middle son, Jack, followed almost two years to the day later in September 1999, and their youngest, Micheál, was born in the run-up to Christmas 2003. Mary and Martin only had three bedrooms on their side of the house, so Tommy took a room on his nana's side of the house. The three generations rubbed along side by side, a happy family.

Martin, a dedicated father and husband, was also keen to make his mark in agricultural circles. He joined the Irish Farming Association's (IFA) Tipperary town branch and in 2002 he held the joint roles of chairman and registrar. During his time in office, membership of the branch was said to be at an 'all-time high' due to Martin's popularity among fellow farmers. In 2002 he also won the IFA/FBD Scholarship Tour award for South Tipperary and joined forty-nine others in an investigative tour of the Baltic farming states of Latvia and Lithuania. During his time abroad he learned about pioneering farming techniques he could implement at home. At that time, Mary was working full-time in the local credit union, but she soon turned homemaker as their family grew. The children were her job and Martin ran the farm.

The close family circle included Martin's sister Imelda, who had married Pat Quirke, a local dairy farmer who lived close by at Breanshamore, known locally as Breansha, about six miles from Fawnagowan. Martin performed the duty of best man for Pat when he and Imelda married in September 1995 in St Michael's Church in Tipperary town. The reception was held in the Aherlow House Hotel, just above Pat's farm in Breansha, the same venue where Dolores O'Riordan of The Cranberries had celebrated her wedding the year before.

Martin and Pat had much in common. Just like Martin, his friend and brother-in-law, Pat had inherited the family land when his father signed it over to him before his death. Also like Martin, Pat was ambitious for his holding and his own standing in the agricultural community. But while Pat was concerned with one-upmanship when it came to his livelihood, Martin, say friends, 'would never have asked another man how many acres he had, or how many cows were in his herd. Those things weren't important to him.'

As their farms were located so near to each other, the two farmers pooled their resources. They bought the best farming equipment, which they owned jointly. They shared knowledge, sought out the newest technologies and ideas and helped each other out on the land as and when needed. It was a good friendship and partnership.

Their wives, Mary and Imelda, were in each other's company often, but were different in many ways. Imelda held the power in the friendship and was considered the 'tougher' and more dominant of the two. They were both into keeping fit and played tennis together at the local Rosanna Tennis Club. Mary, who was extremely sporty, saw her involvement as more of a social pastime, while Imelda became known for being fiercely competitive on the court.

When they were pregnant, the two women went swimming together, their matching bumps protruding from their slim frames. Both women kept themselves well turned out and cared about their appearance, attending the same local hairdresser, where, for a time, they had the same style of dark-haired bob dyed and cut. Imelda was said to be the more 'glam' of the two. She liked the finer things in life and would splash out on designer brands and high-end must-haves.

'Imelda likes her style,' said one local. She was slightly more aloof and guarded than Mary, who was described as more 'free-spirited' than her sister-in-law.

With three sons each, the two women had much in common when it came to the demands of motherhood. Their boys, through family tradition, were absorbed in all things GAA from a very young age. Imelda and Mary settled into their roles as GAA mums, ferrying their boys to training and cheering them on from the sidelines. Mary's boys followed in their father's footsteps, playing junior hurling and football for Arravale Rovers, while Imelda's boys lined out for their local team, Lattin–Cullen. There was a playful rivalry between the families, but the close bond they shared ensured they always supported each other.

Martin and Imelda had always been close as brother and sister, and now their spouses added to that enjoyment, sharing a friendship that was important to all of them. They were involved in each other's lives through friendship as well as family ties, and their close bond made life easier and better for everyone.

As can often happen, just when things seem to be coming together nicely, life can deal a hard blow. In 2005, two years after their youngest child was born, Martin began to suffer from a pain in his knee. He reckoned an old footballing injury was the cause and did his best to get on with things, in spite of the nagging ache. After a year and a half of pain, however, which was showing no sign of going away, in 2007 he went to his doctor to get it checked out. The family was shattered by the diagnosis he received: cancer. Martin had osteosarcoma, a type of bone cancer that often shows up first in the bones around the knee.

Over the course of the following difficult months, Mary was by his side, attending his medical appointments in Dublin and looking after him at home. The trips were daunting for Mary, who had rarely been out of the county and didn't have the confidence to drive into a big city on her own. She was nervous about travelling on the train, so when he could, her brother Eddie took her to see Martin in the Mater Hospital in Dublin city centre.

They hired extra help on the farm and Mary herself started to help with the daily milking. As the prognosis worsened and the cancer spread to his lungs, the family had to come to terms with the possibility that big, strong Martin Lowry might not win this fight. Although he was in great pain, those who knew him say his concern was never for himself, only for his family and friends. Despite his illness, he insisted on attending the juvenile games his sons were involved in at Arravale Rovers, right up until his death.

As he became weaker, Mary nursed him at home with the help of nurses from the local hospice. Martin passed away at home in his beloved Fawnagowan, on 23 September 2007. He was just forty-three years of age, a man who should have had a long life ahead of him. Mary was a widow at forty-one, with three heartbroken children who were aged just ten, eight and three and a half years old. Her mother-in-law, Rita, was still living next door, and the whole family was united in a terrible grief for the son, husband and father they had lost.

Hundreds came to pay their respects at the Lowry farm in the sad days after Martin's death. Mary was surrounded by her own family, but Martin's sister Imelda, although dealing with her own devastation over the loss, supported Mary and the boys as the initial grief took hold. At the funeral, the Arravale Rovers Club provided a guard of honour from St Michael's Parish Church to the adjacent graveyard, where Martin was laid to rest alongside his father, John. In the *In memoriam* card given to friends and loved ones shortly after his death, the image of Martin shows him smiling and squinting at the camera. The backdrop to the headshot was a photograph of the farm at Fawnagowan, with dairy cows grazing in the green fields. On the back, a short tribute carried the following lines:

> *A Tribute to Martin*
> *A dearest son, brother, brother-in-law, nephew, cousin, uncle, god-father, husband & wonderful Daddy and friend,*
> *I know you would not want any fuss but you deserved to be fussed about.*
> *A man who was born to be a farmer, father and friend,*
> *A shy smile with plenty of time for everyone, always there to lend a hand & always there to see the good in everyone and everything,*
> *Even through your pain and suffering you still managed a smile.*
> *Our family circle is broken but we know you are helping us through with God beside you lending a hand,*
> *We always love and miss you.*

Despite his ailing health as he succumbed to the ravages of cancer, Martin's thoughts were for the future of his young family. Just one month before he died, he made his will, leaving everything to his wife so that she had the means to take care of their children. There were a life insurance policy, a substantial investment portfolio and, of course, the family farm at Fawnagowan, which was a very valuable asset.

The farm, which had been meticulously maintained by Martin, was located in the Golden Vale, an area of premium-quality agricultural land that is unrivalled anywhere else in Ireland. Stretching across north Munster from east Tipperary to west Limerick and through north County Cork, the rich soil in the area is free draining and among only 3 per cent of its type in the country. However, the real value of Fawnagowan lay deep below its fertile soil. Locals in Tipperary talk of a sheet of land that stretches from Tipperary town all the way to Cahir, about thirteen miles away. Once the rich topsoil is stripped back, all that can be seen is gravel – a quarryman's dream. The Lowry farm sits on a section of this gravel-rich sheet.

There were already two quarries next to the farm, one belonging to the O'Dwyers and the other owned by the Kinnanes.

At the height of the 'Celtic Tiger' economic boom, when land with quarrying potential drew big money, Fawnagowan had been valued at just under €3 million. In spite of this, even after Martin died there were never any plans to sell it. It was still Rita's home, and home to Mary and her three boys, who might later choose to follow in their father's footsteps and farm the land themselves. So, for now, Mary had to take up the burden of working the farm as best she could, even though running a farm was the last thing she wanted to do.

She probably wasn't aware of it then, amid her grief and the burden of trying to keep hearth and home together, but her role as farm owner put her in a new position. She was now, thanks to Martin's careful planning, a wealthy widow. From the outside, she would have seemed a very good catch – the farm, the assets, the money. Mary Lowry was sitting on some of the finest farming ground in Tipperary. It's likely she didn't realize that this made her vulnerable, but it did.

Fortunately for Mary, her husband's partner in farming, his brother-in-law, Pat Quirke, was there to offer much-needed help. He had made a promise to the dying Martin Lowry that he would be there for his family, to help them in the dark times that would come after his death. Now that that had come to pass, Pat stepped up to keep that promise.

Pat offered to rent sixty-three acres of Martin's land and also to assist Mary with some of the financial investments her husband had made when he was alive. He and Martin were both in a local farming discussion group called the Tipperary Discussion Group and had shared off-farm investments, of which Pat had detailed knowledge. He tried to bridge the gap left by Martin, making himself useful at every turn. He became a daily presence on the farm, always there to give advice. He was the rock Mary leaned on during this most difficult period of her life.

Almost three years after Martin Lowry's death, Mary walked into the Times Hotel ballroom with her friend, Eileen.

Back in those days, Sunday night in the Times was a mecca for patrons of the social dancing scene in Tipperary town. John Buckley, the man selling the tickets at the door, knew the big names that would draw a crowd – The Indians, Robert Mizzell and Jimmy Buckley, to name a few. It wasn't the most glamorous of places, but countless marriages were sealed and an equal number of hearts were broken inside its walls.

The ballroom had an old-world feel, with its step-down dancefloor and decorative ceiling. There was a long corridor on the way into the venue, where the raised stage at the top of the main room was the focal point of the evening's entertainment. John sold the tickets at the entrance, greeting his regulars by their first names as they piled in through the door.

The women, mostly middle-aged, wore tight miniskirts and high heels, and the men came clad in a variety of checked shirts and faded denims. It wasn't like the dancehalls of old, where all the men would be on one side and the women on the other. The tables were mixed, men and women, young and old, separated and married.

John could always spot an unknown face and would tell the ladies who were new to the scene to sit up at the bar. That way, he would tell them, a man could walk up to the counter under the guise of buying a drink rather than running the risk of walking across the floor, getting turned down and having to walk back red-faced. John had the measure of his crowd and knew exactly how to make the evening hum.

Bobby Ryan was one of the regulars at the Times. He had taken up social dancing after his marriage ended in 2005, mastering the jive and the waltz after considerable effort. He mixed well with the crowd. He was the kind of man who could walk into a room full of strangers and engage with them with ease. He was also a man of modest means. He often lived pay cheque to pay cheque, rented a small house and spent little on grand personal possessions. He worked as often and as hard as he could. His main job was as a truck driver for the local Killough Quarry, but his other source of income was as a part-time DJ, going by the stage name Mr Moonlight. It was the music that was his real passion in life.

At the time he met Mary Lowry, Bobby was working as a quarry driver and also had a regular Saturday night slot in Fox's, a famed pub on the Main Street in Cashel owned by the former Tipperary hurler Pat Fox.

'Saturday night was Bobby's night,' a colleague from Fox's recalled. 'He would come in with all his old-school CDs and set up near the back. He played all the eighties classics and would take requests from the punters in between songs. He was a great man for getting the crowd going and the craic would be great. Everyone just loved him, he was full of craic, never in bad form.'

As well as DJing in Fox's, he played at birthday parties and other functions, ferrying around his beloved DJ equipment, his 'disco kit' as he called it, in his silver Citroën van. It had his moniker, 'Mr Moonlight', emblazoned across the windscreen and he kept it immaculately clean, inside and out.

When Bobby turned up at the Times for his usual Sunday night dance on an August evening in 2010, he spotted a woman he'd never seen before sitting on a bar stool. He made his way over to her and asked her to dance. A delighted Mary Lowry readily accepted.

'We got on like a house on fire,' she would later say.

Mary told Bobby that she was on the hunt for tickets to the All-Ireland hurling final on 5 September, so her boys could see Tipperary play Kilkenny. He offered to help her with the tickets and they exchanged mobile phone numbers.

It was a chance encounter, but it was the moment when the cloud of grief that had engulfed her finally lifted. In Bobby Ryan, a man with a carefree, happy-go-lucky attitude to life, Mary Lowry saw a chance of happiness once again. Bobby was approaching fifty-two, almost eight years older than her, but he had the mind and spirit of a teenager. He loved life and he loved dancing and so did Mary. He was a breath of fresh air in a world that had felt stagnant for so long.

They were from very different backgrounds, Mary Lowry and Bobby Ryan. She was a wealthy, land-owning widow with three young children and he was a modest truck driver with few responsibilities. She played tennis and volunteered for charity work, he played music and lived for the moment.

But Mary had a wild streak – a giddy personality and an untameable spirit. Fate, a shared love of dancing and an undeniable spark drew her to Bobby Ryan.

As her friend Eileen minded their drinks and watched her friend dancing, she smiled to see Mary laughing once again. She and Bobby cut a dash around the floor. It wasn't going to come as a surprise when the two started to see each other regularly.

After that evening in the Times Hotel, it was a few months before Eileen saw the couple again. Bobby was DJing in Fox's pub and Mary asked Eileen to accompany her to see him. She went along as a show of support, glad to see that life was moving on for her friend. Some time after that, on St Patrick's Day 2011, she met them in the Ballyglass Hotel.

'Mary seemed very joyous and Bobby as well,' she would later recall. 'They seemed very, very happy.'

One of the difficult things about a new relationship in later life is the number of people it can affect. Where there are children, even adult children, they are sure to have an opinion on their parent's choice of partner. Mary and Bobby had families to consider, which meant they had to tread carefully and respectfully.

The Ryan family weren't terribly enthusiastic about their father's new girlfriend. Bobby's only son, Robert, didn't think the relationship was serious in the beginning and didn't read much into it. His father had had girlfriends in the past and he didn't think this one would last long. It was a bit of dancing and a bit of fun, that was all.

Bobby was very close to his daughter, Michelle. It was during one of her father's DJ sessions that Michelle first met Mary. She would later say that on that particular night in

Cashel, Mary was watching her father like a hawk. It was so intense that Michelle spoke to Mary, advising her that if she was the sensitive type, she wasn't the woman for her father, because he wasn't shy. Mary laughed it off.

While others may have doubted them, Mary and Bobby were sure of each other. Everything about the relationship suited Mary. Bobby could call to her house during the week. He might stay over, or he might not, there was never a big plan. It was an easy-going and flexible arrangement that worked perfectly for them.

Mary was mad about Bobby and eager to introduce him to her in-laws when the time came. For any young widow, the thought of introducing a new boyfriend to her husband's family is daunting. For Mary, there were added pressures. The Lowry family had long since established themselves as one of the most well-respected families in Tipperary town, both in farming circles and through the GAA. Rita, a native of Ballygarvan in County Cork, had moved to the town in 1948 to work in the post office. She was the woman who founded the Sean Treacy Camogie Club. She played in the Munster final for Tipperary when they defeated her native Cork in 1952. She was a close friend of Christy Ring, one of Ireland's greatest ever hurlers. She maintained a scrapbook dedicated to Ring's life, as well as amassing a huge collection of GAA photos and news clippings. Down through the years her home in Fawnagowan became a shrine to hurling through her love of the game. Her three boys, Jimmy, Johnny and Martin, played football and hurling for Tipperary at various grades.

The Lowry name carried with it great honour and pride, but it was also a name that had to be upheld and protected. If there was ever a problem within the family, that's where the problem stayed. They were close-knit, guarded and intensely private. There was an unspoken understanding that no one brought disrepute on the family in word or deed. So how would they react to the news that Mary was in love with Bobby Ryan?

The family had rallied around Mary and her sons after Martin's death, knowing how much she had loved Martin and how devastated she was by his loss. Even though she was now the owner of Fawnagowan, it remained as it always had been: the home place for all the Lowry siblings. All of Martin's brothers and sisters continued to visit Rita frequently, so the farm still felt like home, and Mary didn't want to disrupt that.

Given that Rita lived next door, Mary was conscious that the appearance of Bobby around the farm, a strange man in Rita's eyes, may have given her mother-in-law cause for unease. So, on the nights he stayed over, Bobby always parked the van in the farmyard, where Rita couldn't see it from her window. He and Mary were careful to be discreet at all times. But Rita Lowry, who Bobby once told a friend had mistaken him for a gardener, was a woman of the world, and Mary knew she would quickly figure out what was going on.

When she felt the time was right, Mary went to Rita and told her that she was seeing someone. It was a mark of respect to her mother-in-law to give her the news in person.

'There was no problem,' Mary would later say. 'She received it well.'

Mary might have been nervous of having that conversation with Rita, but Rita was delighted for her daughter-in-law. She knew the heartache that Mary had suffered after Martin's death and she was big-hearted enough to be happy for Mary's new-found happiness. It was Rita who told Johnny and Mary, two of Martin's siblings, about Mary's new relationship.

They were both happy for her, with Johnny calling her and Mary sending her a text, wishing her well.

News of Mary's relationship with a part-time DJ from Cashel filtered out to the rest of the extended Lowry family soon afterwards. Then, in February 2011, Aoife Lowry, the daughter of Martin's brother Jimmy, held a party to celebrate her eighteenth birthday. Invitations were issued, and Mary and Bobby were invited together as a couple.

Mary was reluctant to go initially, but then realized that the event presented an opportunity to introduce Bobby to her in-laws face to face. She went to the party, which was held in Jimmy White's pub in Bohertrime, with Bobby, her sister, Margaret, and her brother-in-law, John. Jimmy Lowry met Bobby at the party and briefly spoke to him after they were introduced. Like his siblings, he was happy for his sister-in-law.

By that stage, Mary's three boys had also met Bobby. She had introduced them to him after Christmas 2010. In those early days, Jack, who was eleven at the time, felt uncomfortable. He thought Bobby was taking over his father's role and responded in the way a child would, by slagging him off for being bald. But when he realized that his mother was very happy, he soon changed his mind. Bobby was kind to the boys. He took them away on trips, on one occasion to Tramore in County Waterford, where he brought them on carnival rides and into arcades. Later on, their mother's boyfriend also went with Mary to buy a 'field car' – a 1987 Toyota Corolla for Tommy to learn how to drive.

Everything seemed to be falling into place for Mary. In Bobby Ryan, she had got a new lease of life and, perhaps, an unexpected chance to be happy again. Now that their relationship was out in the open, she could relax and enjoy being together with Bobby. She had been honest with everyone – her children, her own family and the Lowry clan. The road ahead was cleared of obstacles, and she could finally enjoy her happiness.

The Ballyglass Hotel, located just outside Tipperary town in five acres of lush green gardens close to the beautiful Glen of Aherlow, was Pat and Imelda Quirke's local. Their home and adjacent farm, a modest holding of sixty-seven acres, were just a few miles away, in Breanshamore. Imelda's family were regular patrons too. Her mother, Rita, played cards there every Thursday night, and Imelda's brothers, Jimmy and Johnny, were also known to frequent the hotel. The Ballyglass is a small, family-run hotel in a nineteenth-century house and its private dining room, the Coach House, was often booked by the Lowrys as they celebrated special occasions down through the years. The dining room was small and intimate, with a homely interior that provided the perfect backdrop for their close-knit gatherings.

One Sunday at the beginning of December 2010, Rita, her sons and daughters, and all their children came together for dinner. Mary Lowry was there too, enjoying the company and the chat, when someone made a passing remark about where she had been the night before: 'Did you have a good time in Cashel last night, Mary?' It was a throwaway line, lost on most around the table, but someone in earshot was paying very close attention to this conversation.

As Mary was questioned about her night out, Pat Quirke strained to hear her answers. He maintained a careful poise, hiding the effect of Mary's words on him. Inside, he was seething with rage. In the middle of this family gathering, there was a dark secret that had to be protected at all costs.

No one present was aware of it, but it took an effort of will-power for Pat Quirke to stay in his seat and carry on as normal, talking to his wife and her family.

He watched as Mary chatted happily about Bobby Ryan. He knew, of course, that she was friendly with Bobby, but he had passed it off as a social relationship, a dancing buddy for those nights out in places like the Times Hotel. But here was Mary being asked about Bobby as if he was a fixture in her life, as if he was important, as if people who knew Mary saw him as her boyfriend. Worse still, he hadn't a clue about where she'd been last night – why hadn't she told him?

Mary Lowry's brother-in-law listened hard and took it all in. The chat and clatter of cutlery rattled on around him, but for Pat Quirke there was only the voice of Mary Lowry, as she talked animatedly about going out with Bobby Ryan. Everyone else present seemed delighted for her, but Pat wasn't. Mary Lowry was his lover, the woman with whom he was having a passionate affair, and here she was giggling about another man. What the hell was going on?

2. Land, sex and money

Patrick James Quirke was born on 22 November 1968 in Tipperary. His mother, Eileen, was a housewife and his father, Patrick, or PJ as he was known, was a farmer with a modest sixty-seven-acre holding about 3.5 miles from Tipperary town. The farm sat below the Aherlow woods and the entrance to the Glen of Aherlow, about five miles from the Lowry farm at Fawnagowan. Eileen was the quintessential farmer's wife. Her interests included home baking and knitting and she was heavily involved in the local Mount Bruis Guild of the Irish Countrywomen's Association (ICA). She ran a strict home regime, had a great flare for homemaking and was extremely proud of her respected standing in the community. Her father, John Dore, was a detective garda in Tipperary garda station. He died in 1972 when Pat was just four years old.

The couple had four daughters and Pat, their only son. The five children received an equal primary education, attending Mount Bruis National School near the family home in Breansha, but it was clear from the start that only one would inherit the family farm. As the sole male heir, Pat was to lead a very different life from that of his four sisters.

'Pat was very entitled, and I think that goes back to what happened when he was young,' said a former close friend. 'His father took a stroke when he was in secondary school and could no longer man the farm. Pat's four sisters were at boarding school. Pat was kept at home and they all went to university. Pat always had it that people had it easy compared to him. It was a case of *poor Pat, woe is me.*'

Pat received his farming certificate in 1989 and officially took over the lands at Breanshamore in 1993 while his father was still living. Around that time he was dating Imelda Lowry, one of the four sisters at Fawnagowan. Imelda, like Pat's mother, was active in the ICA. She was quiet, well brought up and had a keen interest in farming because of her own background. They were childhood sweethearts whose romance blossomed in their mid-teens through Macra na Feirme, a voluntary rural youth organization of which they were both members. Pat was seen as a bit of a loner, who never really socialized, and Imelda quickly became his closest friend.

'All they knew was each other,' said one local farmer. 'They were the type who sat outside the disco eating ice creams while everyone else was inside dancing.'

The couple married on 2 September 1995 and Imelda's brother Martin, who was seeing Mary Lowry at the time, was Pat's best man. The two families were delighted with the match.

After they got married, Pat and Imelda – Imelda worked as a sales rep in car finance for Woodchester Finance – built a house on the land at Breansha and tried to borrow as little money as they possibly could. They took out a small mortgage, and saw the property appreciate greatly in value, mostly due to the property boom of the 1990s. Meanwhile, Pat's mother remained in the old, run-down family farmhouse on the same land – the same sort of shared living arrangement that Imelda's mother, Rita, would enjoy over at Fawnagowan.

While his sisters pursued careers in teaching and banking, Pat devoted himself to the land and the farm. His neighbours described him as a 'gruff, cool character' who they believed considered himself to be a cut above the rest.

'He would barely lift his head to you, never mind talk to you,' said one.

The feeling was that his easy acquisition of the farm and lands gave him a sense of entitlement that spilled over into the rest of his life, that he was the 'gentleman-farmer', the landowner, the man at the head of the table, and he expected to be well treated because of this.

'His father was the same, dour,' one of his neighbours remarked. 'Pat was a very cool character, not friendly at all in fact. He would have kept to himself over the years, apart from his involvement in the farming community. He wouldn't have been a man for the pub, just the farm and his family, that was pretty much it.'

Pat took his role as farm owner and manager very seriously, always looking for a way to increase the revenue generated by his business. He had a number of farm workers who helped him over the years and the feeling was that Pat spent much of his time in the office, his time consumed with the myriad of investments he was involved in. Off the farm, he was a consummate networker and prided himself on his reputation and his ability to turn every situation to his advantage.

'Pat used to always say that if you had an idea that you wanted to get through, that you would have your ground-work done initially,' said a former friend. 'He would say you had to have an established level of support before you put a proposal on the table. Make what you like of that, whether Pat would be pressing the flesh or whatever.'

Talking to the people of Breanshamore, the feeling is that Pat was the type of person who was always working to an agenda, who had an ulterior motive tucked up his sleeve. Country people tend to be very wary of anyone who seems to have a public face and a private face. They value straightforward honesty in all dealings, and particularly in business and farming matters. There was a general belief that Pat Quirke was not a man who dealt in straightforward honesty.

In December 1997, Pat's father passed away. Imelda gave birth to their first child, a boy they named Liam, in June 1998. A year later, in 1999, Pat and a friend set up the Tipperary Discussion Group and asked Leonie Foster, a New Zealand dairy consultant, to facilitate it. Martin Lowry was also a member of the group.

'Pat was one of the main founders,' a former member of the group recalled. 'He introduced rules, that was typical Pat, all about control. Any farmer who missed three meetings would be thrown out. People who had the best of reasons for missing a meeting were put out and it caused serious division. It would be up to the chairman's discretion, if a fella came along with his excuses, and of course Pat was chairman for the first two years. He was very controlling. He was always agitating, always wanting things his way.'

Together with Imelda, Pat vied for a position in the upper echelons of the farming world. Theirs was a marriage of equals. Pat was in constant competition with his neighbours, obsessed with getting more land and more cows. Imelda, say those who know her, held the same steely ambition to have a farm that was bigger and better than everyone else's.

Speaking at the Positive Farmers Conference at the South Court Hotel in Limerick some years later, in January 2005, Pat said that the formation of this discussion group 'heralded the start of a huge personal development phase' in his life. He told the audience how he and Imelda had decided that they needed a financial plan for retirement, and how this in turn led them into the world of financial investments. He put it very simply: 'We had to make more money.'

In an attempt to achieve this goal, in 2000 Imelda and Pat attended a two-day introductory course on the topic of shares. Run by a well-known dairy farmer, Mike Murphy, and an agri-business consultant, Lynaire Ryan, among others, the course ran over two days and was described as an 'introduction to investments'. The course wasn't billed as expert guidance, but simply as a general overview to allow attendees to gain some insight and then go off and learn more.

One farmer who also attended the course said it was 'basic stuff. In terms of a legitimate qualification for anything, it was literally just an explanation. How you set up a share account, how you get information, that sort of thing. It wouldn't remotely equip somebody to go off and invest heavily. Not remotely qualified to advise others what to do with their money.'

Upon completion of the two-day introductory course, Pat dived straight in and started purchasing shares. Around the same time, he and Imelda bought three buy-to-let houses in the Tipperary area, two in Cashel and one in Tipperary town. This gave them a rental income separate from the farm income. Their plan was being put into practice, with an eye to their future. Alongside this, Pat worked to establish himself within agricultural circles, both in Ireland and abroad. By 2001 he was chairman of the IFA Dairy Committee in South Tipperary and also a member of the advisory committee of Tipperary Co-op Creamery. He was also now a father of two as his second son, Alan, was born in February 2001.

In late 2001 Pat was successful in his application to become a Nuffield Scholar. The Nuffield Farming Scholarships are awarded by Nuffield Ireland to allow for study, research, and promotion of agriculture and rural development. It's essentially a travel and study bursary that allows the scholar to travel, research, participate in international conferences and then present their selected topic of study at the end of a two-year period. It's a fiercely contested competition and an honour to be selected to join the elite ranks of scholars. Pat was awarded one of just three scholarships in 2001 and chose as his field of study the co-operative movement worldwide. He spent time in New Zealand, Europe and the US while researching and writing his thesis. For this he received a bursary of €5,000 and after the two-year period he submitted a thesis on *Lessons for the Dairy Cooperative Industry*.

Upon his return from New Zealand, Pat started to look in earnest for investment opportunities, with a focus on investments that mature on a shorter term and generate cash. In 2002 he attended the annual Positive Farmers Conference in Limerick, where he heard a Cork farmer and investor, Michael Scully, speaking about an opportunity to invest in commercial property in Poland. It seemed to be exactly what Pat had been looking for.

'The first building Pat got involved in was Bliski Centrum,' said a fellow shareholder. 'It was an office building bought for about ten million euros. Michael Scully wrote to us and said we could have shareholder representatives and, because of the discussion group and other contacts, we succeeded in getting Pat Quirke in. In reality, I don't think he had much pull, but in fairness to him he brought a lot of information about what was going on. The building was bought for about ten million euros and there was a lot of money lost. We all lost a lot of money.'

Ultimately, Pat made three Polish property investments via Michael Scully. The second investment was a €21 million office building called Antares, which was a ten-year project. The third was a €32 million Cirrus investment, another office block, and it had a hundred shareholders. It was eventually sold in 2014. According to another shareholder in the scheme, Pat Quirke had invested €100,000 in it and got about 55 per cent of that back. That sort of return might have put paid to other people's ambitions of being a financial shark, but not Pat. He notched it up to experience and kept going.

In 2003 Pat managed to secure a land and quota lease on the farm next door to Breansha, extending the milking block to 115 acres, milking 107 cows and producing 115,000 gallons of milk. A year later, in 2004, Imelda gave birth to their third son, Gary, on the same date as her own birthday, 2 June.

Pat's drive to expand the farm operation meant that by 2005 he was operating 164 acres, of which he owned sixty-seven acres, leasing the rest from a neighbour in Breansha. In the same year, Pat, who was now thirty-six and a father of three, appeared as a speaker at the Positive Farmers Conference in Limerick. Farmers were being encouraged not to put the Single Farm Payment (an agricultural subsidy paid to farmers in the EU) into their farms. The message was to 'invest elsewhere', and that message was delivered by Pat Quirke.

In his speech, Pat offered some words of wisdom on off-farm investing, explaining how he and his wife had begun building their financial empire. The aim, he told them, was to 'enjoy life, free from financial worry'. The Quirkes felt they were achieving this enviable goal.

There was an extraordinary development that same year which publicly showed up Pat's money obsession, a revelation that no doubt rankled for a man who so carefully cultivated a respectable public persona. The source of this revelation was his own mother, Eileen, who took the incredible step of calling a radio phone-in show to complain about her son.

The background to this was, of course, the land. When the farm was handed over to Pat in 1993, while his father was still alive, Pat told a friend that his mother joined the EU Farm Retirement Scheme, a programme that gave retired farmers a pension of up to €15,000 a year for ten years.

'Typically in that situation there was an arrangement in relation to extras,' a former friend of Pat's explained. 'The farmer who would inherit the farm would supply a car, he would fill the oil tank, there would be an account run in a couple of places that the former owner, usually the parents, would run in the local butcher's stall and the insurances would be paid. That would be an agreement. Once the EU retirement scheme ended, the older person would get the old-age pension. Whether or not the private arrangement would continue would be an arrangement between the parties. In many cases, that would be tied down legally.'

The scheme could only be drawn down once, so when the ten-year period expired, Eileen began to draw her old-age pension, assuming that her only son would keep supplying the extras. Her son didn't see it that way. The same friend remarked that 'Pat maintained that his commitment to the extras to her ended at that time'.

Eileen wasn't happy. In her eyes, her son had reneged on their deal, and so she sought to lay legal claim to the farmhouse he had obtained through his inheritance. She maintained that while his father had intended that Pat inherit the farm, the homestead was always supposed to go to her as PJ's widow. It caused much bad blood between them, until the day Eileen decided to make a bold move to resolve the issue.

She contacted *Liveline*, the RTÉ Radio 1 show hosted by Joe Duffy that specializes in airing public grievances of all kinds. In her live on-air conversation with Joe Duffy in February 2005, Eileen complained that Pat refused to sign over the family home to her. She asserted that while PJ was alive, he had reached an agreement with their son to hand the farm over to him, but she had insisted on keeping the family home in her name. Her husband died shortly afterwards, and Pat did not put the family house in Eileen's name.

'The farm was transferred with the agreement that the house would be in my name and [Pat] refused to put the house in my name,' she told Joe Duffy and a spellbound audience right across the country. 'After what I would consider a very happy marriage, when my husband died I was left with nothing apart from the widow's allowance.'

Eileen said that an agreement had been reached to hand over the farmland prior to her husband's death, but it was never implemented by her son. She described how a solicitor representing Pat came to the house to go over the agreement with her and her husband, and said the house issue could be dealt with easily enough.

'I wanted the house and the solicitor said, "Yes, that would be no bother." It would cost about €1,000 to take it off map. All the years down along, I tried to get it taken off, but no, it would not be given to me,' she said. 'All I wanted was the house in my own name. I think everybody is entitled to their house.'

Eileen said that Pat's solicitor did ask the couple whether they wanted the legal documents reviewed by their own solicitor, but her husband declined, saying that they were, after all, dealing with their own son, their own flesh and blood. She added that her husband had suffered a stroke several months prior to this meeting, and she questioned whether he had even been capable of making such a decision. She stressed how long and happy their marriage had been, and the fact that the farmhouse was where they had lived and reared their family. Eileen spoke emotionally about the stressful position the situation had put her in, exacerbated by the fact that she did not have the money to pursue the matter legally.

'I have no collateral if I wanted to go to be taken into a nursing home or anything like that. Just nothing,' she said. According to her, she had raised this issue again with her son a year before, but he had refused to put the house in her name. He did, she said, offer to let the house out if she required nursing-home care and put the rental money towards paying for her residential care. She added that had she pursued the matter within 'the due time', i.e. within the statute of limitations, she probably would have got the house, but she hadn't pursued it earlier and was therefore left in a very distressing limbo.

'You would think that everybody would have their own house, but it is not so in a lot of the farming community,' she said.

At the time of that phone call, Eileen was still living in the old farmhouse, on the same land as Pat and Imelda in the modern new-build next door. At the end of this sorry episode, she ended up moving into Tipperary town, into one of the investment properties bought by her son and daughter-in-law.

'Pat was mortified,' said a former friend. 'Half the town heard Eileen on the radio and the other half were told about it. Basically, she said she had a deal with her son and he had reneged on it. I'm a poor widow, the whole lot. She was living in the farmhouse up in the farmyard. Pat, when the pressure was on him, took out the tenants he had in the house in town and reluctantly put his mother into it. He now had to pay the mortgage the tenants had been covering.'

It could be argued that it was a problem of his own

making, but, whatever the truth of the matter, the outcome meant there was financial pressure coming on to Pat's shoulders from all sides. The life he and Imelda were striving towards was tantalizingly close, but it seemed that obstacles kept being thrown up to drive them off course.

All the while, Pat continued farming at Breansha but he was also forging a successful partnership with Imelda's brother Martin Lowry. The two men were young and ambitious and worked hard to run their farms well and ensure their children's futures. The family was rocked to its core by Martin's death in 2007. No doubt Pat was upset by the death of his friend and brother-in-law, but his finely tuned antennae also sensed an excellent financial opportunity: a chance to farm Martin's prime land at Fawnagowan at a knock-down price.

'He [Pat] more or less started farming the land the day after Martin died,' Mary would later say. 'The day after he died, he [Pat] brought cattle on to the land.'

Pat's offer to help Mary Lowry with running the farm turned into a formal arrangement whereby he leased sixty-three acres for €12,600 per annum over a seven-year term. He also took ownership of the Single Farm Payment paid to Fawnagowan, which was worth €11,000 per annum. The various arrangements meant that, in the end, the lease of the fine land of Fawnagowan would cost him just €1,600 per annum. Pat was taking in money from various revenue streams, and he was over at Fawnagowan every day, carefully monitoring his investment there. He was also providing a shoulder to cry on for the widowed Mary, who was distraught at the death of her husband. In time, the arrangement between them would come to involve regular meetings for sex, meetings that no one could ever find out about because it threatened to tear both families apart.

Their 'seedy affair', as Mary Lowry subsequently described it (giving evidence against Pat Quirke), began in January 2008, about four months after Martin's death. It would have been a time of raw, bleak grief for Mary, when she was trying to come to terms with this terrible blow to her life and the lives of her children. 'It was a very difficult time for me and for the boys,' she would later say. 'I tried to be the best mother possible. I always put them first.'

In the midst of the pain and the loss was Pat Quirke, ever present, ever helpful. Over the months, that familiarity and daily contact, coupled with the intense emotional crutch Pat was providing for Mary, developed into an intimate, mostly physical affair. They slipped into a routine of meeting on Monday and Friday mornings in her bedroom at Fawnagowan, while the children were at school. According to Pat, it was 'fifty–fifty' as to who started it. He would later recall exactly what he had told her: 'I have to pull back because I am falling in love with you. Her exact answer was, "I am too."'

Interestingly, Mary would recall the beginning of the affair in a different light. She felt that he had preyed on her vulnerabilities as a recently bereaved woman. 'I was led to have an affair,' she would later say. 'I was a very vulnerable young woman with three small children. I was lost. I loved my husband to bits . . . my life had fallen apart . . . Pat Quirke tried to come in and control everything.'

In the beginning, Mary was glad to have Pat's help in dealing with the various off-farm investments. This was an area Martin had always looked after and something of which she had little understanding.

'I wouldn't have known much about the farming business or the off-farm investments,' she later said. 'That's what Martin dealt with, so I was very much lost when Martin died. I didn't know where to start to look for anything. Martin left the bank accounts fairly well sorted, but there would have been a lot of shared investments that I wouldn't have been involved in and wouldn't have known how to sort. Pat Quirke would have been involved so he offered to help me with these. He advised me on different things. I would have considered him to be very good to me in the beginning. A lot of people wouldn't have known what to do but he was very familiar with Martin's goings on.'

For Mary, the grief of losing Martin was overwhelming. Her brother Eddie, to whom she was very close, would later say that 'she found it very difficult to cope and get on with life' after Martin's death. He felt that she needed to talk to someone about it, but she didn't talk to him. Pat, the knight in shining armour, was more than happy to listen. 'He was on the farm every day and we got to be friends, I suppose,' she would later say. 'We chatted and talked and got involved with each other.'

In the midst of her affair with her brother-in-law, Mary still clung to Martin's memory. In July 2008, and for several years after his death, she organized a 'Walk for Martin' in his memory. At the inaugural walk, almost a year after his death, she was joined by Martin's family and friends as they set off on an hour-long Sunday afternoon walk that began at the Aherlow House Hotel, close to Bansha Wood. Her secret lover, Pat, was there too, with his wife, Imelda, holding buckets for a collection on behalf of the South Tipperary Hospice. As everyone gathered to remember Martin and raise funds for a worthy cause, Pat and Mary successfully kept up the pretence of being just good friends.

Their affair carried on right under the nose of Imelda and his in-laws for almost three years after Martin's death. It might seem impossible that nobody realized what was happening, but it's common for people not to notice what's right in front of them, especially if they don't want to see it. Certainly, no one would have expected it to happen, given that Pat and Imelda were happily married and Mary's heart belonged to Martin. Johnny Lowry did notice that Pat and Mary had grown close over those months, much closer than before. He had his suspicions that something might be going on, but he never brought it up. The Lowry family way was, after all, discretion in everything.

Rita was best placed to observe all the comings and goings at Fawnagowan, and she too noticed that something was different between her son-in-law and her daughter-in-law. She was worried, but she brushed aside her suspicions, hoping that she was wrong. Unfortunately, as in many things, Rita wasn't far off the mark at all.

Mary may have entered into the affair of her own free will, but certain things about her lover's temperament worried her. She found him overpowering and controlling, always dictating the terms of their relationship and questioning her every move.

'He was continuously around, but I used to go to town or stay away,' she would later say. 'He was very overpowering.'

If she was late to meet him, he would not be pleased. Any time he saw her leaving the farm, he would ask her where she was going and who she was meeting. He would lecture and gesticulate, annoyed that she had failed to follow his regimented ways. It came to feel claustrophobic, which only added to the weight of guilt that Mary felt.

They were both very much aware of the deep betrayal involved in their illicit liaison, Mary maybe even more so than Pat. She was deeply troubled by their affair, knowing that he was married to her friend and Martin's sister Imelda.

'I felt very guilty,' she would later say. 'I knew Pat Quirke was a happily married man.'

It was a deception that cut right through the family ties that had sustained her all those years. Suffocated by guilt, Mary tried to end the affair many times, but Pat always managed to manipulate the situation back to his advantage and convince her to carry on.

'I tried to finish this relationship many, many times,' Mary would later say. 'But Pat Quirke would say, "If you tell your friends you've had this affair, none of them will talk to you and your family won't stand by you." I like people to like me. I like people and I felt very ashamed of the whole thing.'

Friends of Mary would say she was at 'rock bottom' during the period he had control over her. She was insecure following Martin's death and lacked the confidence she had before. Pat ensured it stayed where it was, on the floor. He could be persuasive because he knew Mary had a weak spot. He knew she hadn't had a sexual relationship in years because Martin had been so sick. It was this void, the lack of intimacy in her life, this heavy loneliness, that Pat exploited to its fullest.

Once this intimacy was established, Pat became more and more involved in Mary's life at Fawnagowan. He had already offered to assist her with running the farm and managing the bills, and now the self-styled financial guru took it upon himself to advise Mary about the need to draw up a new will. She agreed, appointing him and Imelda guardians of her children in the event of her death and, at Pat's suggestion, leaving her in-laws €100,000 to extend their home to accommodate the three boys should this come to pass.

Pat also helped her to manage her late husband's investments: commercial property investments in Poland worth

€200,000, investments with Davy Stockbrokers, shares in banks and Ryanair, and investments in contracts for differences (CFDs). Pat had a soft spot for CFDs. These are a very flexible form of trading that allow the buyer/seller of securities or assets to gamble on the price of the securities/assets either rising or falling. The buyer doesn't actually buy or own the asset, but trades on the margins on the opening and closing prices of the asset or security. This is considered an advanced form of trading, one for expert investors, given that it's high risk and with no certainties or comeback. It is not allowed in the USA but remains a popular form of investment trading in other countries.

Pat, said a farmer who knew him at the time, 'had got mad into CFDs. He didn't seem aware of the risk. He was also encouraging other members of the Tipperary Discussion Group he was involved in to invest in CFDs, to the extent that an outside party was brought in to try and "talk some sense" about the decisions they were making.'

'Pat was stubborn,' one individual recalled. 'Someone had to go and talk to them before they absolutely broke themselves. They were warned not to touch CFDs with a bargepole. Most of them were frightened after that and got out of CFDs afterwards. Pat wouldn't have any of it. Before that I would have described him as a very conservative farmer, but he couldn't be talked to [about CFDs].'

Those who knew Pat Quirke personally describe a man for whom money had become his world, his primary focus. In Mary Lowry, a wealthy widow, he had found his very own cash flow on tap. At one stage he convinced her to give him €80,000 to invest in CFDs. He would manage the investment on her behalf and they agreed to a 50/50 split on the profits. They made €40,000 each in eighteen months, gaining back her original investment and then a further €80,000 that was split between them, as agreed. He bought a new trailer and jeep with his cut.

Triumphs like this ensured that Pat saw himself as something of a financial whiz. Despite previous warnings, he was still swanning around meetings with the Tipperary Discussion Group, badgering other farmers to plough their money into CFDs. Those who knew better started to avoid him. Others could only watch as he started to financially implode.

'Pat was CFDing like mad,' a former friend recalls. 'He used to ring people up at night, encouraging them to get involved. Anybody he knew he was encouraging and pressuring to take on high-risk investments. He rang me one night, wound up about the fantastic deal that was to be had buying C&C shares. The shares were €5 and they collapsed to €2. Pat was slaughtered. He had put €840,000 in. Then, in 2008, C&C announced a profit warning. The share price fell 33 per cent in nine minutes. Pat lost 33 per cent of €840,000 in nine minutes in 2008.'

With Ireland on the edge of an economic bust in 2008/9 after the heady boom of the Celtic Tiger years and his financial investments spiralling into freefall, Pat concentrated on his affair with Mary. Their secret trysts at Fawnagowan continued, but now they occasionally went out for lunch together. They had to be discreet, careful not to be seen in the same place too often. Pat told Mary things he had never told anyone before, and he believed Mary had truly confided in him: 'She'd have told me about her upbringing, that was probably difficult for her to tell.' They also discussed 'day-to-day things', such as problems she would have at work or with the boys, as well as financial difficulties – just like a normal couple.

Whatever about behaving like a normal couple, they were

both old enough to know that there was no future in the affair. It was completely impractical, given their family situations. Pat was still happily married to Imelda, and Mary wasn't in love with her lover. They each saw it for what it was: for Mary, a sexual relationship that had the added bonus of safe familiarity and companionship; for Pat, a lucrative arrangement that gave him cash and sex on demand.

Pat played the mistress game with aplomb. An aficionado of luxury hotels, he liked to turn on the style, whisking his lover away for a night to five-star luxury hotels like the Lyrath Estate Hotel in Kilkenny and the g Hotel & Spa in Galway. Her brother Eddie or a friend would normally mind Mary's boys and Pat would tell an unwitting Imelda that he was off on farming business, when in reality he was wining and dining Mary.

Imelda was at home on the farm at Breansha, keeping his family life, the one with the smiling children and the contented wife, all ticking along nicely in his absence. Although Pat was playing away from home, it wasn't because his physical relationship with his wife was lacking. While he was sleeping with Mary, he was also still sleeping with Imelda. According to Pat, Imelda may have had an 'inkling' about the affair, but never said so if she did.

Against a backdrop of sex sessions at Fawnagowan and secret weekends away, Pat was coming under increasing financial stress. He was constantly asking Mary for money and, all too often, she was giving in to his demands. Pat's control over her was extraordinary. Those who knew her say he also preyed on her openly generous nature.

'Mary probably felt indebted to him,' said her friend. 'That would be her, feeling like she had to show gratitude for the help he gave her in the beginning.'

'He was always asking me for money,' Mary would later say. 'He always mentioned investments and he seemed to be stuck with investments. He continuously asked me for money.' According to Mary, by the summer of 2010 she had had enough of the affair and called it off with Pat.

But he still pestered her for money. Following Martin's death, Pat helped Mary sell off as much of Martin's dairy herd as he could: with the milking operation at the farm no longer in use, there was no need for the animals. Most went to one of Martin's brothers and a farmer in Galway, while Pat bought two of the animals himself and added them to his own milking herd back home in Breansha. In October 2010, Pat discovered that his herd had been infected with bovine venereal diarrhoea (BVD), which he alleged had come from Martin's cows. He estimated that he had by then lost twelve cows to the disease and was due compensation from Mary.

'He was very forceful on this,' she would later say. 'It was continuous. He made me feel guilty about it. He said, "Martin wouldn't see me stuck, he'd have paid up."'

Unconvinced by his arguments, Mary made inquiries, reckoning that if the cattle had not caused the disease in his herd, then she did not owe Pat Quirke anything. He served her with a piece of paper upon which he had made calculations of the money that he said was owed. It concluded that the cost being claimed for the infliction of the disease was €16,500. The note said that this was not a request for compensation but was to be used 'as a guide only'. Pat later asked for the document back, but Mary took a copy before returning the original.

According to Mary, in December 2010 she wrote out a cheque for €20,000, made payable to Pat and Imelda Quirke, after he kept badgering her for money. He told her he needed to repay a bank loan and that he would have to sell shares at a loss to cover it.

'It was continuous,' she would later say about the cheque. 'He was looking for money all the time from me. It had become such a common occurrence. He seemed to be looking for money all the time.'

According to Pat, Mary gave him the €20,000 and told him she didn't need it back until her children started going to college. He would later say that Mary suggested he didn't have to repay this loan of €20,000, but instead could keep it in lieu of compensation for the loss of his cows. Mary was certain she had said no such thing. Ultimately, she never saw the money again.

While some might feel guilt over pressuring a widow for money, Pat didn't seem afflicted by such sensitivities. When it came to money, he was single-minded in the extreme. In fact, he had form when it came to lining his pockets by deceitful means. Although he had a carefully crafted reputation as an upstanding farmer, those who really knew him had seen a different side to him down through the years.

One former friend tells a story about a series of massive electricity bills that Pat traced to a faulty fridge-freezer. 'He put it in the local paper and he caught a young lady that was after buying her first house for it,' he recalled. 'He was proud about the fact that he had sold that dodgy freezer on, didn't give a damn that someone else was being done.'

The same friend also recalled how Pat had boasted that he could sell a BVD-infected cow to another unwitting farmer, without any qualms. Prior to compulsory BVD screening for newborn calves being introduced in 2013, it had long been the practice that once persistently infected (PI) calves were detected by a farmer, they were not to be sold on. PIs are the animals in the herd that do not respond to vaccination. Instead, they shed the infection and, although they pose no risk to humans, they can devastate a herd. It was up to each farmer to test for the disease and dispose of the animal accordingly. Sending the animal for slaughter at a factory would typically only earn a farmer around €200. Pat had openly boasted to other farmers that if he had a PI, he would provide his milk-producing charts, which would show that the animal had a good milk supply record, and sell it on for €1,200–€1,400, even though he knew full well that this would destroy the buyer's herd.

One farmer put it very succinctly: 'Pat didn't give a shit about the consequences.'

He had also told a friend that in order to save money when he was investing heavily in 2005/6, he had stopped spending money on vaccinating his herd: 'He told me his cows had gone zero-converted. In other words, they had built up enough immunity from a year-after-year process of vaccinating that they should be safe now. He said the vaccines were costing him around €2,000, so he cut them out. I told him he was off his trolley.'

The consequences of his actions – the investments, the affair, the loans and the badgering for money that wasn't his – did not matter to Pat. His affair with Mary carried on. He was never going to leave Imelda, and Mary had never asked him to, but nonetheless he was happy to continue with the betrayal, no matter what Mary argued. She often brought up the question of ending it, but Pat insisted that if she told her friends about them, they would abandon her, no one would talk to her and her family wouldn't stand by her. He said no one else would have her and her three boys. He made it sound like she had no choice but to keep seeing him, even if she now found the whole affair 'seedy'. She would later say that she had 'regard' for him but essentially saw him as a friend.

By the time Mary finally ended the affair in the summer of 2010 she had tired of all the secrets and lies and would later say: 'I finished it and I wanted to just enjoy my life and get on with looking after my children and not feel guilty or make excuses or tell lies. There was nothing nice about having an affair, nothing.' She told Pat it was over for good. Pat didn't take the break-up well, she would later say. She 'lent him an ear' and thought that by her being nice to him, he would get over the break-up and move on, but Pat wouldn't let go.

Pat would later claim the relationship didn't end until December of that year, after he discovered she was seeing Bobby Ryan. In his version of events, he realized she was being 'untruthful' to him when she revealed at the dinner in the Ballyglass Hotel that she had been in Cashel with Bobby the night before.

Pat might have been cavalier about consequences, but, sitting in the Ballyglass Hotel as Mary Lowry giggled about her night away with Bobby Ryan, he cared very much about the consequences for him of what she was saying. It was clear that Mary had no emotional connection to him. Up until now, this hadn't been a problem, but that gap between her head and her heart now posed a direct threat to him and their arrangement, an arrangement that benefited him far more than it did her. The idea of Mary falling for Bobby was appalling. Pat had invested so much time and energy in Mary Lowry, he had done everything possible to replace her husband in every way, taking his farm, his money and his wife. He couldn't let someone else waltz in and undo all that good work, no matter what Mary Lowry might think she felt about him. No, their relationship had to keep on going, regardless of her feelings.

The problem was, Pat Quirke was nothing like Martin Lowry. Moreover, he was nothing at all like Bobby Ryan.

Pat said nothing about Mary's shocking revelation in the Ballyglass Hotel, carefully biding his time until he felt it was the right moment to broach the subject. Later that week, he went into Mary's bedroom in Fawnagowan. According to Pat's version of events, they had sex, as usual. Afterwards, they lay on the bed, enjoying the post-coital glow. When Mary got up from the bed, Pat reached under her pillow and slid her phone out. He quickly accessed her text messages and began scrolling through them intently. It took only a moment to see the long list of texts to Bobby Ryan. If he had doubted it before now, this was stone-cold evidence that Mary and Bobby were mad about each other and in the throes of a passionate relationship. Pat was furious.

He deleted all the replies from Bobby Ryan. Then, he stabbed at the screen with his finger, bringing up a new message box. Into it, he typed a message to Bobby, telling him that Mary hadn't been honest with him, that she had been seeing himself for the past three years. He pressed Send.

A minute or two later, the phone started to ring. It was Bobby Ryan. He had no idea about the affair going on between Mary and Pat, and now he'd received this strange message from Mary's phone. He rang back to find out what was going on.

Pat answered the phone and spoke one sentence: 'Sorry, but I'm the man.' Then he ended the call, cutting Bobby off before he could respond.

Pat's white rage was met with equal fury from Mary when

she realized what he had done. According to him, they had a heated argument in the bedroom. 'I more or less left,' Pat would later say about the incident. 'I was angry . . . it's very hard to remember what was said. I must have accused her of lying. She said we were finished.' He stormed out of the house, her phone still clutched in his hand. He hopped into his jeep and took off out of the farmyard, taking her phone with him.

According to Mary's version of events, she and Pat were in the kitchen, not in her bedroom, when a text came into her phone from Bobby. Pat saw the name 'Bobby' flashing up on the screen and grabbed the phone. 'I thought you weren't having anything to do with him?' she would later say Pat said to her.

She asked him to give her back the phone and he refused: 'He wouldn't give it back to me. He drove away with it and rang Bobby.'

Mary said Pat was 'very angry', but that he eventually returned to the farm with the phone. 'He said he'd rang Bobby and that Bobby didn't want anything more to do with me. He [Pat] said to him, "She's mine", even though our relationship had well and truly ended.'

Bobby told a friend that Pat threatened him during this conversation, warning him to stay away from Mary because she was with him.

Pat's actions bore all the hallmarks of bitter jealousy, but he would later insist that he was not jealous, just angry. He was deluding himself. His were the actions of a scorned man, seething with rage, a man who appeared to be losing control.

Mary desperately tried to ring Bobby, but he wouldn't answer. She raced over to his house in Cashel that night in a desperate bid to try and save the relationship. There, she finally came clean about everything, explaining to Bobby how she and Pat had started an affair and letting him make up his own mind about it. She was honest and reassured him that she would be honest in the future – no more secrets.

'He was very frosty,' she said later. 'He didn't know what was going on . . . I told him the whole story . . . I told him I had a relationship and it had ended and that I was having difficulty with Pat Quirke.'

Bobby told a friend that he was furious when he found out about the affair. Moreover, he was deeply hurt. He was under the impression that he was the first man to have been intimate with Mary since the death of her husband.

'He told me she was in tears crying,' said the friend. 'Crying and crying. Bobby was just a big softie and couldn't deal with it. She told him it was all over and he felt sorry for her and he ended up carrying on with the relationship.'

Now that her guilty secret had been shared with Bobby, and he hadn't hated her for it, Mary was hugely relieved and happy once again.

Pat, on the other hand, was still angry. The whole situation was galling to him. He was angry because she was happy, and it seemed to him that Mary didn't care one bit if he was 'happy, sad or indifferent'. In his eyes, all the help and support he had given her after Martin's death were forgotten about, discarded, worthless. After all he had done, in swooped Bobby Ryan, the cheerful DJ with the twinkly eyes, to reap the rewards. There was no way Pat Quirke would just stand aside and let that happen. No way at all.

3. Love rivals

Bobby Ryan knew what it was to be heartbroken over a woman. He had gone through it himself, after the break-up of his own marriage to Mary Ryan (maiden name and married name), the mother of his two children, in 2005. While he might have been expected to be furiously angry with Pat Quirke and his meddling, instead he was sympathetic because he recognized a fellow soldier in the war of unrequited love.

Bobby Ryan was born on 11 December 1959. He grew up in Upper Friar Street, Cashel, with his brothers, John, Jerry and Eamonn, and sisters Ann, Majella and Mary. He came from a proud working-class family. His mother, Ellen, or Nellie as she was known, was a housewife and his father, Edmond, known as Neddie, drove a lorry carrying lime from Killough Quarry in Thurles to various farmers around Tipperary. Bobby's school years were spent at Christian Brothers in Cashel, and one of his later jobs was in the Medite factory, a fibreboard-manufacturing plant in Clonmel.

The nine members of the Ryan family lived in a small, two-storey terraced house situated on a road that faces directly on to the Rock of Cashel. The house was a two-minute walk from the town centre. Bobby's parents had seven mouths to feed and times were hard, but the family were honest and hard-working. They were regular Mass-goers and all seven children were instilled with traditional Catholic values. The Ryans were a well-known and much-loved family and the few neighbours who remain in the area remember Bobby as a happy child who grew into a decent, kind and honourable man.

In the same way that music and dancing would bring him into Mary Lowry's life in August 2010, Bobby met his wife, Mary Ryan, on a similar night out in Tipperary many years earlier. The venue was a place called The Ragg, a bar in Bouladuff, just outside Thurles, about five miles from Tipperary town.

In those years single women were still strictly chaperoned on nights out, and Mary was under the careful watch of her cousin Phil the night she met her future husband. When Phil left his post momentarily to go to the toilet, Bobby made his move. He asked Mary up to dance and she gladly accepted. When Phil returned from the toilet, he tapped Bobby on the shoulder and asked him who he was. He told Mary to get back to her seat, but she refused.

'Do you know him?' Bobby asked her, nodding towards Phil.

'I've never met him in my life,' she answered, collapsing into laughter.

Despite Phil's best efforts, Mary and Bobby spent the night dancing and chatting and were instantly drawn to one another. They met again the following week and quickly became an item. Marriage followed on 22 March 1986, and their first child, Michelle, was born four months later in July. Bobby was working as a forklift driver at the time and the couple were living in Cashel. Their second-born, Robert, named after his father, was born in June 1987.

'Bobby wouldn't have changed a nappy, but he was good with them,' Mary recalled. 'Shelly came first and when she was born I had to jump into the back seat. That was the way it was. Robert came along a year later and [Bobby] was delighted to have a son.'

While Michelle, or Shelly as her family call her, was the apple of her father's eye, he also had a strong bond with Robert. When he was young, Bobby took Robert to the Tipperary Raceway at the village of Rosegreen every Sunday to watch the car racing. Father and son were also regularly spotted inside Bobby's haulage truck, which was always lovingly cleaned to perfection. It was Bobby who taught Robert to drive, taking him to the local quarry, up passages and into fields as he learned how to handle a car properly. He might have been shy of nappies and the like, but Bobby was a good father and his children adored him.

When the children were still young, Bobby began to DJ. He already had a love for music, teaching himself how to play the guitar and performing in a band called Dropzone, so this was a natural extension of that first love. He started out playing the guitar at trad sessions in the Moore Lane Tavern on Thursdays and Fridays and then would DJ there on Saturday nights under the stage name 'Mr Moonlight'.

Mary stayed at home, minding Michelle and Robert, so that Bobby could pursue his musical passion, and as a result she rarely went to see him perform. On the few occasions she did, she was met with the sight of a bevy of women vying for his attention at the DJ box, something she had the confidence to brush off, fully aware that it was part of the job. Bobby, the consummate crowd-pleaser, always laughed it off too and played along.

As his children got older, they came to share their father's love of music. Once he had his driving licence, Robert drove his father to gigs around Tipperary, helping him to carefully load and unload his 'disco kit' at each venue. He would never finish on time on those nights, the crowd yelling for 'one more' from Mr Moonlight. Michelle went one step further than her brother by taking up DJing herself. She went under the name 'Shelly Moonlight', a moniker given to her by her father on the first night she had a proper gig.

By now, Bobby had established himself as a steady hand on the decks and had a regular side-earner as a DJ to supplement his wage at the quarry. He was DJing in other venues around Cashel, in places like the Brian Boru pub and Mikey Ryan's bar.

As couples often do, Mary and Bobby drifted apart over time. They decided to split up when Michelle was nineteen and Robert was eighteen years old. By that stage, they were leading separate lives anyway. They jointly made the decision to separate, following which Michelle and Bobby went to live with their father in a rented house in Cashel.

Despite the fact that there was no ill-feeling between the parties, Bobby took the break-up very badly. He had spent nineteen years as Mary's husband and now he struggled to adjust to life as a single man. He was engulfed by a depression, to the extent that Michelle became concerned for his mental well-being. She became his confidante during those dark days, giving him a quick phone call every twenty minutes just to check that he was all right. Michelle was his confidante and his constant, unwavering support and she was determined to see her father, the man who was always the life and soul of the party, happy again.

It took nine long months before Bobby eventually turned a corner and began to emerge from the darkness that had surrounded him. Finally, Michelle could properly say, 'There's Daddy again.' The old Bobby was back. In all those months, he had never missed a day of work and he had kept putting on a smile and playing his music to make others happy. Most people probably never realized that Bobby was going through such a difficult time in his life over those months, but Michelle knew. She was aware of the full heartbreaking extent of it. That was what made her so determined to ensure that Bobby was surrounded by good people now, people who would lift him up and make him feel good, so that he never again descended into that darkness.

Her father had a few girlfriends at that time, including Mary Glasheen, the woman he dated before he met Mary Lowry. They also met on a night out in the Times Hotel and loved dancing together. Mary Glasheen was a good companion for Bobby and they enjoyed fun times together before deciding to go their separate ways. But they remained friends and continued to enjoy each other's company socially. And then Bobby met Mary Lowry. From the bits he told her about his new girlfriend, Michelle wasn't convinced that this match was as good for her father. She watched carefully as the romance blossomed, trying to gauge where this was going.

The brief phone call with Pat Quirke must have been a shock for Bobby, given that he had no idea that Mary Lowry was involved in an affair with her brother-in-law. Afterwards, he and Mary had an open and honest heart-to-heart and she explained everything to him. She described Pat's upset over the end of the affair and his unwillingness to let go. Remarkably, Bobby's response was one of compassion and understanding. He felt that he might be able to find common ground with his love rival, and so he offered to help. At Bobby's request, Mary asked Pat to meet with Bobby at the Hayes Hotel in Thurles, neutral turf, where the three of them could talk it out and hopefully clear the air. He probably didn't appreciate just how daunting a mountain there was to climb to convince Pat Quirke to relinquish his claim on Mary Lowry and not be 'the man'.

On 5 January 2011, Bobby parked his Mr Moonlight van outside Cusack's Bar in the Hayes Hotel in Thurles and made his way inside. It was a cold and bleak winter's day. Mary had travelled with him from Fawnagowan and as they walked towards the hotel his phone rang and he answered it. Michelle. Bobby had told her all about the Pat and Mary situation and she was not happy with the idea of her father going toe-to-toe with this man who had caused all the drama. She thought her father was acting like a fool and feared that he would be humiliated or insulted, walked over like a doormat.

'I was like a tyrant,' she would admit later when describing that unorthodox meeting.

She was angry that her father wanted to see Pat Quirke in person and also that he had not asked her to accompany him to it. She couldn't understand why he would go alone; nor could she understand what, if anything, he was hoping to achieve by it. But, Bobby being Bobby, in his optimistic and generous way he thought he could build a bridge between himself and Pat Quirke. He had no way of knowing there was no bridge in the world long enough or strong enough to cross that gap.

No matter what she said, Bobby was not for turning, so Michelle told him to call her directly after the meeting. He told her that he would.

The venue was Bobby's choice. It was handy in that he needed to bring his lorry in for a service and the hotel was along the route to the garage, but it's likely he also liked the neutrality and anonymity of Cusack's Bar. It was a big, modern bar with cosy, tucked-away corners – the perfect location for conducting business discreetly.

Bobby and Mary walked into the bar and joined Pat at a table. The waiter brought menus and Mary and Bobby ordered supper; Pat ordered a glass of water, nothing else. For the next hour, they talked. At least, the two men talked. Mary was unusually quiet, something that irked Pat. Bobby spoke about the break-up of his marriage, trying to forge that common ground. He told Pat that he had nearly become an alcoholic after the split and that he had gone through a very hard time, but he had come out the other end.

Pat apologized for the shock of the incident with Mary's phone. This was a positive start to the proceedings. They talked about Mary and Bobby's relationship, that they were mad about each other, and that Mary stood by her decision to end the affair with Pat. It was very simple: Pat was out, and Bobby was in, it was unfortunate for Pat, but it couldn't be helped.

After the hour, Pat stood up from the table and said his goodbyes. He and Bobby shook hands. Then Pat walked away and out of Cusack's Bar as Mary and Bobby left together. Pat later described this meeting as a good talk, that he wished the happy couple well before leaving and that he was unexpectedly impressed by Bobby, whom he had written off as a nobody. He was, he later said, happy that he had got the chance to let Bobby know he wasn't 'a monster'.

'I was happy enough with the meeting because he didn't see me as someone who had it in for him.'

Depending on which way this was meant, it could be seen as a statement of honest conciliation, or a statement of sinister intent. Did he mean that the air had been cleared between them, there was a clear understanding and Bobby could rest assured that his relationship with Mary was not going to be derailed by Pat Quirke? Or did he mean that under the guise of the appeased ex-lover he could handle Bobby Ryan more effectively – that Bobby would drop his guard and leave himself vulnerable?

Bobby later told a friend that he had used the meeting to warn Pat to leave Mary alone: 'Bobby basically said, "Mary is single and I am single, so we are doing nothing wrong." He told Pat that he had a wife that he should go home to and concentrate on and that if he didn't leave Mary alone, he would tell the wife about the affair. He told Pat to get professional help and Pat said he would.'

Whatever Bobby thought about Pat, the meeting had given Pat a unique chance to size up the opposition at close quarters. Would his conclusion be that he should leave Bobby and Mary alone? Or would he reckon that he had a fighting chance of scuppering their relationship and reinstating himself in Mary's Lowry's affections – and life? No doubt Bobby and Mary hoped that it would all blow over now, but only time would tell what Pat's reaction would be.

In January, Mary's relationship with Bobby became intimate and he sometimes stayed with her at her home. He kept the van out of sight of Rita's house by parking in the farmyard, but someone might have noticed it there.

One morning that same month, Mary went out walking with a friend after dropping the boys to school. When she returned home, she found her front door standing open. The children were at school and Rita would never enter her part of the house and leave the door open, and Mary was sure she had locked it when she left, as she always did.

She stepped cautiously through the front door and into the porch. Mary loved plants and the porch was covered from floor to ceiling in greenery. As she navigated her way around her potted plants, everything appeared to be in place. All was quiet. She moved towards the second door, leading into the main house and the kitchen, when she suddenly saw

Pat standing behind that second door. Mary was startled to see him and asked him what he was doing and how he'd got in. She had definitely locked the front door.

'He said I had left the front door open,' she would later say. 'I didn't believe that, but what could I do? He said he was looking for me, even though my car wasn't there.' Mary wasn't happy with this explanation. 'If my car wasn't there, then I wouldn't be there.'

She rang him half an hour later and asked him again how he'd got into her house. He told her she had left the front door open.

Now that she was finally free from his clutches, Mary's eyes were beginning to open to the truth of the situation, but she still hadn't realized the full extent of Pat's obsession. She told a friend about the incident in the kitchen and how his story about the door being open was making her doubt her own mind.

Afterwards, Mary decided it was time to take some precautions. Pat's behaviour was odd and strange, but this latest incident felt threatening too. She called her brother Eddie, who worked as a carpenter, and asked him to change the locks on her front door. Eddie called around with his toolbox and changed the barrel. He gave Mary a set of keys to the new lock, which she kept safely in her possession. With the locks changed and secured, she could rest easier in her bed at night. Or so she thought.

4. Dear Patricia

The end of an affair is always a difficult time, but for Pat Quirke the situation was compounded by a number of factors. He was annoyed about the way he had found out about Bobby Ryan, through an overheard remark. He was angry that Mary didn't care about his feelings in the matter. It was clear that she had moved on, without him. Moreover, there were no longer any secrets between her and Bobby, while Imelda was still in the dark about his affair. It meant that he and Mary no longer shared a secret, so he had lost a handy method of persuasion. His position of control over her was slowly crumbling away. This was galling enough on its own, but coupled with the stress of running the farm and the knowledge that several of his high-risk investments had gone south, it was a nightmare situation. The Bank of Mary was in danger of running dry just when he needed it most.

The whole situation – Mary, the meeting with Bobby, his financial precariousness – was causing him deep anxiety and coming between him and his sleep. At night, he lay awake, obsessively mulling it all over in his head, adding exhaustion to his list of grievances against his ex-lover.

Eventually, he had turned to his GP, Dr Ivor Hanrahan, for help and a listening ear. In a consultation with Dr Hanrahan in September 2010, Pat mentioned a number of work- and finance-related stresses that were causing him to have difficulty sleeping. He didn't mention anything about his illicit affair with Mary Lowry and how it had unravelled. Dr Hanrahan suggested medication, but Pat wasn't keen on the idea, so his doctor referred him to a counsellor.

Around mid-September, Dr Hanrahan received a phone call from the counsellor who had been working with Pat. As a result of that conversation, the GP prescribed mirtazapine, which is an antidepressant, although in this case it was prescribed primarily to help Pat's sleep, which was still disturbed.

This was the private face of Pat, though, the side no one ever saw. On the surface, it was business as usual. That same month, from 13 to 15 September, Pat was in Warsaw checking on the progress of the Bliski building with some of his fellow investors. While there, he met with the letting agents, who informed him that there was some difficulty getting a tenant for 410 square metres of empty space in the building. It had been empty for twenty months, costing everyone money. Separately, while he was there, a new lease was negotiated with the main tenant in the building, to rent 70 per cent of the property until January 2017. The rental market in Warsaw was slow at the time and Pat and his fellow directors didn't want to run the risk of having a vacant building, so they entered a deal for a lower-than-expected rent from the tenant. The move resulted in a significant depletion of the cash reserves available to the property syndicate. The long-term plan remained to sell the building for a profit at a later date, but Pat knew that accepting a lower rent on the building would affect the selling price over the next few years.

Towards the end of 2010 and into January 2011, Dr Hanrahan had a series of phone calls with his patient. Pat was deriving minimal benefit from the medication and remained upset and distressed. He told the GP that there were a number of issues bothering him, but that he did not want to elaborate on them. Dr Hanrahan suggested a face-to-face meeting, which Pat attended on 3 February 2011.

During that consultation, Pat revealed that he had been having an affair, but asked the GP not to document it on his file.

'We discussed the issue at some length and by that time he was not taking medication any more,' Dr Hanrahan later said. 'I don't think it had helped him too much and we just discussed the impact it had on mental health and well-being. He said the affair was with Mary Lowry, who was his wife Imelda's sister-in-law.' The doctor learned that the affair had ended because Mary was seeing someone else and that Pat was 'quite hurt and upset that she had become involved with someone [else]'. He believed Pat was suffering from an adjustment disorder, stemming from stress. An adjustment disorder is a group of mental health symptoms, such as stress, feeling sad or hopeless, and associated physical symptoms and can occur as a direct consequence of a significant life event. He was prescribed sedative antidepressants to help him sleep, although he was not diagnosed with depression.

Pat had alluded to his fragile mental state to Mary. At one stage, he texted Mary and told her that he felt like driving his car into a ditch when on the way home from a tennis match.

'Obviously I was concerned,' Mary would later say. 'I wouldn't be a human being if I wasn't concerned.'

In the same text, Pat told her he wouldn't bother her any more and that he was finished.

'I was extremely worried about this text,' Mary said. 'I felt he was very down and was maybe going to commit suicide. I showed the text to Bobby and he was the same.'

Mary knew her ex-lover wasn't dealing with the break-up very well and did her best to ease the fallout caused by the end of the affair by remaining on friendly terms with him. He was still very much part of her life, through their family ties and his daily presence at her farm. He normally arrived at Fawnagowan around 10 a.m. and tended to his dry stock for a few hours before returning to his own farm in Breansha. Given this proximity and their long family history, even as she moved on with Bobby, Mary also listened to Pat and tried to support him, thinking he would eventually move beyond his downheartedness and leave their shared past behind.

But Pat's feelings about Mary's new relationship were running high and, unknown to her, he was more intent than ever on calling a halt to her new-found romance with Bobby Ryan. He made a decision then that would reveal to Mary the shocking true extent of his bitterness and show her, in no uncertain terms, just how misleading his reaction to the meeting with her and Bobby had been.

On 4 February, the day after meeting his GP, Pat made a phone call to the Health Service Executive (HSE). He requested to speak to the Social Work Department. Deirdre Caverley, a qualified social worker who worked for the South Tipperary Social Work Department, took the call. She listened as Pat disparaged Mary Lowry as a mother. He told Caverley that Mary's children were being left unsupervised for long periods of time, between the hours of 4 p.m. and the early hours of the morning, usually at the weekend. He said this had been going on for about three months and was down to the fact that Mary had 'lost the run of herself' and become fixated on an intimate relationship. He said that Mary 'had recently entered into a new relationship' and was spending time with her boyfriend while her children were alone in the house. Mary was 'failing to take into account the emotional needs of her three children,' he added, expressing concern for the 'well-being and safety' of Mary's three boys.

He said that the 'wider paternal family' were also concerned about her children, but they were afraid to confront her about what was going on for 'fear of repercussions'. In particular, he said that her mother-in-law, Rita, was very worried about the welfare of her grandchildren. The social worker suggested to Pat that Mary might be using childcare while she was away and asked whether their grandmother could be looking after them. Pat told her that Rita was not asked to look after the children.

These were serious allegations of neglect. Whether he had properly thought through all the possible consequences or not, Pat was certainly hitting Mary where it would hurt by calling into question her mothering, her priorities and her devotion to her children. It was an allegation that could not be ignored. Ms Caverley advised him that given the fact that the alleged neglect was taking place at the weekend, when the Social Work Department was closed, he should contact the gardaí if he had urgent concerns about the children's welfare. She then told him that she would follow up the call by opening up a report and carrying out an assessment. At no point in this conversation did Pat divulge his relationship with Mary, or the fact that the 'new relationship' was one that she had chosen over him.

After this phone conversation, on 10 February Ms Caverley made an unannounced visit to the Lowry home. There was no one present in the house, no car in the drive and she met an individual on the property who did not identify himself.

'I asked [him] was Mary Lowry at home,' she said later. 'He said she was not and provided no indication of when she would return.'

Following this visit to Fawnagowan, Ms Caverley phoned Pat to tell him that the unannounced visit was unsuccessful. She told him it was a long drive from her office in Clonmel, County Tipperary, and asked him for advice on when would be the best time to make a return visit. Pat suggested she should call after 4 p.m. as the children would be home from school and Mary did volunteer work during the day.

Ten days after the original phone call, Mary received a formal letter from social services claiming they had received a report alleging that she was not taking care of her children properly. As if Pat had planned it, the letter arrived on St Valentine's Day.

'I can't tell you the shock and surprise I got,' Mary said later about the incident.

Mary called the department that day and made an appointment to meet one of the social workers. They visited the house and spoke to her in person. Ultimately, social services found nothing untoward going on in the Lowry home.

'Everything was cleared up,' Mary later said.

Nevertheless, in his second attempt to scuttle her relationship with Bobby, Pat had knowingly crossed the line. This was a betrayal. He knew that Mary would protect her children at all cost. He also knew that Bobby stood no chance if the HSE got involved and Mary had to choose between him and her children.

After she got over the initial shock of the letter, Mary immediately felt that Pat must be behind the complaint: 'I blamed Pat Quirke for it.' She confronted him outright. He denied all knowledge of it. He would later say that he was 'afraid of what she would do. I was afraid of how angry she would be.'

The incident with social services had a devastating impact

on Mary. She was living in a community where a small section of people believed that a young widow should behave in a certain way. Mary wasn't adhering to the rules by their standards and, long before the call to social services, judgement was being cast on her behaviour. It was a case of small-town thinking, but in rural, land-owning Tipperary, the widow Mary belonged at home on the farm, not out dancing and enjoying herself and moving on with her life.

Pat, of course, knew all of this and was more than happy to add fuel to the fire. In the cruellest way possible, he had added to her growing sense of insecurity as a single mother.

She told Bobby about what had happened and tried to put it aside but one night when they were out dancing, she ended up crying about it in the ladies' toilets. Bobby sent a friend in to comfort her. From that point on, any time Mary needed to pop out in the evening, Bobby was on hand to mind the boys.

Meanwhile, Pat had confided in someone else about his inner turmoil. After all, Mary had Bobby to talk to and even though he had told his GP about the affair, he hadn't been completely honest about his thwarted love. His next step might seem unusual for a middle-aged man: he wrote a letter to the *Sunday Independent*'s resident agony aunt, Patricia Redlich. Of course, his mother had no qualms about writing to newspapers or phoning radio talk shows to raise personal issues publicly, so it might have seemed a very logical step to her son to seek help in this manner. There was likely another agenda at work here too. Pat knew that Mary liked to read the problem pages in the Sunday newspapers. She bought the *Sunday Independent* religiously every week. Therefore it was highly likely that the target of his emotional outpouring would read it herself. It's hard to know what outcome he hoped this might provoke, especially coming after his HSE stunt. It suggests that at this stage Pat was losing his grip on the situation, scrabbling about desperately for the thing that might bring about a change in Mary's thinking. His desperation is clear in the fact that he thought a letter to a problem page would be that thing.

Pat's letter appeared on the 'Dear Patricia' page in the *Sunday Independent* on 20 February 2011. It gave a fascinating insight into the mind of Pat Quirke and into his interpretation of events:

I've made a right mess of my life and I need help on how to go forward. It all started four years ago, when my best friend died. This man was also my wife's cousin and a close family friend. He left a wife and a young family after him.

I coped by throwing myself into doing all I could for my friend's wife and children. There was much sorting out to do in relation to his business. Unfortunately, this led to an affair with his wife, and I fell deeply in love with her. It lasted three years and came to an abrupt end recently when I found out that she was seeing someone else. When I confronted her, she claimed that she had fallen out of love with me and was waiting for an opportunity to end 'us'.

This was a defining moment for both of us. She no longer depended on me, and quickly forgot about me by putting all her energy into developing this new relationship. This man promised everything that I couldn't. She introduced him to everyone in the family, including my wife, and they were all delighted that she had found love again.

My problem is that I am broken-hearted and angry at how well things have worked out for her, despite her lying and cheating on me. We meet on a constant basis as we have a business connection as well as the family connection. She refuses to discuss our affair and says it is in the past. She has confessed it to her new lover, while I have no closure and am forced to carry this dark secret alone. I now feel a tremendous amount of grief, and shame, for a lost love – and am possibly suffering postponed grief for a dead friend – all in silence.

I know I have done wrong and let my wife down badly. I contemplated telling her, but feel it would do nothing to relieve my burden while it would devastate her.

I have been diagnosed with depression, but none of the medication is working. My wife has been a tremendous support and loves me deeply. Ironically, this almost makes things worse.

Unfortunately, while I love [my wife], I am not in love with her. I'm still in love with my ex-lover even though I accept that the affair is over. I wish I wasn't, and wish I could transfer the feelings I have for her back to my wife. How do I begin to rebuild my life?

In her reply, Patricia Redlich didn't have much time for Pat's complaints. He had painted himself as the victim in his letter, but if he thought he would illicit any sympathy, he was very wrong. The agony aunt responded in strong terms, calling out his self-pity without qualm:

You could begin by ditching the self-pity. Don't you know the most basic rule in life, namely that the wrong-doer doesn't get the luxury of saying he's having a hard time? And he most certainly can't feel sorry for himself.

You chose to have an affair. It's gone south. Tough.

And that's letting you off lightly. We could tell this story differently. You made a move on a newly widowed woman, who not only saw you as a support because you were her husband's friend, but who also depended on you for business reasons. She was vulnerable.

Even if she made the first move, a kind man would have sidestepped, allowing her time to get back on her feet.

A married man with any decency would definitely have backed away.

It could be argued, in short, that you've broken faith with two women. Not to mention the fact that all of this is effectively happening within the family, so very definitely in your own backyard. Not nice.

There's something else you apparently don't understand. As her married lover, you had no claim on this woman at all. She didn't cheat on you. She simply found someone else. Just as you hung on to someone else, namely your wife.

. . . The really troubling thing is that you are so self-absorbed. Not to mention the fact that even now you're failing to take responsibility for your own actions.

You say you unfortunately had an affair, as if it were entirely beyond your control.

And while you mention shame, it doesn't ring true, to be brutally honest.

Sometimes happiness is simply a question of taking stock. And then being grateful for what life has given you.

You're getting a second chance, an opportunity to make good.

Pat didn't include his name with the letter, but it was close enough to the truth for it to be easy enough to figure it out. The *Sunday Independent* has a wide circulation in Ireland, so it wasn't the quietest way of seeking out professional advice. From the outside, it looked like a ploy to let Mary know that he was heartbroken, but that he was also capable of outing her and letting her suffer the consequences.

That Sunday, Mary settled down to read the paper as usual. When she began to read Patricia Redlich's page, she recognized the details of the problem immediately.

'I couldn't believe it was so similar to my story,' she would later say. 'I knew who it was, I thought, I know who wrote this. Pat Quirke.'

She was angry. She contacted Pat and asked him if he had written it. 'I asked him the next day because I was fuming. I was very cross about this. I asked did he write it and he admitted he did. He said he had nobody to turn to and that I had just dumped him.'

Mary asked him if Imelda had seen it and he said no, that he had removed the supplement from the paper before she had a chance to read it.

For Mary, this was a further shock and she was starting to see that he just wasn't going to let go. He had spoken fine words of reconciliation in Thurles, but the day-to-day reality for her was very different. He was on her farm every day, an irritating presence, he had made a false allegation against her to the authorities and now was parading their sorry secret in the Sunday papers. It was worrying behaviour. Furthermore, his physical presence around the farm and house was becoming claustrophobic, with that same sense of a man unhinged and unpredictable. He was always in the background, lurking, waiting for an opportunity to sabotage her relationship with Bobby.

Mary wasn't the only one who was starting to realize that Pat's behaviour wasn't normal, even if other people had no clue about the cause of it. Eddie and Mary saw each other most weekends, getting the cousins together for a play. He also helped his sister with various jobs around the house, including putting in a new en-suite bedroom and installing a drainage system. While tending to these various projects, he often saw Pat about the place. On one occasion when he bumped into him, after the HSE incident, Eddie tackled him about it. He told Pat that 'someone hadn't much to do' if they had time to make a bogus report against Mary. Pat appeared unperturbed by the comments and didn't bother responding. Eddie knew full well that Pat had no time for Mary's new boyfriend because Pat had made that very clear. He told Eddie that Bobby was 'a man for the women' and stayed out late at night and that he should talk some sense into his sister.

Eddie responded by saying, 'You know Mary as good as I do. Mary will make up her own mind what she wants to do and you or I won't change that.'

Pat's attempts at turning Mary's closest brother against Bobby and their relationship didn't work. Eddie was happy to see his sister getting on with life, especially after all she had gone through after Martin died. He had no issue with Mary and Bobby Ryan.

By this stage, Mary and Bobby were in a full-blown relationship. The courtship was well-known about the place and they were being invited to events as a couple. They were having a good time and, as she would later put it, 'she loved him to bits'. She did her best to ignore Pat's remarks and possessive behaviour, choosing to focus instead on her future with Bobby. That was all that mattered now. The affair with Pat belonged in the past and she was eager to distance herself from it and move into a better time.

The tie that continued to bind Pat to Mary and, unfortunately for her, Mary to Pat was money. It's not clear how much Mary knew about his financial situation, but at this time his money problems were becoming a burning issue. His investments were crashing and, according to one co-investor, he had racked up losses amounting to hundreds of thousands of euros. He was under pressure and he could see only one solution: Mary and her money.

Even though they were no longer lovers, he still repeatedly asked Mary for money. In one text, sent in early 2011, he said that the financial situation he was in was 'detrimental' and that he really needed the cash.

'He said [in the text] that he really needed this money and was I going to give it to him or not,' Mary recalled. 'I got the option [to reply] yes or no. I said no.'

Sometime in 2011, his demands for compensation over the BVD-infected animals culminated in an unsettling incident.

'One day we were in the kitchen discussing it,' Mary said. 'I refused again, and he pushed me against the table. My three children were in the sitting room. There was nobody else in the kitchen. My children ran out to see what happened. I said I was fine. I didn't fall . . . I just got a shock.'

Pat apologized the next day. He would later deny the incident ever happened.

Mary's eyes were fully open now. She had been blinded by grief before, but time and her new relationship with Bobby had reminded her of what she did and didn't want. Bobby provided her with something her clandestine relationship with Pat could not – a conventional, open, normal, loving relationship. She had been tolerant of Pat's behaviour at the start, but now she had had enough of him making her feel awkward at family gatherings and badmouthing her to her family. She had put his nasty ways down to heartbreak, but he was a grown man and he was taking it too far and for too long now. Mary began to fight back silently.

Unbeknownst to Pat, she went to her solicitor and changed her will. In the event of her death, her children would be entrusted into the care of her brother Eddie. The earlier provision, the one that had bequeathed €100,000 to her ex-lover, was removed. Mary Lowry had hoped this would all blow over, but now she realized that might not happen. Pat's possessiveness and his financial woes made him a sinister presence in her life. But if he felt he knew her weak spot, she certainly knew his: his need for her money. It was time for Mary Lowry to take a stand against Pat Quirke.

5. Save the last dance for me

The love affair between Mary Lowry and Bobby Ryan was now public knowledge, but it wasn't a relationship that always ran smoothly. By her own admission she was mad about Bobby, but that didn't mean they didn't argue or fall out. Mary had an impulsive streak and a temper that could combine to create a stormy atmosphere. Laidback, easy-going Bobby was sometimes caught up in the turbulence of her moods, trying to ride it out as best he could.

There was an event coming up that month that Mary had her heart set on attending. It was a performance by The Indians, a country showband Mary loved. She had seen them perform many times before, and now they were doing a 'dancing show break' to celebrate forty years in the music business. The celebration concert would take place in the Allingham Arms Hotel in Bundoran, County Donegal, known as the showband capital when it came to venues. The hotel was offering a number of deals, including a one-, two- or three-night stay at the hotel with dinner one night and entry to the weekend dances thrown in. It coincided with Mary's forty-fifth birthday, and the only gift she wanted was a weekend of romance with Bobby, dancing to the raucous beat of The Indians in the beautiful coastal setting of Bundoran.

Mary spent a lot of time organizing the weekend, opting for the two-night package for the last weekend in May. She booked it but Bobby, as he always did, insisted on paying his half. She was keen for Bobby and her to spend time together as a couple, away from outside distractions and from the oppressive presence of Pat and his machinations against them. She couldn't wait for the final Friday in May to arrive, but a few days before that she had to endure one last inter-action with her scorned ex-lover.

On her birthday, 25 May, Mary went to Pat and Imelda's house with her three sons. One of the Quirke boys was mak-ing his Confirmation and there was a celebration at the family home in Breansha. During the gathering, Mary's sister-in-law asked her if she had any nice plans for the week-end. Mary, excited to be heading away with her boyfriend, told her that she and Bobby were off to Bundoran to cele-brate her birthday with some dancing. Everything was well out in the open when it came to Bobby and her in-laws at that stage and she had no problem being upfront with them. Just as in the Ballyglass Hotel, Pat was within hearing dis-tance, craning to hear Mary's response. She would later say that she felt uneasy and unwelcome in his house that day. She felt his behaviour was very strange and unfriendly and that he kept hovering in the background, trying to listen in on her conversations. He later told her she looked so lovely in the dress she was wearing that he couldn't talk to her.

Two days after the Confirmation party in Breansha, Mary was finally able to escape Pat when she and Bobby packed the car and set off for Donegal. Bobby had taken the Friday off work and had asked his boss at the quarry, Niall Quinn, for an advance on his wages.

While Mary was looking forward to a romantic weekend away with her boyfriend, Bobby unwittingly nearly scotched her plans when he invited his former girlfriend, Mary Glasheen, to join them on the trip.

The two Marys had been in each other's company several

times before, including an occasion in the Times Hotel when they seemed to have got off on the wrong foot. Bobby was out with his new girlfriend that night when he took to the floor with his ex. Afterwards, Mary Lowry passed a comment that she knew Mary Glasheen was present because she heard her laughing. Mary Glasheen thought it a bit of a bitchy comment. She was aware that she had a loud laugh but felt that Mary was cutting at her.

Just before Christmas 2010, Bobby moved out of the house he was renting in Cashel to a new house in Boherlahane. Michelle helped her father to decorate and furnish his new home, and Mary Glasheen bought him a mirror as a housewarming gift.

Bobby wanted the women in his life to get on, so in an effort to forge some sort of friendship between them, he organized a night out shortly after he moved into the new house. He was DJing in Fox's and rang Mary Glasheen to ask her to come along, that Mary Lowry was going and it would be good fun. When Mary Glasheen said no, he told her that Mary Lowry wanted her to go, so she went. Bobby picked up Mary Glasheen at her house in Tipperary town before going to collect the other Mary in Fawnagowan. The two women sat side by side in the pub that night as Bobby entertained the local crowd, and after he was finished, himself and the two Marys went back to his house for a few drinks. Mary Glasheen ended up sleeping on the sofa while Bobby and Mary slept upstairs.

Luckily for Bobby, given Mary's ideas about their weekend away, Mary Glasheen politely declined his suggestion that she accompany them to Bundoran. She later admitted that she might have considered going along if someone else was going too, but she didn't want to be the only person with a couple.

So Mary and Bobby set off alone for Donegal on the Friday, with her driving and Bobby in the passenger seat giving her directions. He knew most of the roads in Ireland from his trucking and was the man who knew where to go, as she would later put it.

It was a long drive, almost five hours from Tipperary town, but it gave them an opportunity to chat. They both loved dancing, loved The Indians and were looking forward to the days ahead. For Mary, after nine months together it was a chance for them to get to know each other better. Up until then, when they were out together, usually at dances around Tipperary, there were always people they knew about. Bobby seemed to know everyone and would always engage in lively chat or a bit of banter, leaving Mary to feel like they were never alone. Now that she finally had him to herself, she wasn't going to waste a minute of their time together.

After arriving at the hotel and checking into their room, they went for something to eat before kicking off the weekend with night one of The Indians. The Allingham Hotel was packed to the rafters with showband revellers for this ruby anniversary of the band, and they responded enthusiastically as the band kicked off their set. The heaving crowds of women closest to the stage swayed from side to side, their hands flailing in the air as they screamed out the lyrics. Sticky beads of sweat had glued their clothes to their skin and as they frantically tried to fan air under their blouses, the opening chords of 'Wigwam Wiggle' sent them into hysterics.

The Indians were one of the country's leading showbands, and for diehard fans of the social dancing scene it promised to be a night of unrivalled nostalgia. The group, formerly known as The Casino Band, were famed for their Native

American costumes, which complemented their country and western songs, as well as their equally apt stage names.

Since the 1970s the group's lead singer, known as The Chief of the Indians, had changed five times. The original Chief was Flaming Star, Noel Brady, who was succeeded by Rising Son, Paul Brady. In 1999, Golden Eagle, Kevin Kearney, took over. From 2002 to 2006 it was White Cloud, Stephen Proctor, on vocals, and then the reigning Chief, Geronimo, Raymond Kelly, took over the mic. To mark the ruby anniversary, all five incarnations of The Chief were appearing together on stage.

On guitar that night in Bundoran was Dull Knife, aka Tommy Hopkin, as well as the original drummer, Kevin McKeown, who was known as Long Arrow. On keyboard was Sitting Bull, Eamon Keane, while Crazy Horse, Brian Woodful, was on bass. Dressed in full eagle feather headdress and mock-buckskin fringed coats they strutted the stage, belting out the favourites with their faces covered in warpaint. They played all the classics, songs like 'Running Bear' and 'We're Just Indians', as well as a few covers like 'Can't Help Falling in Love' and 'Save the Last Dance for Me'.

Mary and Bobby had a fantastic night. Their romance had started in the ballroom of the Times Hotel and so it continued as they twirled around the dancefloor to the chants of The Indians. It was exactly as Mary had hoped it would be – romantic and, most of all, great fun. The jive had become their signature dance, and that night they performed it to perfection. They could never have known that they had just danced their last dance together as a couple.

On Saturday morning, Bobby complained of feeling unwell. They went for a walk along the beach to help clear his head. Later on, they were in the hotel, getting ready for night two with The Indians. It wasn't shaping up to be the same great fun as the previous night. By the time the doors had opened and it was time to dance, Bobby was still feeling unwell and said he didn't feel up to dancing. Mary was in great form and didn't want to be an onlooker for the night, so she asked him if it was okay for her to take to the dancefloor with someone else. Bobby was happy for her to go off and have a dance. When Mary returned to their table, she found Bobby chatting to another woman and flew into a rage.

'I wasn't at all pleased,' she would later say. 'I was disappointed he chose to talk to somebody else for what seemed like hours.'

During an almighty row that she would later admit was a complete misunderstanding, Mary argued with Bobby for the duration of the five-hour journey back to Tipperary the next day. 'I gave out to him the whole way back from Bundoran. His ears must have been fairly reddened.'

Bobby later told a friend that he had been 'mortified' by Mary's behaviour on the dancefloor and that he couldn't believe she had reacted so badly: 'He wasn't happy at all about what happened. He told me it was a case of "all picture, no sound" the next day and that because she had driven them up there, he was stuck having to travel back to Tipperary with her.'

Mary later realized that Bobby was in fact talking to a woman who used to own a pub in Tipperary where he used to DJ. They had been catching up on old times when she'd returned to the table and got the wrong end of the stick.

After the explosive fallout and the exhausting arguing, Bobby said that he needed to give the relationship a break and they decided to call it off for a time. It was certainly not the way Mary had expected the weekend to go. Later she would say that it was silly to be falling out over something so innocuous at their age. She realized that she had overreacted about what happened in the hotel and that 'Bobby was just being Bobby, just being friendly'. At the time, though, she was furious with him, and their romantic weekend ended their relationship.

On Monday morning, Bobby returned to work at Killough Quarry as normal. His boss, Niall Quinn, said he seemed to be in good form after the weekend away with Mary, giving no sign of how he and his girlfriend had fallen out. The next day, after work, Bobby went with his son, Robert, to Fox's pub, to pick up his DJ equipment. After several years playing in one pub, Bobby had decided to spread his wings and move on. He had ordered a brand new van, in black, and he planned to put a hitch on it so Robert could take his racing car to the hot rod races. Ever since he was a child, Robert had gone to the Rosegreen racetrack in Tipperary with his father to watch the rally car racing. It was here that Robbie developed a love of hot rod racing, a version of the NASCAR stock car racing so popular in the USA, with drivers competing on a quarter-mile oval track. As he got older, he bought his own car and often participated in local races.

Robert had never really talked to his father about Mary Lowry, but he sensed something bad had happened between them in Bundoran. He was there in his father's house in Boherlahane the day himself and Mary had returned, on the Sunday. Mary had driven them to Donegal, so she had to leave Bobby back home, even though they were no longer speaking. When they arrived at the house, Robert noticed the atmosphere between them. Mary didn't hang around.

When he later learned about the row, it fitted with his belief that Mary had a tendency to become jealous. For this very reason, Robert had made a point of not telling Mary whenever Mary Glasheen, with whom he remained friendly, called to the house to see his father. Robert, his partner, Leanne, and their baby daughter, Amy, who were living in Ovens, County Cork, often travelled up to stay with his father in Boherlahane. During those visits Robert noticed other things, like the fact that his father's phone would be 'hopping' with text messages in the evening, which he seemed 'pretty pissed off' about.

On another occasion Robert and Leanne were watching a match in the sitting room, while his father and Mary were in the kitchen. His father was coming in and out, watching bits of the match. He kept asking Mary to come in and watch it with them, but she wouldn't. Robert sensed something was off between them, but he didn't pry. On the Tuesday after the Bundoran trip, Bobby rang his daughter, Michelle, to tell her about what happened in Bundoran and to ask her honest opinion about his relationship with Mary Lowry. They had an open and frank discussion and Michelle, straight-talking and direct as ever, advised him to 'P45 her'. She had already cautioned him about getting involved with Mary Lowry after he told her about the three-way meeting at the Hayes Hotel. And now she reminded him of another run-in with Pat that had always troubled her.

Bobby was a huge Brendan Grace fan and had agreed to go to a gig he was doing in the Clonmel Park Hotel after Mary said she had heard an advertisement for tickets on Tipp FM. According to Pat Quirke, he suggested to Mary that it would be good for him and Imelda to go along too, to help promote harmony between all parties. The gig was on 20 January, just a few weeks after the meeting in the Hayes Hotel. Pat would later say that Mary and Bobby already had tickets, so himself and Imelda bought theirs at the door.

According to him, when the Quirkes arrived inside the venue, Mary and Bobby had kept them two seats.

Mary's version is somewhat different. She said that one day on the farm Pat seemed very down, so she suggested he take Imelda to a dance or a show. Separately, she had booked tickets for herself and Bobby to go to see Brendan Grace and when they arrived into the show that night, Imelda and Pat were at the same show, with seats directly behind them.

'I don't know how that happened,' she said, remembering the evening as 'very awkward'. During the interval she introduced Bobby to Imelda. Her sister-in-law and her boyfriend chatted happily to each other. Bobby and Pat talked too, and Mary 'thought everything was fine'. But when Imelda and Mary were at the bar getting drinks, Pat leaned over to Bobby and issued a stark warning: 'Stay away from Mary.'

Bobby had told Michelle about the confrontation. He said he wasn't aware that Pat was even going to be there until that night and that he didn't feel comfortable around him at all. He had also told Mary that what happened at Brendan Grace was never to happen again. He did not want to be in Pat's company. Now, after hearing about Bundoran and telling him what she thought he should do, Michelle was relieved as she believed the relationship with Mary was over for good. That was a good outcome for her father, as far as she was concerned.

The news that Bobby and Mary were no longer an item wasn't floating around for long before it became outdated. Michelle's relief was very short-lived, as it turned out. Even though they had agreed to give things a break and not see each other, Bobby and Mary did talk to each other and decided that they didn't want to be apart. The argument in

Bundoran was pushed into the past and a line drawn under it. Bobby, it seemed, had put Michelle's advice to one side. He and Mary would forget it and start again.

Later, on Tuesday night, the Mr Moonlight van travelled the backroads towards Fawnagowan, where Mary was waiting. They'd make up, pick up where they left off and all would be well again.

6. The short goodbye

On Thursday, 2 June, it was Robert Ryan's birthday. He planned to spend the day with a friend, out with his racing car at New Inn, a nearby village, and he set off in the early afternoon. He spoke to his father a few times on the phone that day and Bobby asked him to cut the lawn. Bobby suffered from entomophobia, an irrational fear of insects, and couldn't bear to be in an environment that might bring him into contact with any creepy-crawlies. It was a source of amusement for his children, who often teased him that he had the nerves of a small child.

Leanne, Robert's partner, was in the house that evening when Bobby came home from work at about 5.30 p.m. It had been an extremely hot day, so he changed out of his work clothes, leaving his boots at the bottom of the stairs, and went upstairs for a shower to freshen up. When he came back down, he cooked something to eat and then played on the floor for a while with Amy, as he always did when he came in from a day in the truck. He was known affectionately as 'Grandad Bob' to his grandchildren, and he found great enjoyment in spending time with them.

Leanne would later describe how his phone, which was charging in the living room, was 'going off and off and off' and he was 'kind of giving out' because he had to repeatedly go over to check it. After watching the soap operas with her on the sofa he left the house at 9 p.m., saying, 'I'd better go across and see what's wrong with her', and asking Leanne if she would be okay on her own in the house. Phone records would later show that Mary sent Bobby just two texts that evening. Records also showed that he contacted Mary Glasheen at 6 p.m. Mary worked as a cleaning lady in a school and told him that she was helping out with the refreshments at a graduation Mass that night. She said she would be home at about 9.30 or 10 p.m. He told her that he was going up to Mary Lowry's and might call into her house afterwards. Mary Glasheen texted him later, at 10 p.m., to say that she was finished work and was at home, but he never replied, which she found unusual.

After he left Leanne and Amy at the house, Bobby hopped into his Mr Moonlight van, still loaded with his DJ equipment from Fox's pub, and made the thirty-minute journey from Boherlahane to Fawnagowan. The likely route he took that evening, the one that he always took, led past the shadow of the Rock of Cashel, through familiar country roads into Golden and Bansha, and finally up the long, steep lane that brought him on to Mary's farm.

He parked, as he always did, in the farmyard area behind the sheds at the back of the house, where Rita wouldn't see his van. Rita was out playing cards in the Ballyglass Hotel that evening and while she knew all about the relationship at that stage, Bobby still stuck to the old routine.

As he made his way towards the house, dressed in a navy tracksuit and white runners, he had his phone pressed to his ear, although phone records would later show that he didn't speak to anyone at that time. Perhaps the person he was trying to call didn't pick up. Bobby walked into the Lowry house at about 9.30 p.m., where Mary was with two of her boys. The eldest lad had gone to a friend's house in nearby Galbally after school and was staying the night there. She jokingly remarked on his clothes, 'You look snazzy tonight', before they both sat down to a cup of tea.

After spending some time chatting and listening to music, the couple decided to go to bed around 11 p.m. The heat of the day had left Bobby exhausted, having spent the day in the truck with no air conditioning. He asked Mary to put his black Nokia phone on the charger and set his alarm for 6 a.m. He had an early start the next morning because he had a long journey to make in the truck. With another balmy night ahead, Mary opened the window in the adjoining en-suite in an attempt to ventilate the room. Bobby took off his clothes, dropped them on the floor as he always did and slid under the purple sheets of Mary's bed.

Rita returned home at 11.30 p.m. and went to bed, like Mary opening a window to get some relief from the warm night air.

Back in Boherlahane, it was 11.30 p.m. by the time Robert got home. His father was not at the house and his van was gone, so he assumed he had gone over to Mary's house. He would catch up with him the next day, no doubt.

As darkness descended on Fawnagowan, everyone inside the houses was in bed and asleep by midnight.

Someone else was celebrating their birthday that day. In Breanshamore, Imelda Quirke woke up on Thursday morning to her forty-second birthday. She was getting a very special gift from her husband. Pat usually wouldn't go away at this time as it was one of the busiest periods in the farming calendar, but this year he had made an exception and booked them a two-night stay in the five-star Heritage Hotel in County Laois to celebrate her birthday. They would be going the following day, Friday, and returning on Sunday. The package, which cost €641, was booked on 8 May. It was a surprise trip, although, as Pat would later say, Imelda knew they were going away somewhere but she didn't know where.

Earlier that day, Patrick O'Donnell, who worked as a contractor baling silage and spreading slurry on Pat Quirke's lands, had cut grass and baled silage at both Pat's home farm in Breansha and at Fawnagowan. The subject of bales, namely 10–15 bales that were seen wrapped in plastic on Mary Lowry's farm in the days that followed, would later come into sharp focus.

On Thursday evening at around 8 p.m., Pat set off on the forty-minute journey to the Horse & Jockey Hotel, located in the village of Horse and Jockey, to attend a meeting about one of his doomed investment schemes in Poland. Through Property Strategies BV, a holding company formed in the Netherlands, Pat and about thirty-five other farmers, including the late Martin Lowry, had invested funds in purchasing a commercial property in Poland. Cirrus, a ten-storey office tower on Rzymowskiego St in the Mokotów business district of Warsaw, had been purchased for €31 million in 2006. Pat was a paid director of Property Strategies BV and had personally put €100,000 into the Cirrus scheme.

The meeting at the Horse & Jockey, which was described as 'heated', had been called to discuss how the property in Mokotów was being handled. The investors congregated in one of the hotel's meeting rooms, where chairs were arranged in rows, with an aisle dividing the room into two sections. Henry Walsh, a farmer from Oranmore in County Galway, and Michael Healy, from Thurles, were seated at the top table. The two men had shareholder representative roles in various projects in which the syndicate was involved. The group would normally meet in Limerick and this was the first time the meeting, which began at around 8.15 p.m., had been held in the Horse & Jockey Hotel. It was also the first time Michael Healy had chaired a meeting. Pat Quirke arrived late, at about 8.40 p.m., according to others who were there.

'A shareholder revolt was called in the Horse & Jockey Hotel in Tipperary,' said one of the investors who was present at the meeting. 'Michael Healy called it to get support to get [Cirrus] up for sale. There was huge anger and support for Michael and outrage at another shareholder who wanted to hold on to the investment. Pat swept into the meeting, as he does, whether or not it was deliberate, but it was like, *Do you all see me, lads?* He sat up near the front. We were sitting in lines of chairs like at a school concert, facing forward. Pat sat facing out on to the aisle, as was his habit.'

Pat waited until the end before he decided to speak. He told the group that they should have listened to his advice in the past with regard to the investment. By the time the discussion concluded, the decision was taken to sell the building. Cirrus was eventually sold in 2014 to a Polish commercial real estate company, Adgar, and renamed the Adgar Wave. Pat eventually lost just under €50,000 on the original €100,000 he had invested in the project.

After the meeting concluded at around 10 p.m., some of the shareholders went into the bar for a few drinks. Pat stayed behind and chatted to Henry for about an hour before the two men eventually went their separate ways.

Pat's drive home in his Volkswagen Passat took him from the village of Horse and Jockey to Cashel and then on to Tipperary town and back to Breansha. When asked about this later, he reckoned it could have been 11.30 p.m. when he left the hotel and made the forty-minute journey home. He hadn't seen Mary that day because, as he put it, they weren't getting on at the time and would not have had reason to meet.

When he arrived back at his home farm in Breansha, Imelda, whom he described as being a night person, was in bed but awake. He would later say that he presumed they talked about the shareholder meeting before going to sleep, getting their rest to be fresh and ready for their departure the next day for their weekend trip.

As the hands of the clock crept past midnight, the temperature was building towards a day that would see the mercury hit record levels. The night air, stale and sticky, hung in a humid cloud over the hills of the Golden Vale. It was now Friday, 3 June – a day no one in Fawnagowan or Breansha would ever forget.

7. Friday, 3 June 2011

Bobby Ryan crept quietly out of Mary Lowry's house just as the morning sun began to burn the edges of the surrounding farmland at Fawnagowan, sending up a heat shimmer that blurred the green horizon. As he pushed his way through the door of Mary's bungalow, stepping outside into the muggy, motionless air, the early-morning sun warmed his shoulders. It was to be the hottest day of the year, with temperatures reaching 26 degrees Celsius in some parts of the country and record sunshine hours clocked in others. The smell of summer, mixed with the familiar odours of the farm, greeted him – the sweet, perfumed scent of fresh hay and the evocative aroma of newly opened blossoms, infused with a waft of manure and the pungent stench of agricultural diesel.

Bobby was feeling relaxed and energized. He had woken earlier and made love to Mary, their disagreement from the previous weekend long forgotten. Then he had left his lover's bed, got dressed and left the house as silently as possible, so as not to disturb Mary's sleeping children.

As he walked towards his Mr Moonlight van, the loose gravel in the yard crunched loudly beneath his feet with each step. He crossed the driveway at the back of Mary's house and made his way towards the farmyard, where the van was parked. On his right, he passed a lush green playing field where Mary's boys had two sets of goalposts and, on the left, an aged aluminium storehouse sometimes used for drying clothes.

It was a new day. There was a smell of growth, of a newness that only summer brings and a sense that the months ahead held promise. He was one day's work away from the June bank holiday weekend and the weather looked set to hold up until Monday. Life, for a man who enjoyed its simple pleasures, was good.

Bobby walked towards his van, ready for the day ahead. Moments later, before he reached the driver's door, from behind he felt a thud to the back of his head. There were several more blows. He fell heavily to the ground.

Then, Bobby Ryan's world went black.

As always, Mary waited for the familiar sound of Bobby's silver Citroën Dispatch rattling over the cattle grille as he left her sprawling farm. He always left very early, so that her sons would not be aware that he had stayed the night. Whenever she heard the reassuring thud of van wheels crossing the metal barrier, she knew he had made his exit unnoticed. Mary could then relax.

But on 3 June 2011, as she lay in bed, Mary waited and waited for the tell-tale sound. It didn't come when she expected it. It was maybe seven to eight minutes longer than usual, she reckoned, before she eventually heard the van drive off.

Apart from the sound of Bobby's van clattering over the grille, there was no noise: no raised voices or cries for help, no sudden smack as each blow was dealt, no thud as a battered body hit the ground. Not a thing was heard by Rita through her open bedroom window or by Mary, lying in bed but wide awake. Just like any other day at Fawnagowan, there was nothing to be heard but the mundane, muted sounds of the animals outside in the fields and a house slowly stirring from slumber.

Earlier that morning, Mary had stretched out in bed and watched as Bobby got dressed. He had left his clothes on the floor the night before, as he always did. He was slow pulling on his navy tracksuit with the white stripe, his white runners and a heavy navy jumper. She remembered saying to him about the jumper: 'What are you doing with that?' as it had been 'a very warm few days'. He replied, 'It's the easiest way to carry it.'

It was around 7.45 a.m. when Mary eventually rose to make breakfast and prepare packed lunches for her boys. A short time later, at about 8.30 a.m., she looked out of the window and saw Pat Quirke's jeep passing up the driveway.

'Usually I wouldn't pay any heed, but when I saw his jeep, I thought, where's he going at this hour of the morning? It would be ten o'clock when he'd normally start.'

At around 8.45 a.m., Mary headed outside with her boys and her mother-in-law, Rita, who always took a lift to town on a Friday. As she loaded the children into the car for school, she noticed Pat nearby in the farmyard. He was wearing green overalls and looked very 'hot, sweaty and bothered'. They did not speak.

Mary headed off and dropped the boys at school and her mother-in-law at an appointment with her GP, then she returned home to Fawnagowan at 9.30 a.m. and sat outside to enjoy the peace and quiet of her surrounds in the heat of the morning sun.

Earlier that morning in Boherlahane, Robert had noticed that his father's work boots were still in the hallway. Leanne also noticed that his lunchbox was where he had left it in the kitchen the night before. The two of them laughed, assuming Bobby had got up late at Mary's and gone straight to work from there, without the essentials. He normally came home first and collected everything before heading to the quarry, but time must have got away from him this morning.

A short time later, Robert left Leanne at home with their young daughter and headed off to a friend's house. By the time he got back, Bobby's boss, Niall, had called to the house, wondering why his usually diligent and punctual employee had not shown up to drive his truck from the quarry that day.

Robert phoned his sister, Michelle, who was on her way to her aunt's house in Borrisoleigh, to find out if she had been speaking to their father. She had no idea of his whereabouts but guessed that he might have gone to the beach with Mary and her boys because it was such a beautiful day. She told her brother not to panic and tried her father's phone herself, but to no avail.

Robert felt in his bones that something wasn't quite right. There was no real reason for it, but he felt unsettled. He went straight to the quarry and saw for himself that his father's van wasn't there, then he sent Bobby a text at 10.44 a.m.: *Da, are you not working today?*

He never got an answer because the message never reached Bobby. Fifteen minutes earlier, Bobby's phone signal had pinged off a local mast before it was lost for ever. His phone would never be found.

After discovering that the Mr Moonlight van wasn't at Killough Quarry, alarm bells started to ring loudly for Bobby's two children. Michelle knew that if her father had indeed decided to take the day off, he would have told his boss so that someone else could drive his lorry. He had never and would never let Niall Quinn down. This was entirely out of character. What had happened that Bobby hadn't gone about his day as planned?

*

At Fawnagowan, at around 10.30 a.m., while Mary was still basking in the sun, she got a call from Michelle. Mary told her that Bobby had stayed over at Fawnagowan the previous night and left her house earlier that morning on his way to work. Michelle, distraught with worry, told her that she was reporting her father missing at Tipperary town garda station. Mary arranged to meet her there.

Before she could leave, Robert pulled into the Lowry farmyard, also looking for his father. He looked in his rear-view mirror and saw Mary, shaking and upset, approaching his car just as he reached one of the outbuildings. He rolled down his car window and when he asked her where his father was, she told him she didn't know. She asked him if they had searched the rivers or lakes. The reason she alluded to suicide, she would later say, was because Bobby had spoken to her before of being depressed and contemplating taking his own life. What Mary did not know was that although Michelle was aware of this side of Bobby, Robert was not.

Before driving off at speed, Robert immediately dismissed her suggestion, angered by the implication that his father might have done something to harm himself.

'Daddy never said anything to me about a fucking river,' he said.

He refused to give her his mobile number and said that if she heard anything, she was to contact Michelle. Then he pulled out of Fawnagowan, rattling over the cattle grille noisily, to continue his search for his father.

Once Michelle had established that Bobby wasn't at Mary Lowry's and wasn't at the quarry and wasn't answering his phone, she and her aunt, her mother's sister Ann Stapleton, started to search for him themselves. Michelle was too upset to drive, so Ann's husband, Liam, ferried them in Michelle's car from Borrisoleigh to Tipperary town.

Michelle couldn't explain why, but she had a feeling that her father was in a wood and she asked Liam to stop in Bishop's Wood, Dundrum, to check for Bobby's van. She had already called South Tipperary General Hospital in Clonmel to see if he was there and was told that he wasn't. By now, she was in a state of very real panic.

After they checked the wood and found nothing, Michelle was again overcome with an uneasy, sick feeling in her stomach. She asked Liam to take her to Tipperary town garda station straight away. They arrived there at lunchtime, and Michelle and Ann went inside together to report Bobby missing. There, they met Garda Thomas Neville, who would later say Michelle was in a 'very distressed state', and that Ann told him Michelle was concerned her father may have taken his own life. Michelle had been ringing and ringing her father's phone and knew it was out of character for him not to return her calls, especially if he thought she was in a panic. She was desperate to find out where he was.

After getting a description of Bobby and noting his last movements, Garda Neville created a 'missing-person high-risk' incident on the Garda PULSE system.

This action logged the incident nationwide. It formed the starting point for a record that would be kept in connection with Bobby's disappearance. Garda Neville took as many details as possible from Michelle, including a physical description of her father, his eye colour and build, approximate height and weight and details of what he was wearing when last seen. A description of his van, including the number plate, was also noted, as well as a list of places he frequented regularly. An alert was then given out divisionally, with details of Bobby's appearance and the van he was driving. It meant that if a garda on the beat stopped a vehicle matching the description of the one Bobby was driving, it would be flagged on the system as being associated with a missing person. The alert was put out to patrol cars all over Ireland.

That day, as officers came on duty in Tipperary town garda station, they were briefed about a missing person, who was categorized as high priority. There are different initial categories for people who are reported missing, and not all are considered high risk. People with special needs or highly vulnerable people are usually considered to be more at risk than others. In Bobby's case, the fact that he hadn't been seen since 6.30 a.m., that he hadn't shown up for work and that Ann and Michelle said there were concerns that he may have taken his own life automatically put him in the high-risk category. It was a bank holiday weekend, a period during which gardaí often deal with reports of missing persons. More often than not, they turn out to be cases of young people who didn't make it home after a night out, only to show up safe and sound some time later. But Bobby's disappearance didn't fit that category, either.

As Garda Neville input all of Bobby's details into the PULSE system, the first official step into the investigation of Bobby's disappearance had been taken. A picture of the missing DJ would later join the faces of the many missing people on the website of the National Missing Persons Bureau, where it would remain for twenty-two months.

After leaving the garda station, Michelle rang and spoke to Mary again, who suggested that she come out to Fawna-gowan in a bid to try and settle her. Michelle told her that they were on the way. En route to the farm, Michelle stopped in at Mary Glasheen's house in a nearby housing estate to see if Bobby was there. Mary Glasheen wasn't at home and there was no sign of the Mr Moonlight van.

Meanwhile, Mary Lowry guessed that Michelle might have gone to Mary Glasheen's house to check for Bobby. So, Mary Lowry drove over there, where she met Michelle, Ann and Liam. Bobby going missing like this was a bolt from the blue and it was clear Mary Lowry was upset and worried. She wanted Michelle to come to her house, 'just to calm down and see', she said to her.

Michelle could see that Mary was distraught, so she got into Mary's car and told Ann and Liam to follow behind. They weren't sure where the farm was, so it was easier to follow Mary. As they made the short three-mile journey from Tipperary town out to Fawnagowan, Michelle, once again overcome with a foreboding feeling that her father was in a wood, asked Mary if Bansha Wood was near her farm. She knew it was in the vicinity, but didn't know how close it was to Mary's place.

She kept saying, 'I think he's in a wood, I think he's in a wood', as Mary steered the car around the winding road from town. Such was the effect of her chant-like repeating of those words that Mary forgot to turn into her driveway. Instead, she continued on the N24 towards Bansha village and then kept on going, taking the right turn into Bansha Wood, known locally as Kilshane Wood.

As Mary's car descended through the entrance of the horseshoe-shaped car park, an amenity area for walkers using the local woodlands, the beaming early-afternoon sun faded from view. Tall stands of oak and long-needled pine trees loomed overhead, with only a few shards of sunlight breaking through the leafy canopy that shaded the ground below. It was under this twilight of hanging pine branches that Michelle spotted her father's silver van. Before Mary's car had even come to a standstill, she frantically jumped out, leaving Mary at the wheel in bewilderment.

Michelle ran across the car park, calling out 'Daddy' as she stumbled towards his van. She caught hold of the handle of the driver's side door and pulled it. The door opened. The van was unlocked. Inside, on the passenger seat, she noticed her father's driving licence and diary. She went to the back of the van, which was facing into the woods, and began shouting and screaming for her father.

There was no answer.

Mary, shocked at the unexpected sight of Bobby's van in the woods a mere two minutes from her house, had by now run to the back of the vehicle and pulled opened the rear doors. She saw Bobby's DJ equipment in the back, neatly stacked, waiting to be unloaded and used to deliver another great night out. She knew that Bobby would never leave his precious equipment in an unlocked van.

Meanwhile, Ann and Liam had pulled into the woods behind them. Like Michelle, when Ann saw the Mr Moonlight sticker emblazoned across the windscreen of the silver van in front, she knew straight away it belonged to Bobby. She had the number of Tipperary town garda station saved on her phone from earlier and she called now to let them know about the discovery.

Michelle went to the front of the van, climbed into the driver's seat and burst out crying with her head on the steering wheel. It was then that she noticed something very odd. She had driven her father's van many times and knew exactly how he left it when parked. The scene she found herself in was anything but familiar. The driver's seat wasn't in its normal position and neither was the rear-view mirror. As she placed her hand on the gear stick, she noticed that the van was in gear; Bobby always put it in neutral when he parked. And, like Mary, she knew well that he'd never leave his valuable disco kit in an unlocked van. Everything felt wrong and out of place and she knew in her gut that her father wasn't the last person behind the wheel, driving.

Grabbing her father's diary and clutching it tight to her chest, she ran off into the dense forest, screaming for him over and over and over again.

Garda Neville was on his way to Mary Lowry's home to investigate the newly opened missing-person inquiry when a message crackled through his patrol car radio to say that Bobby's van had been found at a car park leading into the nearby Kilshane Wood, so he drove there instead.

When he arrived, he found Mary and Michelle, the two women at the centre of Bobby's world, screaming for him all around the wood. Robert arrived a short time later, followed by what Mary would later describe as a blur of people who had come to help them search for Bobby. Among them were Mary's sister and brother, both upset for her and willing to do anything to help the search.

'It seemed like there was action straight away,' she would later say. 'The place just filled up. It seemed like minutes, but obviously it was more than minutes.'

They searched for hours in the silent wood, finding nothing. There was no clue whatsoever as to where Bobby might have gone after leaving the van.

As night fell and darkness enveloped the wood, Mary finally returned home to the farm at Fawnagowan. Bobby was gone, and no one could explain it. Her world, one that had seemed to be finally coming together in happiness, had taken on a sinister feeling that nothing could shake.

Breda O'Dwyer, an artificial-insemination (AI) technician from Annacarty, County Tipperary, had been working for Pat Quirke for over fifteen years. Like most of her clients, Pat was big into breeding. He got more money for the highest-yielding cows and it was all about producing the best milk.

Farmers would usually order the semen online, and when AI season started, around 20 April each year, Breda would go from farm to farm with straws of semen stored in nitrogen and administer it herself. Most farmers would request her to service cattle for six to eight weeks, so every day, after dropping her children to school, she worked out her route and drove to each client in turn. The majority had around a hundred cows, therefore expected to breed 20–25 replacement heifers for the following year. It was all about making money, Breda would later say. She carefully organized her route in advance to avoid zigzagging around the countryside and wasting diesel.

Pat was always the first or second farmer on her list and the time at which she would arrive at his farm each year never really varied. Breda had known Pat for years. He had gone to school with her sister and she had done some relief milking for him in the past. She had a well-established routine when it came to visiting his farm to inject his cows.

First and foremost, Pat wouldn't be there when she arrived. He would normally be cleaned up and gone, the machinery in the milking parlour would be switched off and the whole place would be spotless. In his absence, he would have left a Post-it note for her, detailing the number(s) of the cow(s) to be inseminated, the 'straw' (semen) that had to go into it and the date. It was a well-honed routine and Breda knew it off by heart.

On Friday, 3 June 2011, when Breda arrived at Pat's farm in Breansha at about 9.30 a.m., there was an immediate and notable change to their routine: inside the milking parlour, standing in the pit beneath the cows, she saw Pat in the process of milking. Her diary showed that she inseminated two heifers that day, a process that would have kept her on the farm for about fifteen minutes. When she left at around 9.45 a.m., Pat was still in the pit milking his cows, not off having breakfast at home, where he would usually be by then. Something, or someone, had made him late that morning.

When questioned later, Pat gave a different version of the morning's events from Breda O'Dwyer. According to him, on 3 June 2011 he got up at around 6.15 a.m. He could not be sure of the time because he never set an alarm nor checked the time. He had to collect the mobile calf-feeder from a nearby field, so he jumped on his quad and brought it up to the milking parlour to start the morning milking. He began milking his herd of 120 cows at around 7 a.m. and was almost finished when he got a text from Sean Dillon, Imelda's fourteen-year-old second cousin. Sean had been helping Pat on the farm since he was seven years old and received a bullock each year as payment for his labour. The only time he received financial reward for his time was three years later, in 2014, when he was seventeen, and Pat paid him €3,000 to cover the insurance on his car.

That morning, Sean texted Pat to say he wanted to bring in the haybales so Pat 'made use of him', as he would later phrase it, and told him to come down to the farm in Breansha. When he got there at about 8.30 a.m., Pat was on the second-last row of cows. He got Sean to take his place, leaving him free to go to Mary Lowry's farm to collect two bulls that he planned to leave with his cows over the weekend. He wanted to introduce the bulls while the cows were in the parlour rather than out in the fields. He used a cow box and a 4x4 to transport them from the shed at Fawnagowan to the milking parlour in his own farm. There were a number of routes from Pat's farm to Fawnagowan. The two most accessible were the narrow country road from the farm across Cordangon, which passed along a number of farms and fields. The other, over the Longford bridge, was a busier route along a main road that skirted around the edge of Tipperary town. Pat would later say that he travelled the route he normally did, over the Longford bridge, and not across Cordangon, to arrive at Mary's farm at about 8.45 a.m. There, he saw Mary Lowry getting into her car with the children.

'I didn't stop to talk because I was rushing,' he said. 'I was probably on the farm for twenty minutes because of the box. I wanted to get in and out fast.'

He took the same route, over the Longford bridge, as he travelled back to Breansha. He drove straight into the farmyard, dropped off the bulls and helped Sean finish milking the cows before washing down the parlour. The cows were put back in the paddock, with the bulls following. He then made his way to the house, where he ate breakfast at about 9.30 a.m., the time at which Breda said he was in the milking parlour, alone, milking cows.

'I was conscious I wanted to get on the road [for Imelda's birthday trip] so everything was done a bit faster,' Pat would later say about finishing up the milking before breakfast at 9.30 a.m.

Sean Dillon, who was a friend of Pat and Imelda's three

sons, would later say he wasn't sure if he was at Breansha at all that day.

According to Pat, at midday he and Imelda set off for her birthday weekend in the Heritage Hotel in Laois, leaving Sean to bring in the bales alone. Imelda had arranged for her sister to collect their three sons from school and look after them while she was away.

The phone records would later show that Pat's phone pinged off masts in Portlaoise from 1.56 p.m. on 3 June 2011 until 4.50 p.m. on 5 June 2011. Pat drove off with his wife, away from the eye of a storm that was gathering over the Golden Vale. He was far away when the storm broke and wreaked havoc in the lives of Bobby Ryan's family and in the life of his lover, Mary Lowry.

Bobby probably didn't have time to realize what was happening. It is believed his murderer took him by surprise, coming at him quickly and delivering the first brutal blow without warning. Wielding a blunt object, possibly a baseball bat, his attacker brought it down on his skull with so much force that he was immediately rendered incapacitated and unconscious. That left him unable to defend himself from the blows that rained down.

He suffered more blows to the face, the force of them smashing his cheekbones and shoving his nasal bone back into his skull. A blow to his upper leg was so powerful that it fractured the strongest bone in his body. The keys to his beloved Mr Moonlight van and his phone, which he usually kept holstered to his waist, were snatched and later discarded, never to be seen again.

His battered body, bloodied and swollen after the fierce, unprovoked assault, was then stripped of every item of clothing he had put on that morning, right down to his socks and underwear. All of these items would also disappear without a trace. The only item that wasn't removed from his body was his gold watch, which remained strapped around his left wrist. Other than that, he was left naked.

At some stage after that, as the blazing sun rose higher over Fawnagowan, Bobby's cold and lifeless body was to suffer one final indignity. Only a small number of people knew about the underground run-off tank behind the old milking parlour on the Lowry farm. In the 1970s John Lowry had built it using cavity blocks and his own bare hands, when his boys, Martin, Jimmy and Johnny, were approaching their early teens.

The tank could be accessed by removing two slabs of concrete that covered about one-third of the entire tank. The rest of it was covered by poured concrete, which was not designed to be removed. Each removable slab weighed well over twenty stone (130 kg). It was designed to collect water that was then used to wash down the nearby milking parlour, but it hadn't been used since Martin's death four years earlier. Apart from the Lowry men, only one other person connected to the family knew that the tank existed.

This was the place to which his murderer brought Bobby Ryan's naked body, the place where his body was thrown into the suffocating darkness. It formed a concrete coffin, 1.6 metres deep, 3.6 metres long and 1.8 metres wide. For now, at least, Bobby Ryan would lie undiscovered in a secret tomb hidden beneath the ground, sealed tight overhead by a carpet of grass and soil and then covered again by 10–15 haybales, while the lives of those searching so desperately for him slowly fell asunder.

8. Missing

Just beyond Bansha Wood, on a forest road that leads to the southern side of Slievenamuck ridge, there is a statue called Christ the King. Cut from white marble and standing on a circular stone plinth, it was erected on the road between Tipperary town and the Glen of Aherlow in 1950 to mark the Roman Catholic Church's Jubilee Year. The monument sits facing the majestic Galtee Mountains, its right hand raised over the people of the Glen below to give a blessing over everyone living there and over everyone who passes through.

It was here, at this isolated, eerie spot, that Michelle Ryan found herself seeking solace the morning after her father had disappeared. As a new day dawned and the search parties congregated at the entrance to Bansha Wood to continue the search for Bobby, she drove off alone to search for her father.

Michelle had spent the night before in a car parked outside the forest car park. Earlier, as gardaí closed off the entrance to the wood by lowering the barrier that barred access to cars, her mother, Mary, who by now had joined the search effort, pleaded with her to go home and get some rest. Michelle couldn't be persuaded to leave. She had gone to the local shop in Bansha before it closed and bought her father a bottle of Lilt and a Cadbury's Fruit & Nut bar in case, by some miracle, he appeared out of the woods. She would keep vigil outside, with her mother and several others, until daylight the next morning.

As she walked along one of the narrow trails leading off from Christ the King, thoughts of her father swirled around Michelle's head. With the clarity of a new day, she knew that he wouldn't have taken his own life, that he would never leave her and Robert in despair. She believed that something sinister had happened to him and that someone else was responsible for his disappearance, but before she could explore that terrible possibility, she had to find his body.

Michelle didn't know it at the time, but the road that sweeps past the statue, rising for a short while before start-ing its descent towards Tipperary town, also branches off to the left towards the townland of Breanshamore. Pat Quirke's farm was a mere five-minute drive away from where she stood. The Quirkes lived in an area steeped in history and folklore. In ancient times, the Glen of Aherlow was an important pass between the counties of Tipperary and Lim-erick. Its remoteness and the cover provided by the Galtee Mountains and Slievenamuck led to several bloody struggles for its possession, and the many caves in the foothills of the Galtees were used as hiding places by those fleeing from the warring factions. There was a dark history to the Glen, and now Bobby's fate was added to it. Michelle did not know that the answers she sought lay so close by.

Over at the Heritage Hotel, word had filtered through to Pat and Imelda that Bobby Ryan was missing and that an extensive search was underway to find him. Imelda had received a call on the Friday night, shortly after they had arrived at the hotel. As they discussed what was happening back at home, Pat told Imelda that he didn't believe Bobby had taken his own life. People who commit suicide want to be found, he told her confidently.

As the searches of the dense forest at Bansha continued

over the next few days, every available agency was called upon to try and locate Bobby, but it seemed he had disappeared without a trace. The Garda air unit and a Coastguard helicopter circled the skies above, and gardaí search teams, on foot and on horseback, worked their way through the vast network of trees, dizzying ridges, corrie lakes and narrow gullies. They were joined by army units, members of the civil defence and local volunteers. All of it came to nothing.

Bobby's van was removed from the wood on the day it was found by Michael Noonan, who ran a car recovery service in the town. At the time, he had the contract with the local garda station to provide storage for vehicles seized by gardaí, and on the odd occasion, in the case of more serious crimes, he would transport them on request to Dublin for forensic testing. He held Bobby's van in his garage on the Limerick road until it was tested at Templemore on 15 June. Fingerprints were taken from it, as well as from Bobby's driving licence and diary, but nothing would ever come of it. There were no forensic clues to give them a lead or an insight or even a shred of hope.

As part of their routine inquiries into Bobby's disappearance, gardaí had taken statements from everyone he had been in touch with before he disappeared. They had spoken to Michelle and Robert, and to his boss at the quarry, Niall, as well as to Mary Lowry, the last person known to have seen him.

Pat and Imelda returned from their break on the Sunday and headed straight for Mary's house in Fawnagowan. When they walked in, she was in the kitchen, deeply distressed and worried, waiting on news of Bobby.

Meanwhile, teams of gardaí were still searching the woods, trying to find any clues to tell them what might have happened to Bobby. Checkpoints had been set up on the surrounding roads, where gardaí were stopping drivers and showing them a picture of Bobby, asking them if they recognized him. As Bobby was a missing person, there was no incident room as it was not a criminal investigation. The gardaí had opened a jobs book on the case, detailing the first report, initial sightings, background on Bobby, etc. The jobs book follows a natural line of inquiry, taking in reports from search teams and house-to-house teams. It was reviewed weekly and any fresh information followed up on. Among those involved in the initial stages of the missing-persons investigation was Detective Inspector Paddy O'Callaghan, a local garda who had taken up a post in his home town just a year before in 2010. He would prove an important member of the team in the course of the investigation.

As the chaos of the search operation continued, Mary turned to her brother Eddie for support. Her home at Fawnagowan became a focal point for people to congregate at, sitting down for a cup of tea or using the toilet in between searches. Eddie himself organized searches, calling on friends from Newport to lend their time in the effort to locate Bobby. During one search on 6 June, bank holiday Monday, he went out with Pat Quirke, who was driving his car, and with Jimmy, Mary's brother-in-law.

There wasn't very much said while they were driving around, until Jimmy referenced Bobby Ryan and said: 'This wouldn't have happened if Martin Lowry was alive.'

Eddie didn't like the remark and slammed the car door shut as he was getting out. He would later say that he felt the blame was being put on Mary.

Eddie knew more than anyone just how desperate Mary was to find Bobby. He had driven his sister to meet a psychic in Nenagh, County Tipperary, in the hapless search for clues. 'She wanted to see if it would help in any way,' he later said.

The woman, who was well known in psychic circles but was not openly public about her work, had previously assisted various families in a number of high-profile cases, including the murder of a Limerick man, Roy Collins, in 2009.

When she spoke to Mary that day, she gave her very specific information about what had happened to Bobby, leaving Mary with no doubt in her mind that something terrible had occurred. The psychic told her that Bobby had been struck from behind and that he was dead. She also told her that the DJ had met her late husband, Martin, on the 'other side' and that there was no animosity between the two men. But she couldn't tell her where Bobby's body was.

The searches of the wood proved fruitless and it was clear Bobby was not going to be found there. So now gardaí looked to the last place Bobby had been seen alive. The case was still a missing-person inquiry and there was no criminal offence associated with it. To a certain extent, the hands of the gardaí were tied in terms of what they could do. Searches at this stage, without any evidence of foul play, had to be carried out with consent. This was an intelligence-led inquiry, and as the missing man's van had been found in the wood, the initial searches had focused on that area. With no sign of a body, or any suggestion that Bobby had been murdered, the focus moved back to the place where he had last been seen alive.

On bank holiday Monday, 6 June, Paddy O'Callaghan took possession of the mobile phone belonging to Mary Lowry, and Garda Tony O'Brien conducted a forensic examination of the handset. The data retrieved from Mary Lowry's phone showed that she had made at least six attempts to call

Bobby on 5 June 2011, two days after his disappearance. Garda O'Brien went through the handset to search for anything that might assist the gardaí with their investigation, but he found nothing he deemed relevant and the phone was returned to Mary. On Tuesday, 7 June, an eight-person team of gardaí from the Divisional Search Unit went to Mary's farm and, with her full permission, searched every inch of her land, without interference. By now, the blistering heatwave of the bank holiday weekend had subsided, giving way to torrential rain. The Garda search team, led by Sergeant Cathal Godfrey, started the methodical search at Fawnagowan at around 9.30 a.m. They combed the sheds and outhouses first, before splitting into two teams of four to search the surrounding fields. As they walked up and down the land, searching in ditches and under hedgerows, they were told to bring anything that could be of evidential value to the investigation to the attention of Sergeant Godfrey.

Although it was of little significance that day, Garda Conor Ryan and Garda Tom Finnan noticed more than half a dozen bales of hay, each about five feet high and wrapped in black plastic, stacked in an area of grassland behind the milking parlour. Garda Finnan would later say that he recalled the heavy rain 'hopping' off the plastic.

During the search, Sergeant Godfrey noted the open slurry pit at the back of the farm, but the amount in it was too minimal to contain a body. Garda Michael Fitzgerald saw a gold Toyota Corolla in one of the larger sheds he searched. He got into the car to have a look inside and noticed that the boot was open. The search, which extended into the disused quarry next door, finished just before midday, yielding no further clues.

Even though the gardaí had conducted a thorough search,

Mary's brother Eddie organized a group to comb the farm and all the fields around it for a second time. The grass was trampled down where the gardaí had already searched, but they did it again anyway. 'We could see the tracks of people [who had searched already],' Eddie said. They searched the two slurry tanks, the one in the slatted shed and the open tank, but found nothing.

Meanwhile, Michelle had taken matters into her own hands. In the immediate days after her father's disappearance she scoured the internet looking for missing-persons groups that might be able to help. There, she came across a group called Searching for the Missing, a voluntary organization headed up by Tosh Lavery, a retired member of the Garda Sub-Aqua Unit, and a former policewoman, Catherine Costello, who had worked with the Metropolitan Police in London and had been involved with the group for more than ten years. Michelle rang them and asked them if they could come to Tipperary to help find Bobby.

After the request from Michelle for assistance, Catherine had called on Abbeyfeale District Search and Rescue, a voluntary search organization she had enlisted the help of many times before, to co-ordinate searches. Two volunteer members, Christy Kelleher and Jimmy Cahill, made their way to the wood to carry out an assessment of the area on Tuesday, 7 June.

'We went to the site where the van was found and had a good look around,' said Christy.

'We needed to access the wood in advance of planning any search. Once that was done we sent out a text to all of our members to try and get a team together to take part in a search the next day.'

On that same Tuesday, Catherine met Michelle at a quarry

next to Mary's farm, where she was in the middle of a spiritually led search for her father.

Like Mary Lowry, Michelle had also enlisted the help of a psychic, who came to visit the area where her father had gone missing and drew searchers to a quarry next to the farm, where, she told them, she believed Bobby would be found.

There were two quarries next to the Lowry farm, both with entrances leading on to the main road. The first was a disused facility that belonged to the O'Dwyer family and the second was a sand quarry, owned by the Kinnane family. The psychic indicated that Bobby was in the second quarry, and that he was still alive.

Michelle, desperate to believe the psychic was right, had asked another missing-persons group, Trace Missing Persons Ireland, to assist in a search of the quarry. On the Tuesday after Bobby went missing, Joe Blake, the founder of the charity, arrived at the quarry with his two cadaver dogs, Patch and Murphy.

The two dogs ran around the property, sniffing around boulders and rocks, where they detected something under an area of sand.

'One of the dogs found something,' recalled Joe. 'But when we investigated, we found animal bones.'

Acting on the psychic's information, Michelle went to the Garda, begging them to thoroughly search the quarry. During a day-long operation, Garda searchers, assisted by a digger, dug up thousands of tonnes of sand in the hunt for Bobby. They found nothing.

Catherine Costello had pulled up in her car on the Tuesday, when Joe Blake's two dogs were running around sniffing for clues.

While Michelle, Mary Ryan and Joe searched the area

around the quarry, Catherine joined the Abbeyfeale District Search and Rescue in their assessment of Bansha Wood, making her way up to the farm a short time later. When she pulled into the yard, a figure immediately appeared from one of the sheds. It was Pat, brandishing a veterinary syringe and brazenly watching her every move as she made her way towards Mary Lowry's front door.

Inside the house, Mary was seated at the kitchen table, dabbing her eyes with a tissue and struggling to contain her emotions.

'Do you mind if I ask you a few questions about Bobby?' asked Catherine, explaining her role and putting her at ease. It was clear Mary knew her boyfriend intimately, supplying Catherine with details about his weight, height, eye colour and date of birth. A psychological assessment was next. 'Was Bobby depressed?' Catherine asked. 'Had he ever talked about suicide? How was his demeanour the morning he left?' When Bobby had disappeared initially, Mary had been immediately concerned that he had taken his own life. But now, after he hadn't been found, she was beginning to realize that something else might have happened. She knew that he had plans for the future, that he was in good form when he'd left that morning and that he would never do anything to upset his family. So now, when Catherine asked her if there was any suggestion that he might have taken his own life, she categorically rejected the idea. 'Absolutely no way,' she told Catherine, 'he was a happy-go-lucky guy.'

Bobby had told her that when his marriage had broken down seven years previously, it was the worst time of his life and if he hadn't jumped off a bridge then, he never would. His attitude to life was, she said, 'I will get out of this mood as soon as I get into it.'

While the two women chatted over a cup of tea, Mary's three boys were hovering in the vicinity, never too far from their mother's reach.

Mary began to open up to Catherine, explaining that she was overwhelmed by all that was happening and that her brain had gone into overdrive trying to piece together what might have happened. She thought Bobby had parked his car in the wood and maybe gone off with one of his friends to Lisdoonvarna in County Clare. She told Catherine he was 'mad into music'.

The night before he'd disappeared, she said, they had sat up listening to music and Bobby had been in great form. She remembered him tapping his leg up and down to the beat of a new tune. The next morning, after he left, she described how she had sat up in bed to wait for the sound of his van leaving, and that it had taken him longer than usual – maybe five minutes, maybe seven minutes, maybe even longer.

Believing the delay could prove relevant, Catherine carefully noted down the times. These things were playing on Mary's mind now. Before Catherine left, the women exchanged numbers and promised to stay in touch.

On the Wednesday after Bobby's disappearance, Christy and Jimmy arrived at Bansha Wood with a thirty-three-person team of searchers.

'We were up there from 9 a.m.,' said Christy. 'Due to the fact that the van was found in the woods it was assumed that this was a case of suicide. If a person parks a van in a wood they are not going to go two or three miles away to die by suicide, so the focus was on the wood. We combed that place and found nothing.'

Meanwhile, a few days after the Garda search of the farm, Garda Conor Ryan returned to Fawnagowan to meet Pat

Quirke there. Pat had been asked to empty the slurry tanks on the farm so they could be checked, in case Bobby had somehow fallen in. Pat took Garda Ryan to inspect two tanks. One was a tank that collects waste through a slatted floor in a cattle shed, which Garda Ryan noted was empty. The other was an open tank that contained a small quantity of slurry. Pat was on hand to assist with a tractor and a vacuum tanker, so that the slurry could be sucked out and spread in the adjoining fields. While he was there, Garda Ryan, a farmer himself, asked Pat if they were the only two tanks on the farm. Pat told him they were. What he failed to mention to the garda was the existence of another tank, a little-known run-off tank behind the milking parlour. Few people knew of the existence of that third tank, so Garda Ryan was easily misled. Pat had good reason to keep its existence to himself.

As the days wore on and no new information came to light, the intensity of the Garda search operation eased considerably. Locally organized search teams were still out, day and night, searching the woods for Bobby. They had discovered dead calves and dead pigs, and a smell coming from the area close to where Bobby's van had been found caused gardaí to do a dig. They discovered a dead dog, evidently buried there by someone who walked the area frequently with their pet.

The Sunday after Bobby went missing, on 12 June, a search was organized by a group of about 15–20 local volunteers. They set off at 8 a.m., meeting at a number of council-owned water tanks just above the car park. When they finished at about 11 a.m., they again congregated at the water tanks. Few knew the man who appeared from the woods and walked through the crowd, but one person recognized him.

'No one knew him,' said one volunteer, 'but I knew it was

Pat. He had the head down and he was keeping a low profile. He said, "Well, any sign?" and I said, "No."'

Down below, at the entrance to Bansha Wood, where Bobby's van had been found, a local priest had arrived to say a special Mass for Bobby's safe return. Robert and Michelle were there, joined by their mother and other members of the extended Ryan family. They were all frantic for some news on Bobby, but as time went on and their prayers went unanswered, the chances of finding him looked slimmer.

Over the next week or so, Catherine returned to the area on a number of occasions. She was helping co-ordinate searches and speaking to people who knew Bobby, in the hope of shedding some light on his disappearance. One evening, at the end of a day's search two weeks after Bobby's disappearance, Catherine was pulling out of a petrol station in Bansha when Mary Lowry phoned. She wanted to meet and arranged to come down to the petrol station. Catherine's car was full of members of the search team, and when Mary arrived Catherine got into her car so they could talk in private.

Once inside the car, Catherine could see that Mary was extremely upset, sobbing hysterically to the point of hyperventilating. As Catherine struggled to calm her down, Mary confessed the details of her affair with Pat Quirke. Mary told her that she had finished the affair and had confided in Bobby about it, doing the best she could to stem the fallout from it. Pat hadn't taken her decision well, she said, and had made her life a misery in the aftermath of their split. She had now come to the frightening realization, she said, that he had done something to harm Bobby.

Halfway through the conversation, which lasted about thirty-five minutes, Catherine had to go back to her car and tell her colleagues to go and get a cup of tea because she had been away for so long.

When she returned to the car, Mary told her that she had arrived home one evening to find someone had broken into the house. Nothing was taken and the gardaí who attended the scene claimed it was possibly youngsters who had got into the house through the bathroom window because it looked like items on the sill had been disturbed. Mary told Catherine that she believed it was Pat who had broken in because he had been stalking her since their affair had ended and she suspected he had a key to her house. She also told Catherine about the time she had returned from a walk with a friend and found Pat standing inside her house. He had told her the door was open, but she was certain she had locked it.

Mary told Catherine that Pat had warned her 'not to open her mouth' to anyone about the affair. She strongly suspected that he was involved in Bobby's disappearance and told her that she believed Pat was on her farm earlier than he said he was the morning Bobby had disappeared.

Catherine urged Mary to tell the gardaí all of this as a matter of urgency. 'I said, "You have to go to the gardaí, it's vital that you do." The thought of doing that just made her so uncomfortable. I think she was caught. She could see the ramifications for her family straight away. On a social level, it was catastrophic for her. She said she had met a nice female garda named Karen in the woods during the search for Bobby and that maybe she could talk to her.'

With a plan set for Mary to go to the gardaí, the two women parted ways. The following night, at around 7.30 p.m., Catherine rang Mary.

'Have you got in touch with the female garda?' she asked. Mary told her that she thought the garda was on nights and that she was changing shifts at the end of the week. Catherine told her that she could make an appointment for the garda to come and see her, rather than going into the station, if she preferred.

After the conversation ended, Catherine decided to phone the garda station herself. She asked to speak to Karen and was told there were two Karens. 'The blonde Karen,' she told the garda on the phone. He said he had two blonde Karens. Catherine told him she was looking for the Karen who was with Mary Lowry in the woods and that it was vital that she went to see Mary. 'I told him she had really important information on Bobby,' Catherine said. 'I said it was information that could upend the investigation and gave him the brief facts.'

What Catherine and Mary didn't know was that investigating gardaí already knew about the affair. The gardaí were waiting for Mary to come to them with the information herself. They were dealing with a close-knit, rural family and they knew that to go poking around in their business could turn potential witnesses against them. Both the Lowrys and the Quirkes were happily co-operating with the investigation, and although gardaí knew that there was a dark secret between two of them, a tactical decision was made to first try and get Mary onside, comfortable enough to open up to them herself, rather than forcing her hand.

For their part, the gardaí also suspected that Pat Quirke had something to do with Bobby's disappearance, but without a body there was little they could do. Bobby's house in Boherlahane was searched as part of the investigation, but it showed no signs of disturbance or a struggle and offered no clues as to where Bobby had gone.

Meanwhile, the subject of interest, Pat Quirke, was keeping a low profile, but nothing passed him by. He was uniquely positioned, as the master of the farm at Fawnagowan, to see, hear and control everything that went on around the farm. He saw every visitor arrive through the gates, knew where the gardaí were searching, kept tabs on the efforts of Catherine and the search team.

The second weekend after Bobby went missing, 11–12 June, Michelle took a break from the search and made her way up to Mary's house to go to the toilet. As she was making her way back to her car, she noticed a man in a wine-coloured jumper standing at the boot of her car. She introduced herself and asked him if he knew the man who ran the farm.

'That's me,' he said.

Michelle immediately knew, from what her father had told her, that she was looking at the man who had had the affair with Mary, the man who had warned her father to stay away. She was staring head-on at him and it felt like someone had cracked her in the stomach with a rock. Even though she felt incredibly uneasy, she managed to ask him if he had heard anything about anyone prowling around, of if the neighbours or other farmers had heard anything strange.

Pat told her that he hadn't heard a thing, but that the world was full of 'cold' people.

Michelle thought it a very odd thing to say. She found Pat himself to be a cool character. Her immediate gut instinct was that he had something to do with her father's disappearance. As Pat made his way to leave, she issued him with a stark warning.

'I will find my daddy, and I will make sure you get what you deserve for it.'

Pat was still of interest to the gardaí because he had been at the farm on Friday, 3 June, so was connected to the last sighting of Bobby Ryan. On 21 June, Detective Sergeant

Long and Detective Garda Martin Steed went to Pat's house in Breansha to ask him for a statement about what he had seen that morning. Pat had talked to the gardaí before now, but not formally.

At this meeting, he told them he had gone to Mary Lowry's farm at around 8.45 a.m. on the morning of 3 June, where he saw Mary Lowry getting into her car with the children. He didn't stop to talk to her because he was rushing. He was only on the farm for about twenty minutes, he said, because himself and Imelda were going away for the weekend to the Heritage Hotel in Laois. He told the officers that he had met Bobby on several occasions, in January when they went to the Brendan Grace gig, at Killough Quarry in early May and in the Hayes Hotel. He said he had never spoken to Bobby Ryan on the phone. He could offer no help to the investigation whatsoever as he didn't really know the man and had no idea what had happened to him.

Two days later, on 23 June, Mary Lowry admitted the affair with Pat Quirke to gardaí. Following Catherine Costello's call, they contacted Mary and asked her to come into the station. She did so and, after a general chat, she made a formal statement, outlining her affair with Pat. While the details she disclosed established a possible motive, there was no indication that anything untoward had happened and little or no evidence that Pat was responsible.

The summer months rolled by and still Michelle and the Ryans searched relentlessly. Locals in Cashel remember seeing the young mother of four in the town, plastering posters of her father on every available surface. Mary was searching too, and Trace Ireland were often up at her farm, where Pat always seemed to be in the vicinity, listening to what everyone had to

2. Bobby and his granddaughter Amy, Robert's daughter.

1. Bobby Ryan and his son, Robert, on Robert's Confirmation Day.

3. Though Bobby and his wife, Mary, separated in 2005 they remained on good terms. Here they are at daughter Michelle's twenty-first birthday celebration in 2007. Picture shows *(l–r)* Bobby, Michelle, Mary and Robert.

4. Mary Lowry's late husband, Martin, who died in 2007.

5. Mary Lowry with her new love, Bobby Ryan, at a dance in October 2010.

6. Mary in September 2012 at her niece's wedding in Spain. Before she went travelling, her passport had gone missing. Pat Quirke later admitted having taken it. Relations between the two had become toxic.

7. The headstones of Imelda and Pat Quirke's son, Alan, and of Martin Lowry, Alan's uncle, stand side-by-side in St Michael's Cemetery in Tipperary.

8. Bobby Ryan was reported missing on Friday, 3 June 2011. His desperate family plastered the area with posters but gardaí received no substantial information.

9. A garda forensics team and a diver examine the run-off tank in which Bobby Ryan's body was discovered.

10. Mary Lowry's middle son, Jack Lowry (nineteen), was the youngest witness in the trial.

11. Mary Lowry's eldest son, Tommy Lowry, aged twenty-one, also gave evidence at the trial.

12. Patrick and Imelda Quirke on their way into the Central Criminal Court. They took the train to Dublin every morning of the fifteen-week trial.

13. Mary Lowry arriving at the Central Criminal Court.

14. Eddie Quigley, Mary Lowry's brother, gave evidence at the trial.

15. Mary Lowry's house and farm at Fawnagowan, Co. Tipperary.

16. Flor Cantillon, Mary Lowry's boyfriend from 2012 to 2014. Pat Quirke's secret recordings of the couple in Mary's house were played in court.

17. Mary Glasheen, Bobby Ryan's ex-girlfriend. At the trial she described Ryan as bubbly and kind.

18. Breda O'Dwyer, artificial insemination technician. Her evidence contradicted Pat Quirke's account of his movements the day Bobby Ryan disappeared.

19. Chief Superintendent Dominic Hayes (then Detective Superintendent with command of the South-Eastern region), who oversaw the investigation into the Bobby Ryan murder.

20. Superintendent Padraic Powell, then sergeant in charge at Tipperary town garda station when a body was discovered at Fawnagowan, was the first at the scene.

21. Superintendent Paddy O'Callaghan (then Detective Inspector) was the senior investigating officer (SIO) in the Bobby Ryan murder inquiry.

22. Robert and Michelle Ryan outside the Criminal Courts of Justice after Patrick Quirke was convicted of murdering their father.

say. Relations between him and Mary were amicable, but whenever anyone to do with the search appeared, he would be there, hanging around, and she felt increasingly uneasy in his presence. She would later say that herself and Pat talked about Bobby's disappearance, but that Pat never had anything to say about what he thought might have happened to Bobby or where he might be.

At the end of September, a new series of RTÉ Television's *Crimecall* programme appeared on screens. Michelle had been asked to supply clothes similar to the ones her father had been wearing, as well as his shoes and a mobile phone. She dropped them off at Tipperary town garda station in the hope that the programme might trigger someone's memory.

In the episode that featured Bobby's case, gardaí appealed for information, revealing that a male matching his description had been seen walking along a country road at Cordangan, Tipperary town, at approximately 10 a.m. on the morning he went missing. A local woman, Siobhán Kinnane, had come forward to say that she had seen a man fitting Bobby's description as she made her way into town that morning. Although it was followed up as a line of inquiry, there were a few issues with what she told gardaí, namely that the person she saw was wearing different clothing to that worn by Bobby, that she couldn't remember whether it was the Thursday or Friday and that she was very unsure of the exact time. After extensive house-to-house inquiries, gardaí found no one else who could confirm the sighting.

It was a sighting that would later be dismissed as a case of mistaken identity, with many speculating that it could have in fact been Pat Quirke that Mrs Kinnane saw on the road that day. The two men were of similar build, and if Pat had dumped the van in the woods, one of the most likely routes he would have taken on foot back towards a car he had parked in a concealed spot nearby would have cut through the area in Cordangan where the sighting occurred.

Back in September 2011, however, the sighting was still leading gardaí to believe that Bobby Ryan had possibly left the farm alive. A month before, at the annual Bansha Agricultural Show, they had handed out hundreds of missing-persons leaflets on Bobby, hoping that someone there would come forward with information. Again, there was nothing.

By now, Mary Lowry was becoming increasingly frustrated by the lack of progress made by the Garda investigation into Bobby's disappearance. On more than one occasion, usually at the weekend, she phoned the *Tipp Today* radio show on Tipp FM to complain that the authorities weren't doing enough to find him. The show, which was presented by Seamus Martin at that time, had been covering the story since the day Bobby went missing, leading to a flood of calls from locals over the weeks that followed. Mary never made it on-air, but her calls to the station, described as frantic and pleading, showed that she was desperate to find her boyfriend.

Even though she had strong suspicions about Pat's involvement, Mary was still hoping that her worst fears were unfounded and that Bobby was alive. She made two attempts to call him in September 2011. That same month, she received a text message from an unknown number. Written phonetically in text shorthand, it said: *u tink u r so col out partyn lik Bobby nevr existd. We no u hidn somethn nd wer gonta watch u till u crak*. She made a complaint to the gardaí, but the sender was never identified. The phone was unregistered, so gardaí were unable to track its owner or user, but they were able to confirm that it hadn't been used for anything else, so possibly the sender obtained the phone solely to send this message.

Meanwhile, and incredibly, given the circumstances, Pat was badgering Mary to rekindle their relationship. In what would become an unsolved mystery, he made a booking for an overnight stay in the Cliff House Hotel in Ardmore, County Waterford, on 6 September 2011, later telling gardaí that he had spent the night there with Mary. The booking was made under his name but using Mary's email address for confirmation. Mary would later deny ever setting foot inside the hotel, least of all with Pat Quirke.

The investigation continued to try to make headway, but the trail was cold. Nonetheless the gardaí focused on the living witnesses, hoping to find that one crucial piece that might lead them to solve the puzzle of Bobby's disappearance into thin air. Based on their interviews with Mary Lowry, they had started to gather a fuller picture about Pat Quirke's prior contact with Bobby Ryan. In November, Pat was asked to come to Tipperary town garda station to provide a further statement.

Inside the interview room in the garda station, they put it to Pat that he had been having an affair with Mary Lowry, which he admitted as part of his formal statement. He told them that he had started seeing Mary in early 2008, after Martin Lowry's death. They were 'off and on for a while' and they both knew there was no future in it. The break-up, he said, was 'not amicable'. She had met Mr Ryan a few months before and he was 'very angry with her' when he found out. On one occasion, he said, he saw texts from Mr Ryan on her phone and took the phone. He told Bobby that Mary was with him now.

He also described the meeting in the Hayes Hotel between himself, Bobby and Mary, after Mary had confessed to Bobby about her affair with Pat. They talked for about an hour and Pat described Bobby as being friendly and sympathetic, having had a relationship break-up himself. He told gardaí that he was in a bad place himself at the time and was getting counselling.

Pat once again went through his day on 3 June: Fawnagowan at 8.45 a.m., no interaction with Mary or anyone else, gone by 9.15 a.m. and breakfast at home at about 9.30 a.m. Sean Dillon, his helper on the farm, was there, he said. He had heard about Bobby Ryan's disappearance that evening, while he was in the Heritage Hotel. When he returned from his trip on the Sunday, he took part in searches for Bobby. That was it, all he could contribute to the investigation, just as he'd said to them last time.

The gardaí noted it all down, but they had nothing further, so Pat went back to his life, farming at Breansha and at Fawnagowan. Just as after Martin's death, he was a daily fixed presence on the farm, which meant he was a daily fixed presence in Mary Lowry's life. He used that contact to recommence his war of attrition in a bid to get her to agree to take him into her bed once again. He told her that he wanted to rekindle the affair, suggesting they meet just once a month and asking would she be agreeable to those terms. She refused.

In the midst of Mary's struggle to stave off Pat's unwanted advances, Bobby's birthday approached. He was still missing, but the milestones in his life were nonetheless being marked by the ones who loved him most. On what would have been his fifty-third birthday, his brother John and John's wife, Sally, marked the occasion in the local newspaper.

Remembering Bob (Mr Moonlight) on his 53rd birthday and his first away from home on Sunday 11th December.
Where ever you are boy, we hope you are happy.

Will those who think of Bob today, a little prayer to Padre Pio say.
Always in our thoughts —
Sally and John.

As the Christmas lights went up and the year wound towards its end, Pat kept on asking Mary again and again to meet him alone. New Year's Eve came and went, and now Bobby was missing 'since last year', a new and painful distance between him and his family and no answers in sight. Pat kept up his nagging of Mary and, eventually, she relented.

'I was so pestered I said I would go,' she would later say.

It might beggar belief that Mary agreed to go away with Pat, but she was swayed by two convictions: that he might yet divulge something about Bobby's disappearance, and that he still had a hold over her because of the dark secret of their affair.

In January 2012, Mary boarded the train from Limerick Junction and went to Heuston station in Dublin City, then made her way to Fitzpatrick's Hotel in Killiney, south Dublin. She knew the place as she had stayed there years before with her husband. While she was gone, Mary's brother Eddie looked after the boys.

Pat and Mary went to see a play in Dublin at the Olympia Theatre called *The Night Joe Dolan's Car Broke Down*, then back out to the hotel, where they had a double room booked.

'I can't remember a whole lot,' Mary would later say of that night. 'I had a lot to drink. I felt pressure. I didn't want to be there.'

Later that same month, gardaí made a second appeal on *Crimecall* for anyone who had seen Bobby's van on the morning of Friday, 3 June, to get in touch. They also wanted to speak to anyone who was in Bansha Wood walking and may have seen him there on the morning he disappeared. By this stage, a witness had come forward who recalled seeing a maroon saloon car at 8.10 a.m. on the morning Bobby went missing at the same time as he saw a van similar to Bobby's Citroën van. On *Crimecall* gardaí appealed to the driver of that maroon car to come forward.

Meanwhile, the Ryan family were still living in hope of some news on their father. After the programme aired and there was a muted response to the appeal, they fell back into a state of despair. They had searched and searched for months and, now that the physical searching had stopped, they were relying on someone who knew something about their father's disappearance to come forward. But, as had been the case since that long ago summer morning in June, there was nothing but silence. Not a thing to give them hope.

Pat Quirke had never given up on ensnaring Mary Lowry again. He was unstinting in his efforts to reignite their sexual relationship, constantly trying to convince her that they were good together. But in March something happened that thwarted his deepest desire once and for all.

Mary had a voucher that had been given to her and Bobby for the Gleneagle Hotel in Killarney, County Kerry, which they had never got the chance to use. When the hotel rang her up to tell her that the voucher was about to expire, she decided to take the boys to Kerry for the St Patrick's weekend dancing festival.

The Gleneagle was full to capacity for the three-day event, with acts like Mike Denver and Mick Flavin taking to the stage in the ballroom, where hundreds crowded the floors to dance. That weekend Mary bumped into Flor Cantillon, whom she knew through the social dancing scene, and they shared a few dances and swapped numbers, promising to stay in touch.

When she returned from the weekend in Killarney, Pat quizzed her about what she had got up to there. She told him that she had met Flor Cantillon. Ironically, Pat warned her that it was a bit too soon to be getting into a new relationship.

Flor, or Florrie as he was known by friends, was a part-time farmer from Liscarroll in County Cork. Although, like Bobby, he enjoyed dancing, the two men were very different. Flor was more reserved than the outgoing, fun-loving Bobby, and tended to be more of an introvert. For Mary, say her friends, the new relationship was much less talked about than the one she had with Bobby. They never heard of her talking about things they did as a couple, or places they went to.

As time went on and the courtship continued and Flor visited the farm occasionally, Pat asked Mary if she and Flor were sleeping together. She told him that it was none of his business who she was or wasn't sleeping with. In spite of this, it was obviously clear to Pat that Mary had moved on again and that, once more, he had been left on the sidelines in favour of someone else.

In fact, Pat no doubt knew a lot more about Flor and Mary than either of them could ever have guessed. Although Mary did not know it at the time, Pat was secretly recording the couple in her home. Prior to Bobby's disappearance, the gardaí believe, Pat had installed a number of clandestine listening devices in Mary's bedroom and several other locations around the house. They would later discover recordings on Pat's home computer of interactions that took place in what Mary believed was the privacy of her own home. Now that

Pat no longer had her ear, he made sure he could listen in on every word she spoke. His first motive for bugging her house was to monitor her and Bobby; now he could monitor Mary and her new boyfriend, Flor.

While Mary and Flor continued their relationship, Pat then told Mary that he was finding everything very difficult and that he wanted to tell Imelda about their affair. Mary didn't want him to do that, but she told him that if it made him feel better to go ahead and tell her.

Mary was still feeling immense guilt about the affair. In the midst of all the turmoil of the last few years was Martin's sister, Imelda, a loyal wife to Pat and a good friend to Mary. Imelda seemed to be the one no one gave much thought to as the affair raged and then waned.

In March 2012, after Pat spoke to her about coming clean to Imelda, Mary went and bought a blank card, wrote the word 'Sorry' on it and posted it anonymously to Imelda.

'I felt very guilty about having the affair,' she would later say. 'And I suppose it made me feel better. It just took some of the guilt away.'

Whatever her reasons, the card was gone from her now and making its way into Imelda's hands.

The following day, Pat approached Mary at the farm, his face like thunder. He hadn't, in fact, made a confession to his wife, but the 'Sorry' card had turned up on the doormat and he was furious.

'What the hell did you send that card for and who told you to send it?' he demanded.

Mary told him she came up with the idea herself. Given that Imelda was now looking at this card and wondering what it was about and it was making her deeply suspicious, Pat was forced to follow up and confess to his wife that he had had an affair with her brother's wife. That conversation remains private – neither husband nor wife ever described it to anyone, but Imelda tore up the card and never spoke to Mary again.

The secret was out in the open now and somehow it took wing on the air and found its way into the general stream of gossip. The details of the affair between Pat and his wife's sister-in-law spread like wildfire among an incredulous community.

'There was more shock about the affair than the man who was missing,' said one local farmer. 'People could not believe it. It was all anyone was talking about.'

Everywhere there were whispers and speculation and people watching to see what would happen next. Pat was feeling more and more uncomfortable in the locality. He told a friend that he felt like everyone at Mass was staring at him and he didn't like the looks he was getting. The friend told him to go to another church.

Mary was also the subject of this gossip and speculation and she was beginning to feel the pressure. There was an uncomfortable get-together in May, when she had to be in Imelda and Pat's company for a Lowry family gathering to celebrate Rita's eighty-fifth birthday. A picnic was planned in Glengarra wood in Cahir, and all Rita's grandchildren, including Mary's and Pat's boys, were there. Pat couldn't help himself, secretly approaching Mary and asking her how she was. She told him to get lost.

They had become the source of intense gossip, the butt of jokes, and now Imelda knew it all as well. This was a difficult time for Mary to hold her head up high, but she kept on going, raising her boys and enjoying her new-found love with Flor Cantillon. The attention didn't stop Pat hassling her, though, as evidenced right in front of his wife at Rita's party. For Mary Lowry, the pressure was mounting on all sides.

By the time of the first anniversary of Bobby's disappearance on 3 June 2012, Michelle and a small search team of family and friends went back to Bansha Wood to search for her father. They took a search dog and combed the area close to where his van was discovered, but came away, as before, with nothing. By this stage, relations between Bobby's children and his girlfriend had deteriorated significantly. They had gone from being united in their efforts to find him to Robert and Michelle being thoroughly disenchanted with all the chaos in Mary's life, all of which distracted from the only thing that mattered to them: finding Bobby.

In a bid to jog people's memories and keep Bobby fresh in their minds, Robert and Michelle erected missing-person posters in the Tipperary town area and on the road that passes the entrance to Mary's farm. Mary felt intimidated by the position of the posters so close to her house and phoned the gardaí to complain. She said it was upsetting her three boys, who loved Bobby very much, and she felt that the posters were implying that she had something to do with his disappearance.

On one occasion, Mary phoned the gardaí to state that she had been 'abused on the road' by Michelle. A poster at the end of Mary's road kept going missing, and Michelle had to keep replacing it, until one day Michelle witnessed Mary removing it. She approached Mary and the two women launched into a verbal argument. Michelle told Mary to get her 'grubby hands off my father' and told her that she had a letter in her car from Clonmel County Council giving her permission to erect the poster. Mary told her that she didn't want posters going up at the end of her road because it was upsetting her boys. She didn't mind them anywhere else, pointing out that she herself had put up posters, listing her own mobile number as a contact, and was as desperate as Michelle was for answers. They had a common goal, but with tensions running so high they were no longer able to find common ground. It had been a whole year since the man they both loved had disappeared and, as they argued over posters on the road, the mystery of what had happened to him was no closer to being solved.

Over the course of that year, before they had this falling out, time and time again Michelle had been drawn back to the farm at Fawnagowan, overcome by an inexplicable feeling that the clues to explain what had happened to her father lay there, somewhere. Whenever she could, she popped up to the farm to have a discreet look around. One day she was out searching in the fields at the back of the farm and caught the leg of her clothing in a cattle trough. She struggled to free her leg, ripping her trousers in the process. There were several haybales nearby, stacked, but Michelle had no idea that they were strategically placed to hide the existence of a run-off tank. Nor did she have any idea that all of the answers to her questions were within reach, that her father's body lay just a few feet below where she was sitting. One secret was out in the open, with the knowledge of Pat and Mary's affair now common knowledge, but there was another, much darker secret hidden still. But it was only a matter of time before it too rose up to the surface and broke out into the light of day.

9. Stalker

The first anniversary of Bobby Ryan's disappearance came and went. Mary and Flor were still seeing each other. The relationship was low-key and a more casual arrangement than the one Mary had enjoyed with Bobby, but she was happy in Flor's company. They were regularly seen on the dance circuit together and Flor was often spotted making his way into the farm at Fawnagowan to visit his girlfriend.

Over at Breansha, the Quirkes were still a united couple, although Imelda had not spoken a word to Mary Lowry since the revelation of the affair. The fact that she stayed with Pat and never broke from him suggests that she didn't see him as the main culprit, although what she did think about the affair was and remains a mystery. Imelda Quirke is not a woman to speak loosely, so whatever her thoughts and feelings, she kept them to herself and focused on her marriage and family. She had decided to stand by her husband, determined to keep her family together for the sake of her three boys, and that's what she did.

The Lowrys and Quirkes were already the centre of much attention because of the affair and Bobby's strange disappearance, and now, incredibly, they were pushed into the limelight once again because of a terrible tragedy.

On 8 August 2012, shortly before 5 p.m., Imelda and Pat's middle son, Alan, arrived home with three of his friends. They were playing in the hallway of the family home, looking for water bottles so they could have a water fight. Imelda was in the kitchen, cooking spaghetti bolognese for dinner, and she asked Alan to go outside and take the clothes in from the washing line.

Pat was in the house as well, talking to Imelda at the back door while he got ready to go over to the farm for the evening milking. While he put on his boiler suit, Imelda asked him to organize sausages for supper, so that there would be something to eat when she and Alan returned from under-fourteen hurling training, which they were due to go to later. She stepped back into the house just as Pat was getting into his jeep and trailer, which were both parked at the back of the house.

Alan hadn't taken the clothes in from the line, so Imelda went outside to fetch them herself. Just as she stepped outside again, she saw Pat driving around the corner of the house. She saw Alan's three friends run to put their hands on the trailer and shouted at them to stand back. As she walked to the clothesline, she heard a cry. Straight away she knew something was wrong. She ran around the corner of the house and saw Pat's jeep, stopped.

When she looked at the trailer, she could see Alan caught between the two wheels, screaming for help. He had jumped on the drawbar of the trailer and crouched down as his father had pulled off. He had slipped and the front wheel of the trailer had rolled over him. Imelda was by his side within seconds. He wanted to get out from underneath the wheels of the trailer, but she didn't want to move him. He kept wriggling and shouting that he wanted to get out. As he freed himself from under the wheels, Imelda could see that his left arm was badly damaged. She shouted at Pat to call an ambulance.

Imelda was on the ground, talking to Alan and trying to keep him calm. He told her he was finding it hard to breathe.

While she reassured her little boy, his friends ran into the house and brought out pillows. One of the children called his mother, Breda, who was a nurse. She arrived ten or fifteen minutes later and found Alan on the tarmac, with Imelda kneeling by his side. Breda spoke to Alan and he told her he was finding it difficult to breathe, so she told Pat to call a local doctor immediately. Imelda had a first aid bag, which they opened and found a foil blanket that they wrapped around Alan. As they waited for help to arrive, Imelda kept talking to her little boy, reassuring him that he would be okay and keeping him calm and focused.

When the ambulance arrived, Alan's pulse was weak, so the paramedics gave him oxygen. By now, two gardaí from Tipperary garda station had also arrived, quickly moving the trailer to one side to give the medical personnel more room to tend to Alan. The local GP, Dr Conor Carroll, arrived after the paramedics. The doctor was very concerned about Alan and urged that it was important he get to a hospital immediately.

The paramedics placed Alan on a bodyboard and carefully lifted him into the ambulance. Imelda climbed in with him, all the time reassuring him that everything would be okay. As the ambulance sped off, sirens blaring all the way along the narrow country road that leads from the house, Alan began to get weaker. About five to ten minutes after the ambulance had set off, the machine monitoring his heart started to beep. The paramedics did all they could, but when his heart stopped in the back of the ambulance, all their efforts couldn't resuscitate him.

Alan was pronounced dead at 7.15 p.m. at South Tipperary General Hospital in Clonmel. His father identified his body later that night.

The whole community was deeply shocked by this tragic loss, and Pat and Imelda were utterly devastated. Alan was the middle of their three boys, just about to enter sixth class at Mount Bruis national school. Locals remembered him as a wonderful child with a passion for sport. He played hurling in Lattin–Cullen GAA club and soccer for St David Cullen's. He also played tennis and enjoyed swimming and basketball. He was buried in his Tipperary jersey.

Due to the circumstances of Alan's death, the gardaí were called in to investigate what had happened. As part of their inquiries, Pat's jeep and trailer, bought from a cut of money he had gained through one of Mary Lowry's investments, were taken away for examination. Michael Noonan, of Noonan Motor Factors in Tipperary town, was called in to collect the jeep and trailer on behalf of the gardaí. It was Noonan who had collected Bobby Ryan's van for forensic examination after it was found abandoned in Bansha Wood. On this occasion, the gardaí quickly confirmed that what had occurred was a tragic accident. An inquest would later determine that Alan's injuries were due to vehicular trauma consistent with an accidental death.

Alan's death shocked the tight-knit community of Breanshamore and the surrounding area. The child was laid out at home, on the farm where he grew up, and hundreds came to offer their condolences to Imelda and Pat. Volunteers from the local GAA club came out in droves to direct traffic and to help manage the large crowds who came to pay their respects. The surrounding fields were turned into car parks and neighbours on the narrow boreen that leads to the Quirke farm ferried mourners to and from the house.

A few days earlier, as the family waited for the hearse to arrive with Alan's remains, a neighbour of Pat's called over to the house to deliver some food. He recalled meeting the grieving father outside the house, He embraced Pat, offered his condolences and listened as Pat explained what had happened. He described how he felt resistance under the jeep as he was pulling off.

'Pat, why didn't you stop?' pressed the neighbour.

He thought it was a ball, he said.

'It's been a terrible year,' Pat added. 'It's just been one thing after the other.'

On Saturday, 11 August, the funeral of Alan Quirke took place at the Church of the Assumption in Lattin. The community turned out in force to support the Quirkes at this dreadful time, rallying around them in huge numbers. Farm accidents occur all too often across the country, and every farming family lives in fear of that momentary lapse of concentration that ends in tragedy. Their neighbours felt deeply sorry for the Quirke family.

During the service, a tearful Pat Quirke stepped up to the high marble altar to deliver the eulogy. In front of him, sitting shoulder to shoulder in dozens of pews, hundreds of grief-stricken mourners waited to hear his words about his son. In the carved timber gallery over the main entrance, the choir were still. All eyes were on Pat. As he began to speak, his voice, gruff as it always was, carried up through the vaulted ceiling and echoed from wall to wall.

In what is remembered as an awkward yet heartfelt eulogy, he paid tribute to his little boy, Alan. His manner of speech was unusual, though, and left many in the congregation questioning the wisdom of his approach.

'Pat was trying to tell a story as if Alan was speaking,' a member of the congregation recalled. 'He said that Alan said to him, "Is it true, Dad, that you are one of the top fifty EBI [economic breeding index] farmers in the country?" and Pat said, "Yes, I am." And Alan said, "I haven't thought about it, sure what good is that?" and went back to his fun. It didn't go down well because Pat was seen as being boastful. He was burnt at the stake for that.'

Alan was laid to rest in St Michael's cemetery on the outskirts of Tipperary town, in a plot next to his grandfather John and his Uncle Martin.

John had lived until his sixty-seventh year, but Martin and Alan, Mary Lowry's husband and Imelda and Pat's son, had been taken too soon. The two women, once close friends who had shared family holidays together, now gathered at the same graveyard spot to pray over the loved ones they had lost. They were no longer on speaking terms.

Pat had been a source of talk and speculation because of his affair with Mary Lowry, and now he was an object of fascination for another reason. Among the people who attended the house over the next few days, Pat's demeanour was a cause of much discussion.

'Everyone deals with grief in different ways, but the consensus was that Pat wasn't acting like a grieving father should,' said one mourner. 'He was all business. I was there with my daughter and he very excitedly started to ask her all about how she was getting on at college. It was all very strange.'

There was also a sense that the accident could have been avoided if Pat had been alert to the situation. The farming community are well aware of the hazards of their workplaces and quick to respond to potential threats. There was a feeling among the community that Pat must have had other things on his mind on the day of the accident, that he was distracted and wasn't paying attention. Although, of course, accidents always seem avoidable and inexplicable when examined with hindsight.

What was truly surprising, though, was the fact that the tragic loss didn't recalibrate Pat's perspective. While Imelda was focused on her family and the community was focused on sympathizing and offering practical help to the family, Pat seemed to be concentrating on the reaction of Mary Lowry. In his mind, Mary had withdrawn from him when he needed her most.

Sometime after the funeral, Mary's brother Eddie was doing some repair work on the lead valleys of the roof at Fawnagowan when he was interrupted by the sound of raised voices below. He could see his sister heading towards her vegetable garden, and could hear the voices getting louder and angrier. Pat was giving out to Mary for her lack of support over Alan's death.

'Why weren't you of any help?' Pat shouted. 'This was a very difficult time in my life. I didn't get one text or phone call from you. Nothing.'

Mary fired back, telling him to go home to his wife and children.

Eddie, still on the roof as the altercation began to escalate, sent his nephew Tommy to his mother to say there was a phone call inside and take her away from the situation.

Some weeks later, Eddie was again working on the farm, getting materials for fixing the roof, when Pat approached him directly.

'Your sister is a right bitch,' he seethed. 'She didn't support me or Melly [Imelda] after Alan's death.'

Eddie didn't hesitate with his response. 'Do you not think Mary has enough to deal with?' he retorted.

Pat was furious. He knew it was likely that Mary had by now confided in her brother all the details of their affair.

'I only want family and friends, good friends, at my son's month's mind Mass,' he warned. 'If Mary shows up, I will personally remove her from the church myself.'

'That's your choice, Pat,' came the reply. 'Yours and your wife's.'

It was a public declaration of his mounting feelings of bitter resentment. Up until now, Pat had confined his anger towards Mary and kept it between the two of them. Now, something had shifted and he couldn't keep those feelings under control. He could not accept the fact that she had completely removed him from her life. After all he had done for her, everything he had risked, she had deserted him completely. His love for her seemed to be turning to hate and his behaviour was becoming increasingly erratic.

The following month, Mary and the boys were getting ready to go to Spain for a much-needed holiday. Mary's niece was getting married and all the Quigley clan were going, so Mary decided to fly out a week early and enjoy some time in the sun with the boys.

An anniversary Mass for Martin, who was now five years dead, was planned at the house in Fawnagowan on the night before the flight from Dublin. On the day of the Mass, Mary laid out all the passports and the boarding passes on the kitchen table because she knew they would be rushing out of the door to the airport and she didn't want to forget anything.

As the boys were packing their suitcases and getting everything ready to go, they noticed one of the passports was missing. Mary, she would later say, was 'fit to kill them', until she realized the missing one was hers.

They tore the house apart before the Mass, but there was

no sign of the passport. The boys refused to leave on the flight with their aunt, so Mary had to change all of their tickets and apply for an emergency passport. They finally set off for their holiday a few days later.

Mary believed Pat had taken her passport, but she couldn't prove it.

Soon after she had returned from Spain, Pat confronted her about a ladder he had on the farm that had been moved. He told her not to move his property without his permission.

'Where is my passport?' she furiously asked him.

He told her he had sold it and laughed in her face.

Against this toxic backdrop of theft, accusations and rage-filled confrontations, the search for Bobby Ryan was still ongoing. Towards the end of September 2012, up to thirty gardaí decided to re-search an area of woodland in the Cordangan area, about 2.5 miles from Tipperary town, where a local woman, Siobhán Kinnane, said she had seen a man walking on the day Bobby disappeared. No trace of Bobby was found during the day-long operation. As the investigation team reached another dead end, Bobby's brother John spoke out in a newspaper interview, saying he believed his brother had been killed.

'All we want is closure at this stage. You'd be hoping every day when the phone rings it will bring some bit of news,' John said. 'I believe someone killed him. That's my own belief.'

Widescale searches had taken place for Bobby since he'd disappeared and posters seeking information on his whereabouts were still dotted around the area between Tipperary town and Cashel. Investigators had received many tip-offs and there had been countless reported sightings of the part-time DJ. One person said they had seen him DJing in Lanzarote. Another said he was in Carrick-on-Suir. Still another said he had been spotted in Jurys Inn hotel in Cork. At the more bizarre end of the scale, the actor who posed as Bobby in the *Crimecall* appeal was himself mistaken for the missing DJ after the show aired. Every lead, however implausible, was followed up. They all came to nothing.

In the months following Bobby's disappearance, Eddie had started work on an extension to Mary's house. One of the boys had his bedroom in Rita's part of the property and, as he got older, Mary wanted him to have his own space that wasn't in the granny flat. She applied for permission to extend her house to include a new bedroom and a playroom for the boys, and permission was granted. Eddie did the work over a period of about eight months. He needed a key, so he could get into the house to plug in his equipment, and normally left it in the front-door lock when he was done for the day. At some stage, the key mysteriously disappeared.

As Christmas 2012 approached, Pat's hold over Mary no longer existed. He had no control over where she went, who she spoke to, or what she did with her money. Worse still, their previously amicable relationship had more or less disintegrated and they were now barely on speaking terms. And, of course, Imelda wouldn't utter a word to Mary either. The two families had been ripped apart.

Over the past two years, since 2010, the Eircom Phone-Watch house alarm at Fawnagowan had been triggered seventeen times. At first, it was easy to explain it away as birds hitting the windows or a power surge or cut or a fault in the system, but over time this continual alarm disturbance began to worry Mary. In a bid to find out the cause, in November 2012 Mary had CCTV installed around the property. There were four cameras: one facing the gate leading into the farm; one on Mary's front door that was focused down over the driveway; another monitoring Rita's back garden, where there was a clothes line; and a fourth camera trained on the sheds where the postbox was situated. If the alarm went off again, Mary might just be able to find out why.

On 3 December 2012, shortly before midday, while Mary and the boys were away, the alarm was triggered and its noisy bell rang out over the farmyard. When they got home and realized what had happened, Mary asked her son to help her view the CCTV footage.

They sat side by side, staring at the screen, and they saw the cause. There was Pat, at 11.45 a.m., handling her underwear on the washing line in the sheds, looking in through her windows, then putting a key in the front door that set off the alarm, causing him to run away. He was also spotted over at the postbox, peering inside and checking for mail. Gardaí arrived, reacting to the alarm, but Pat was safely hidden away while they were on-site. He re-emerged into the open once the gardaí were gone and the coast was clear.

Pat had no knowledge of the CCTV system that had been installed because Mary never told him about it. So presumably he left that day thinking he hadn't been seen by anyone, and that he had outfoxed the gardaí. He had no idea that his movements had been caught on camera, providing incontrovertible evidence that he was snooping around and trying to gain access to the house in Mary's absence. What would later emerge was equally interesting – what Pat did later that day.

After attempting to enter Mary's house that morning, Pat later went on home. Shortly after 3.30 p.m., he was sitting in his home office in Breansha, logged on to the family computer, with the private-browsing mode switched on. The computer screen was opened on the Google homepage. Pat slowly began to type the words – *human body decomposition timeline*. His search returned a series of options. He read each one quickly and clicked on www.forensics4fiction.com, a website with an article called 'The five stages of decomposition'. Minutes later, he typed *rate of human decomposition* into the search engine. He surveyed the returned hits and clicked on a website called www.environmentalgraffiti.com.

A third Google search, again for *human body decomposition timeline*, brought him to www.suite101.com, where an article entitled 'How a body decomposes after death' described the changes in a corpse twenty-four hours after death, and from two days to seven days after death, and then the later stages of decomposition beyond that. Embedded on the various webpages Pat was looking at were several links to YouTube videos. These included a link for a YouTube channel with a video of the 'Body farm and beyond', which takes the user on a tour of the 'body farm', showing and discussing 'human remains, skin slippage and DNA analysis'. A second link was to another YouTube video of the 'body farm', which showed a study of human decomposition carried out on real corpses. On the video, the researcher mentions that 'you never forget the smell'.

This wasn't the first time Pat had carried out research on body decomposition, but the flurry of online activity that afternoon showed that he was meticulously estimating what now lay in the run-off tank that had been so carefully sealed eighteen months earlier. There was a calculation being made, and the decision it informed was about to become urgent.

At Fawnagowan the following day, Mary showed the CCTV footage of Pat handling her underwear to Eddie. He was there again the next day, 5 December, when Pat called to Mary's house with a key and a half-baked story about finding it in the yard on the day he was caught on camera. He said he had found the key that day and had just put it in the lock to see if it was her key. Mary would later say that he was 'very shaky and extremely nervous. Very, very strange indeed . . . physically, he was shaking.' Eddie recognized the key in Pat's hand. It was the original key that came with the new lock he had installed months before. He checked to see if the key worked in the lock and it did. Neither Mary nor Eddie told Pat about the CCTV or what it had shown to contradict his story.

On the same day, 5 December, Mary informed the gardaí about Pat's snooping. They called to her house to look at the CCTV footage and to take a statement from her, but she refused to make a formal complaint about Pat entering her home. She had decided against formally involving the gardaí, but Pat interfering with her underwear and the privacy of her home was the final straw for Mary. She wanted him off her land.

'I just wanted the lease to finish,' she said. 'I just wanted to be rid of this man.'

Mary went to see her solicitor, Aidan Leahy in Cashel, and asked him to write to Pat, 'as kind-heartedly as possible' on her behalf. She was very clear on her course of action: she wanted to terminate Pat Quirke's lease, and to do so as soon as possible.

After taking instructions from his client, Mr Leahy drafted a letter to Pat, outlining exactly how Mary felt. There were a number of matters that had continued to cause his client 'considerable concern for some time', the solicitor wrote. He noted that Mary 'would like to come to an arrangement with you regarding early termination' of the lease agreement they shared. Mr Leahy suggested that Pat instruct his own solicitor on the matter and added, 'it does sound as though it would be better for both you and her family if some arrangement could be made in this regard'.

The alarm had been activated at her property on a number of occasions: 'My client wants to make it clear that while she is not making any allegations against you in this regard, she did report it to An Garda Siochana.' Moreover, it was noted that Mr Quirke was spotted on CCTV on 3 December, interfering with her postbox, looking through her windows and interfering with items on her clothes line.

The letter asked Mr Quirke to 'refrain from entering' the property and to confine his activity to the 'farm vicinity' and only 'in daylight hours preferably'.

The letter was delivered to Pat on the morning of 14 December. That evening, he sat down to draft his furious response. In a Word document he saved as 'Dear Mr Leahy', he acknowledged receipt of the letter before adding that Mary had led a 'sustained campaign' against him for the past twelve months. Her teenage son was driving a motor car around the fields like a rally track, he wrote, with 'little regard for my stock, crops or fencing'. He said he had spoken to Mary about his ladders and had told her to 'refrain from moving' them. He complained about a tractor that blocked the entrance to the farm, with no keys in it, and nobody around to ask to move it. 'I believe this was another deliberate act,' the letter said.

Two days later, Pat was back sitting at his keyboard, still in a blaze of white fury. As he read over the letter from Mary's solicitor again, he carried out a series of Google searches for *defamation of character*. Who does she think she is? He wouldn't be intimidated by a solicitor's letter and would show Mr Leahy and Mary Lowry that he knew just as much about the law.

But the die had already been cast. By getting caught on camera, Pat had triggered the curious and fatal chain of events that would ultimately lead to his undoing. He had unwittingly handed Mary the reason and the means to destroy his claim to the farm. The clock was now ticking on his reign at Fawnagowan. He knew Mary wanted him off her land, but he also knew full well what secret that land was harbouring. It was a tricky situation, with much at stake. But by God, he wasn't going to go down without a fight.

10. Land war

Bobby Ryan was now missing nineteen months, and all this time one person knew the answer to the mystery of his disappearance: his murderer. While Bobby's family drove themselves to despair searching and wondering and wishing, the man who knew exactly what had happened to Bobby was skulking about the Lowry farm, stealing knickers off washing lines and acting as if none of it had anything to do with him. It seemed a master stroke – a crime that didn't even look like a crime because there was no body, no definitive evidence of any kind. But, like all 'perfect crimes', it had the potential to be unravelled, and this was now Pat Quirke's greatest fear. The legal wrangling was one way of buying some time.

Pat replied to Mary Lowry's solicitor on 2 January 2013, stating that her letter contained many inaccuracies and insinuations 'that I am not going to comment on or clarify for your benefit but please note I may do so at a later stage'. He pointed out that his mother-in-law lived at Fawnagowan and he wanted to continue visiting her as he had done 'for the last 25 years . . . She looks forward to my visits,' he wrote.

He would consider the termination of the lease if compensation was offered. This would have to take into account the 'forced sale' of his cows and the 'obvious loss of income'.

Pat was willing to go head-to-head with the allegations and the complaints – he had plenty of his own to sling back at his former lover – but he also knew that his eviction notice had effectively been served. Mary wanted him gone, so it was going to happen, it was just a matter of when. Once he was gone, it left the way open for a new tenant to take on the land. The next tenant might want to use the milking parlour and in restarting it might reopen the sealed run-off tank. That was why Pat was researching decomposition of the human body – he needed to know what exactly he was dealing with in the hidden run-off tank.

The solution wasn't immediately clear. It posed a dilemma, and his options were limited. If he did nothing and left Bobby's body where it was, he ran the risk that it would be discovered and he would immediately come under suspicion. He could fill in the tank, but Mary was now watching his every move on the farm and would surely notice if he arrived to Fawnagowan with a truckload of cement and deposited it. There was also the issue of the CCTV cameras, the ones that had sparked the solicitor's letter and were driving his early departure from the farm. They might see the things he managed to hide from Mary. Moving the body to a new location was also out of the question. Again, that kind of activity around the tank wouldn't go unnoticed.

Pat had a strategic way of thinking, and he soon alighted on the best solution. It was daring, but it was the only option that could work: he would control the gruesome discovery and pretend to find the body himself. Who would ever suspect the person who blows the whistle and calls the cops? And so began the devious and cunning plan that would finally solve the mystery of what had happened to Bobby Ryan after he left Mary's house on that June morning in 2011, nineteen long months ago.

First, Pat needed a plausible excuse to open the run-off tank. He came up with a plan to spread slurry on the land, a job that would require huge volumes of water to make it spreadable. He would say he went to the tank to draw the water and when he opened it, he discovered the body. There was a problem with this plan: the milking parlour was no longer in use and there had been little or no liquid flowing into the tank for years. That was easy enough to solve. Pat just needed a surreptitious 'water event' to take place that would cause the tank to fill with water.

As luck would have it, or more likely through a deliberate act of sabotage, a leak emerged in the milking parlour that did just that.

On 13 March, Mary suffered a further loss when her father, Michael, passed away at the Padre Pio Nursing Home in Holycross, where he had lived out his final years. Like his daughter, Michael loved music, and Mary had called on a local musician to entertain him and a few close friends in the days before he died. As she prepared to bury her father, a leak in the mains water system meant there was no running water in the house. The water flowed to the farm first and then to the house, so the reduction in pressure left them with no supply to the shower. Mary and the boys had to go to a neighbour's house to wash.

Pat later claimed that he had spotted the leak in the milking parlour, one he said had been caused by a pipe pulling away from its fitting due to frost, and that he had repaired it himself with fittings he had at home. By the time it was fixed, however, two days' worth of water had been flowing down through the milking parlour, along the underground pipes and out into the run-off tank. Pat could now say that he went to the tank to get water because he believed it would be full as a result of this flooding.

For the next part of the job, Pat needed a tractor and an agitator, a device used to stir slurry so that it can be sucked into a tanker and spread on the fields. He asked his friend and neighbour Pat O'Donnell whether he could borrow his. He was almost ready to make his grand discovery. Before he could do so, events overtook him yet again.

While Mary and her boys attended her father's funeral on Friday, 15 March, the house alarm went off yet again. When she returned home and looked at the CCTV footage, she spotted a man in the adjacent fields, prowling around and acting suspiciously. She knew it was Pat. He had been warned, clearly warned, and now it was time for action. Mary rang the gardaí. She had given him a chance before, but now she was happy to press charges.

Gardaí couldn't identify Pat on the footage from 15 March, but he was clearly visible on the footage from 3 December 2012. Using that, and the evidence that he had taken a house key, on 16 March at 8.45 p.m. they arrested him on suspicion of burglary. He was taken to Tipperary town garda station, where he was shown the footage from December and asked to account for his actions.

During an interview under caution, Pat told Detective Garda Martin Steed that on that day in December he had gone into his mother-in-law's property to turn on the heating. He also rang a doorbell and opened the postbox, but he said he didn't think there were any letters inside. While in the shed area, he noticed there was women's underwear on the clothes line and looked at the label because, he said, he was 'curious'. He took the items of underwear off the line and then pegged them back up again. He said he then tried a key, which he had previously found in the yard, in the lock of Mary's front door. When he pushed the handle, the door opened. He heard the beep of the alarm and 'panicked, having realized what I had done was wrong'. Still in a panic, he said he got in his jeep and drove away.

Pat was later released without charge in the early hours of 17 March. After his visit to the garda station, he engaged a solicitor to convey to Mary his deep regret at the deterioration of their relationship. As he did not want relations to deteriorate further, he was prepared to surrender the letting agreement and forgo any compensation, although he would continue visiting his mother-in-law at the property. A further letter from Mr Leahy suggested 1 July 2013 as the date for termination of the lease and offered that there was 'no difficulty' in Mr Quirke visiting his mother-in-law as long as the visits were 'confined for that purpose only'. After Pat agreed his departure date and his solicitor sent a deed of surrender to Mr Leahy, he secured a lease on a neighbouring farm to Breansha, belonging to Imelda's cousin, Mary Dillon.

After being caught on tape by Mary's surveillance cameras, Pat was in the frame for two break-ins and coming under close scrutiny from local gardaí. As he continued to concoct his plan to 'find' Bobby Ryan's body, he knew he had to be extremely careful. He was bolstered by the belief that he was smarter than everyone around him, the certainty that he could outwit them all.

Pat let some time lapse after the interview at the garda station, then in early April 2013 he contacted Seamus Buckley, a farm machinery salesman from Breen's Farm Machinery who had sold him a tractor the previous Christmas. Pat told him that he was now in the market for a vacuum tanker upgrade. The one he had could take 1,100 gallons of water, but he wanted one that would hold up to 2,000 gallons. Seamus had met Pat at the Ploughing Championships in Wexford the summer before. He also ran a printing business, and after Alan

Quirke's's tragic death he had supplied the *In memoriam* cards for Pat and Imelda. Wearing his farm machinery hat now, he visited the farm at Breansha to look at Pat's current tanker and then returned to his boss to discuss the trade-in and give Pat a value. The sale went ahead, subject to Pat taking the new tanker for a demo period. One of Pat's farmhands picked up the new tanker from Breen's Cashel office on 26 April.

He was ready to open the secret slurry pit.

Now that a date had been settled for Pat to officially vacate the farm, Mary tried to get on with life as best she could. She would only have to endure him a little while longer.

On 29 April, the CCTV cameras outside the house captured the last fleeting hours before the truth of what lay below the surface at Fawnagowan was finally laid bare. The footage, which would later be played in court, showed how the routine comings and goings of day-to-day life and the unavoidable interactions between all involved continued at Fawnagowan, despite the animosity between all parties.

In the garden, beside her mother-in-law's side of the house, Mary could be seen hunched over, her hands firmly gripping the lawnmower as she pushed it across the grass. As she powered over the lawn, bare-legged in a pair of high-cut shorts and a tight-fitting windcheater, the washing on the clothes line fluttered in the breeze.

A short time before, Pat could be seen cleaning his boots and entering through Rita's door. Earlier in the day he had brought his own tractor and vacuum tanker over to the farm to spread the contents of the open slurry tank over the adjacent fields. He would leave both on the farm overnight, in preparation for tomorrow. As he walked inside Rita's home, he found Imelda there with her mother. She had come to drive him home to collect Pat O'Donnell's tractor and agitator and bring them over to Fawnagowan.

While Pat, Imelda and Rita chatted briefly inside, Mary mowed the lawn just metres away. She took long, fast strides, weaving her way up and across the grass with purpose and eventually passing out of camera shot. Seconds later, Pat emerged from Rita's entrance door with Imelda. The pair got into a car and left.

Less than an hour later, at around 5.30 p.m., another camera, this one trained on the entrance to the farm, showed Pat arriving back at Fawnagowan in a blue tractor with an agitator connected to the back. He entered the farm through the gate and disappeared from shot.

Mary, meanwhile, had noticed the unfamiliar tractor and agitator and went over to the farmyard for a closer look. Imelda was by now back on the property too, waiting to collect Pat and drive him home. He would later tell gardaí that just as the couple were about to pull off in their car, he remembered he had left the keys of the tractor he had borrowed from Pat O'Donnell in the ignition. Imelda told him to run back and get them quickly.

In the CCTV footage, he is captured jumping out of the jeep in the pelting rain and disappearing through the farm gate. Imelda waits in the yard, engine running, unaware that her husband and sister-in-law were about to have another altercation.

As Pat made his way to the tractor, he saw Mary walking through the farmyard.

'Are you all right there?' he said.

Mary, sick of the sight of him parading around her farm as if he owned it, launched into a foul-mouthed tirade that would be her parting salvo to the man who had ruined her life.

'You're some c**t and I can't wait to see the back of you and I hope you won't be stealing Mary Dillon's knickers off the line,' she shouted.

Pat, safe in the knowledge that he was about to unleash fresh hell on her, laughed in her face and ran off. Two minutes later, as the rain continued to pelt down, he re-emerged from the farmyard, jumped in beside Imelda and the couple drove off.

Left to close the farmyard gate for the umpteenth time, something that deeply irritated her, Mary can be seen on the footage a few minutes later. That golden date, 1 July 2013, the day Pat would finally have to clear off her farm, couldn't come quick enough for her. But even then, with Rita as his excuse to visit, she knew she would never really be rid of him.

Pat, on the other hand, had taken his fate into his own hands and was looking ahead to tomorrow. When a dead body was discovered on her land, and she could give no explanation whatsoever as to how it had got there, perhaps it would turn out to be Mary, rather than him, who had to leave Fawnagowan behind for ever.

11. A gruesome discovery

It was 1.20 p.m. on a mild spring day and Sergeant Padraic Powell was kneeling down, peering into a small, dark opening in the ground. One of two cement slabs that had been covering the opening he was looking into was leaning against a small stand of hawthorn trees. The other, the one closest to the house, had been partially prised open, just wide enough to push in the suction pipe that was sticking out of it.

As visibility was poor, Sergeant Powell had to position himself low to the ground to get a good look. He crouched down and peered into the darkness below. He caught sight of something gardaí had been looking for since 2011. There, covered in a transparent, algae-like substance, was the partial outline of what could only be human remains.

It was 30 April 2013, and twenty-two months after the inexplicable disappearance of Bobby Ryan, the Lowry farm in the heart of the Golden Vale had just given up its darkest secret.

Earlier on, shortly after midday, the CCTV cameras outside Mary Lowry's home had filmed Pat Quirke, behind the wheel of his silver jeep, pulling into the farmyard at Fawnagowan. He arrived with a shovel, which he used to prise open the run-off tank behind the milking parlour so that he could draw water from it to agitate the slurry in the nearby slatted shed. While he was drawing the water, he saw something in the tank. He rang his wife, Imelda, to come directly to meet him there.

At 12.53 p.m. Imelda pulled into the driveway and drove past Mary Lowry's house and on up to the farmyard, where she parked her car. Pat told her of his find and asked her to take a look. She peered into the dank gloom of the tank and she saw it too. Unmistakeable. At that point Imelda, not her husband, rang a local garda to report the finding of human remains.

Garda Tom Neville, the same garda who had filled out the missing-person report on Bobby Ryan almost two years before, knew Imelda Quirke through the local underage hurling team. He had her number stored in his phone and when she rang him at 1.07 p.m. that day and told him about the gruesome discovery in the tank, he told her not to touch anything, that he would send a patrol car out to meet her at the farm.

Sergeant Powell, who at that time was the sergeant in charge of Tipperary town garda station, was on duty when Garda Neville phoned in with the news that a body had been discovered at Fawnagowan. He immediately made his way to the farm, accompanied by his colleague, Detective Garda David Buckley, who knew the way to Fawnagowan. When they arrived shortly after 1.15 p.m., they found Pat and Imelda sitting close together on a low wall, just past the cattle crush at the back of the farm. Pat appeared quiet and didn't say much, other than speaking to tell the sergeant that he had found a body in the run-off tank. Imelda seemed shocked and bewildered by all that was unfolding before her eyes. As Pat led Sergeant Powell to the tank, he noticed that the farmer was extremely clean, something he thought was odd considering he had been working with slurry. The garda didn't know much about farming, but his father-in-law often spread slurry and he knew it was a dirty job. He noticed that even Pat's hands were clean.

Detective Garda Buckley noticed it too. He would later recall looking the farmer up and down, carefully examining his clothes. He noted that there was no dirt on Pat's clothes, hands or person.

'That stood out in my mind because he was on a farm.'

While Detective Garda Buckley waited at the wall with Imelda, Sergeant Powell went with Pat to inspect the spot where he had found the body. When they reached it, the Sergeant saw an underground tank covered by a concrete slab, with a suction pipe running into it. When he knelt down and peered underneath the slab, he saw an outline of human remains, covered in transparent algae. To the right of the tank stood a tractor, and he saw that one of the slabs on the tank had been pushed aside where the suction hose had been wedged into the small gap that led to the bottom of the tank. The other end of the hose was attached to a nearby slurry tanker that was connected to the tractor.

A short time later, a second patrol car, carrying Garda John Ivers, Sergeant Cathal Godfrey and Garda Conor Ryan, drove up the laneway leading to Mary Lowry's house. They parked the car and made their way into the farm area. Pat and Imelda were sitting on the wall and Garda Ivers noted that Pat looked 'red-faced' and 'anxious'.

When Garda Ryan reached the area around the tank, he noticed that there was no fresh watermark inside it. He also noticed that the vacuum pump handle on the nearby vacuum tanker was in the neutral position, which would indicate that it wasn't sucking at the time of the discovery. He walked around the farm, and into the slatted shed he had visited with Pat Quirke in 2011 when he went to empty the open slurry tanks during the search for Bobby. There, he saw an old tractor and an agitator that had been placed into the tank through the manhole cover outside the shed. He looked inside the tank and noticed that the slurry was heavily crusted.

The slurry system inside the slatted shed at the Lowry farm worked as follows. The shed was floored with concrete slats. Underneath the slats was a tank, 5 ft deep, similar to a septic tank. When the cattle were inside the shed, their manure fell down through the gaps in the slats and into the tank below. The manure gathered until it passed along a pipe that ran underground from the tank, across the yard and into the open slurry pit. From there, it could be drawn out by a suction pipe attached to a tanker and then spread across the fields.

Depending on the type of diet the cattle were fed, sometimes the flow could become blocked. If they were on a high-fibre diet, the manure would be very watery and free-flowing and would therefore pass along more easily. If the manure was thick and unable to flow freely, the farmer would have to agitate it. This required coming in with an agitator, a device that is similar to a whisk, and adding water to make the manure more free-flowing and therefore more spreadable.

At Fawnagowan, the access point for doing this at the slatted shed was through a manhole cover outside the shed. The manhole cover could be opened and the agitator placed inside after water had been added. By adding water and whisking the manure, it slowly became more diluted. The manure would then start to flow underneath and make its way down the pipe and over to the open pit, from where it could be drawn.

The fact that Garda Ryan looked into the tank and saw that the manure was heavily crusted indicated that it hadn't been agitated at all. Moreover, it indicated that the slurry was so hardened, it would require massive amounts of water to get it to flow again. Pat Quirke was coming with a teacup's worth of water to do a job that would have required thousands of gallons of water.

Following a phone call from Garda Neville and Sergeant Powell, Detective Inspector Paddy O'Callaghan from Tipperary town garda station made his way to the scene. He had a small torch in his jeep, which he used to look briefly into the tank. Straight away he believed he was looking at the remains of Bobby Ryan. He had worked on the missing-person investigation and knew the farm was the last place Bobby had been seen alive, so it was logical that these were the remains of the missing man. He would later say that he believed Bobby had been murdered and placed in the tank or else placed in the tank following a serious assault and died there. Detective Inspector O'Callaghan immediately called Detective Superintendent Dominic Hayes, who had regional command of the South-Eastern region at the time, to inform him of the find. Hayes gave him clearance to declare the entire property at Fawnagowan a crime scene, specifically the farmyard and the slurry tank at the rear of the milking parlour, and then he set off to make his way to Mary's farm. Like his colleague Detective Inspector O'Callaghan, Detective Superintendent Hayes suspected that Bobby had been assaulted and murdered on the Lowry farm.

At 1.30 p.m., Detective Inspector O'Callaghan instructed Garda Ivers to cordon off the scene, which was now believed to be the location of a murder. All members of the team were instructed to collect and preserve anything that might be of evidential value. As more and more officers gathered at the scene, the entrance to the farm was sealed off with blue-and-white Garda tape. The same was done at the entrance to the general area of the run-off tank.

Detective Inspector O'Callaghan spoke to Detective Garda Buckley and asked him to invite Imelda and Pat to be interviewed in relation to the circumstances of the finding of the body. Of course, everyone was a suspect at that stage, but given Pat's history with Mary, the burglary arrests and the allegations of harassment, investigating gardaí had a strong suspicion that the man sitting quietly on the wall might have had a hand in murder. They also knew the importance of conducting a cautioned interview with him as quickly as possible.

Detective Garda Buckley went over to the wall, where Pat was in deep conversation with Imelda, and asked him if he would go with him to the station to make a statement under caution, making it clear that he wasn't under arrest, that he was under no obligation to come with him and that he was entitled to speak to his solicitor. Pat said he had no problem giving a statement and as he walked to the nearby patrol car, dressed in his sparkling clean zip-up jacket and trousers, he was followed by Imelda. The couple made the short journey to the garda station in separate patrol cars.

Mary Lowry was in her house when the police arrived and she watched the commotion outside. She had no clue what was going on, but she could see that, whatever it was, Pat Quirke was at the centre of it. Her boys were at school, so at least they weren't witnessing any of this.

She stepped out of her house at around 1.37 p.m. and walked towards the gate before turning around and going back inside her house. Shortly before 2 p.m., once the area behind her milking parlour had been declared a crime scene, Mary had to be told that a body had been found on her land. The task of telling her fell to Detective Inspector O'Callaghan.

He went to her front door and rang the bell. She greeted him and he told her a body had been found on her farm. She was stunned.

He then asked her if she knew of the existence of the run-off tank. Mary had no idea what he was talking about, so they walked towards the farmyard so he could show her. As Detective Inspector O'Callaghan led Mary towards the general area of the tank, he pointed over at the location of the discovery.

'A body was found over there,' he said.

Mary still had no idea what he was talking about.

'Where?' she asked.

'Over there in the tank,' he repeated, pointing over at it.

'There's no tank over there,' said Mary.

Mary was in total shock. Not only had she no idea about the tank, but the chilling realization that the body found in it was, in all likelihood, Bobby came like a bolt from the blue. She saw Pat and Imelda, just before they were led away to the patrol cars. She made no eye contact with either of them, but she would later say that she felt Imelda was 'shook by it' and that 'Pat was not perturbed at all'.

As Mary tried to take it all in, O'Callaghan told her that the farm, including her family home, was now a crime scene that had to be preserved. This meant that she and her children would have to leave so that the various forensic teams could start the hunt for clues.

Mary went back to the house to tell her mother-in-law, Rita, the terrible news about what had been found on the farm. She would later have to bring the elderly grandmother to her sister-in-law's house while the murder investigation got underway.

After leaving that day with just a few belongings in some

black plastic bags, Mary Lowry would never again return to her home in Fawnagowan.

Pat and Imelda arrived at Tipperary town garda station shortly after 2 p.m. They were taken to separate interview rooms, Imelda with Detective Sergeant Long and Detective Sergeant Keane, Pat with Detective Garda David Buckley and Detective Garda Martin Steed. Detective Garda Buckley walked Pat to the interview room, where he handed him an explanatory note on interview regulations. There were two cameras in the room, one behind the door and one on the ceiling. Detective Garda Buckley explained what would happen to the videotapes of the interview before unwrapping three tapes in Pat's presence. They would make three copies of the recording: a master copy that would go into a sealed bag; a copy that would be provided to Pat; and a copy that would be used by investigating gardaí. He then asked Pat if he had a mobile phone, which he did. Pat handed it over to be examined and, at 2.17 p.m., just over an hour after the human remains were found, the Garda interviewers pressed Record on the video recorder and the interview began.

'You discovered a body at the back of Mary Lowry's land earlier today?'

'Yes,' replied Pat.

They asked him if it was right to say that he farmed the land there and he explained that he was leasing it.

'Will you tell us, in as much detail as you can, how you came to find the body?'

Pat began by telling them that he went to empty the slurry tank so that he could 'spread the slurry'.

'I had borrowed a tractor with an agitator to agitate the slurry,' he said. 'The slurry was very thick and needed more water. I also had my own tractor with a vacuum tanker. I knew there was water in the old septic tank because there had been a leak in the milking parlour which services that tank. I went to suck out water. I opened the lid and noticed something down there as I was sucking the water up. I could see plastic, then thought it was a dummy or inflatable doll. The water was all sucked up at this stage, so I turned off the tank and opened the other lid. I could see clearly it was a body. I was shocked. I rang my wife, Imelda. It took three calls to get through to her. I wanted to wait for her until I did anything else. She came on and I tried to tell her as best I could what I was preparing her for before she looked at it. After she got over the shock, she called Tom Neville. We waited, then ye all came out.'

Pat told the detectives that he had arrived at the farm that day at about 12 or 12.30 p.m. He had got the tractor the evening before and 'everything was all set to go'. He added that one of his students, Gary Cunningham from Aherlow, was supposed to be there to help him, but he 'got a kick from a cow last Friday' and had been out of work since.

'Is it the time of year to be spreading slurry?' asked the gardaí.

'Yes, it's late, but the year is late,' Pat replied.

He confirmed that the run-off tank was connected to the milking parlour, which hadn't been used since 2007. They asked about the tank, and when he had last opened it.

'Not since 2008.'

'When you lifted the lids on the tank, which lid did you lift first?' they asked.

'The one nearest the house,' replied Pat.

They asked how he had lifted it.

'I had a shovel with me. I didn't actually lift it. I prised it open.'

Pat's demeanour during questioning, which would seldom change in the presence of gardaí, was that of quiet confidence.

At 2.47 p.m., Detective Garda Buckley left the interview room. When he returned, Pat was again asked about the position of the lids when he first looked into the tank.

'So you hadn't lifted the lid fully off, you only prised it open?'

'Enough to get the pipe in,' he answered.

'Was there enough water in the tank?' they asked.

'I thought there would have been more, a third to a half full, but didn't really know the depth of it,' replied Pat.

'When you saw the body first, on what side of the tank were you standing?'

The next line that came out of Pat's mouth was to be the source of much controversy. The gardaí believe he said, 'It was down through the hole that the pipe was in. I hadn't the other lid lifted off.' In court, however, his defence would argue that he said, 'It was down through the hole the pipe was in. I had the other lid off.' Ultimately, the transcript of the interview, which was later sent to an expert stenography company in the UK, contained the word 'had'. Despite arguments about dialect and accent, this would be the version shown to the jury.

The gardaí then asked him how he got the other lid off.

'I think I just caught it and flipped it upside-down,' said Pat.

He could clearly see it was a body, he told them, so they asked him to describe what he saw.

'I could see his pelvis and what looked like his private area, though he looked to be face down,' he said. 'It was kind of confusing. I couldn't see his face.'

It was at this point, he told the two detectives, that he rang his wife, Imelda.

'You rang her before you had a good look?'

'If you want to put it that way,' he replied.

Phone records would later show that Pat called Imelda's phone at 12.33 p.m., a call that lasted eight seconds. His phone then called a vet seconds later. Within a minute of that, the phone called voicemail and a minute later called Imelda's phone twice more. On the last occasion, the call lasted for thirty-six seconds.

In the interview, Pat described how he tried Imelda a number of times before he eventually got her. He said she told him she was in her sister-in-law's house and he asked her if she could come to the farm. Imelda asked him did he want a lift and he said yes because he didn't want to panic her.

While he waited for her to arrive, which was about ten minutes later, he walked around the farmyard.

'Why ring Imelda and not gardaí?' they asked.

Pat told them he just wanted someone to confirm the find with him first.

'I suppose it was instinctive to ring her,' he said. 'I wasn't even thinking about it.'

'Would agitating slurry not be a dirty job?' they asked.

'I was really only going into the dirty part, by mixing water and that,' he replied.

They wanted to know if he had known Bobby Ryan.

He said 'not really' and that he had only met him three times: the first time was at a hotel in Thurles, the second was at a night out in Clonmel, and the third was in Killough Quarry, where Bobby worked.

They talked about the day he went missing and Pat confirmed that he had previously told gardaí that he was at the farm that morning.

'Would you have been at the tank that day?' they asked.

'No,' replied Pat.

'Did you see anyone at the tank that day?'

'No,' said Pat.

As Detective Garda Buckley stepped out of the room to get some new tapes, Pat asked Detective Garda Steed if he would be able to get his tractor back that evening.

'That I don't know at the moment,' replied the detective.

When Detective Garda Buckley returned to the room a short time later, Pat was again reminded that he was still under caution. The new videotapes were unwrapped and the questions started again.

As the afternoon wore on, the questions asked by Buckley and Steed turned to Pat's relationship with Mary Lowry. They wanted to know how he felt about her relationship with Bobby.

'Well, I'm sure you know I had an affair with Mary Lowry,' he said at one point when asked if he approved of the relationship. 'But to answer the question, I didn't disapprove of it.' He added that there was 'no animosity' between him and Bobby. He admitted the relationship between him and Mary had ended badly, but denied being jealous of her new relationship with Bobby.

'You just took it on the chin?'

'What else could I do but take it on the chin?' he replied.

He told them that he wasn't bothered by the new relationship and that on one occasion he had even taken his wife on a night out with the couple.

Had he met Bobby at Mary's house on the morning that he disappeared?

'No.'

Did he know that Mr Ryan's body was there all along?

'No. These are nice questions now, lads,' he said.

All he knew, Pat told the detective, were the 'things Mary Lowry told me'.

And what were they?

'Different things,' he replied. He said she didn't know whether it took two minutes or ten minutes for Mr Ryan's van to leave her house on the morning that he disappeared. He found that 'strange'. He also questioned 'how she found his van so quick', referring to how Mary and Michelle found the van abandoned in nearby Bansha Wood on the day Bobby disappeared.

'When she showed me the location of the van, I asked her how she could see that from the road,' Pat told them, 'and she replied that she couldn't, she just drove in.'

He told the gardaí that he had asked her if she had heard a car drive into the yard on the morning Bobby Ryan disappeared. She said she was 'certain' a car hadn't entered because she would have heard it. But, he said, he had been in her bedroom when the doorbell rang, and 'you couldn't be certain of hearing a car'.

'I found it intriguing,' he said at one point. 'She had a couldn't-care-less attitude about it.'

He had 'asked questions' and thought the answers 'strange'.

He had a hunch about what happened, like everyone else. 'Everyone had notions, was he attacked? Did he leave for Spain?'

'Have you any idea how the body ended up in the tank?' they asked him.

'No.'

'Did you have any role to play in the body ending up in the tank?'

'No.'

To someone on the outside looking in, they said, he had a motive to kill Bobby Ryan.

'Maybe,' he replied, 'but that's not true.'

He agreed that he probably still had feelings for Mary.

'It couldn't have been easy to see her carrying on with Bobby Ryan, it must have bothered you?'

'No more than it was for her to see me with my wife,' he replied.

After Bobby's disappearance and when the two slurry tanks were emptied, why did he not tell gardaí about the third, hidden tank?

'I didn't think of it,' he said. 'I thought it was laughable [for the gardaí] to be emptying the slurry tank. I thought it was a waste of time.'

'That's because you knew the body was there,' they said to him.

'No,' he shot back.

He told them he didn't know who else knew about the tank and that it was Martin Lowry who had told him about it. It was a tank that he 'wouldn't pay attention to' and he hadn't seen anyone near it.

At 5.03 p.m., after an interview that had lasted nearly three hours, the video recorder in the interview room was switched off.

Shocked and confused about what was going on, Mary Lowry called her brother Eddie. They arranged to meet in Super-Valu in Tipperary town, and Mary made her way there. They drank tea and talked while they waited for the boys to finish school. Mary was visibly upset, Eddie would later recall. They arranged that, while the Garda investigation team took temporary ownership of her home, Mary and the boys would come to stay with Eddie's family in Newport. Even amid the surreal, the practical decisions had to be made.

Detective Superintendent Dominic Hayes made his way to Fawnagowan. The farm was now alive with activity as the investigation got underway. Hayes arrived there at 2.50 p.m., met Garda John Ivers at the outer cordon and was admitted on to the farm. Sergeant Cathal Godfrey directed him to the inner cordon, which was the area around the tank. He walked over to the top of the tank, where the lid was open. To his left he saw the little stand of hawthorn trees and to his right he noticed the slurry spreader attached to a vacuum tanker. He crouched down on his hunkers and looked into the tank, where he could see the outline of a human body, lying face down. He ordered a full team of investigators from the Garda Technical Bureau (GTB) in Phoenix Park HQ in Dublin to examine the scene. The local Scenes of Crime Unit had already been requested to attend by Detective Inspector O'Callaghan, but this was going to be a difficult task and looked like it would require the top expertise at his disposal.

He also made contact with Dr Khalid Jaber, the Assistant State Pathologist, informing him of the discovery of the body and the circumstances of Bobby Ryan's disappearance. Detective Superintendent Hayes asked him to attend, but Dr Jaber didn't see any need to visit the scene. He arranged to do the post-mortem the following day.

After surveying the scene at the tank, Detective Superintendent Hayes walked around the farmyard and found another tractor, with an agitator attached, parked outside the slatted shed. The agitator was inside the tank, having been placed there through the manhole cover. It was full of crusted cattle slurry. It was the same agitator and tractor that had already been noted by Garda Conor Ryan. Going by what they observed, there was little to suggest that the slurry had been agitated at all.

At this stage, discussions were taking place about how best to remove the body from the tank. The remains appeared to be severely decomposed and were therefore in a very delicate condition. Any operation to remove the body from such a confined space would have to be executed with extreme care in order to preserve as much evidence as possible. It would not be a straightforward task. By then, officers from the GTB had arrived, dressed in white overalls, masks and protective footwear. A blue crime scene screen was erected around the tank to protect the removal operation from view. It would be these officers' job to assist in planning the extraction of the most vital piece of evidence, the body. They had their work cut out for them.

Shortly before 6 p.m., Bernard O'Brien, a part-time fire officer, took a call at the local fire station requesting assistance in retrieving the body from the tank at Fawnagowan.

Both Detective Superintendent Hayes and Detective Inspector O'Callaghan had been in and out to the scene all day, and as the focus zoned in on the retrieval effort, they arranged to meet again at the farm.

Detective Superintendent Hayes arrived back at the scene shortly before 6 p.m. with several members of the GTB. They included Detective Sergeant John Grant, a crime scene manager with over twenty years' experience, Detective Garda Sharon Langan from the ballistics section, a crime scene mapper, a fingerprint expert and a photographer. The job of the crime scene manager is to lead the team of crime scene investigators and specialists at a complex or major investigation. He or she will advise the senior investigating officer (SIO) in planning forensic investigation strategies at a crime scene to ensure that the gathering of relevant forensic evidence and data is undertaken in a legal and ethical manner. The crime scene manager's role is to maximize the evidential potential of the scene by supervising the team of crime scene investigators and other specialists to ensure the effective processing of the scene. He or she also has to manage the crime scene staff and other specialists to ensure their well-being and welfare, ensuring appropriate care and support is in place to enable them to operate safely and effectively.

As the team, under Detective Sergeant John Grant's guidance, worked out how best to remove the body, the second lid was removed to get a better view inside the tank. Detective Superintendent Hayes and Detective Sergeant Grant discussed their options, taking into consideration the health and safety risk of entering the tank in its current state.

Bernard O'Brien and his nine-man team of firemen were met at the scene by Detective Inspector O'Callaghan at around 6.15 p.m. When O'Brien looked into the tank it was 'murky and dirty', but he could see the shape of a body. 'I could see an outline,' he said. 'I could see ribs.' Realizing that the men he would be sending in to retrieve the body would be wearing 'bulky' chemical suits to avoid cross-contamination, O'Brien asked the gardaí to widen the space. The tank was covered by a concrete roof that had been poured in place and reinforced with corrugated iron. Peeling it back would require a digger.

Before that could happen, the tractor and the vacuum tanker had to be moved back from the scene within the inner cordon, to allow space for the digger to manoeuvre into position. Garda Ryan, because of his farming background, was asked to move both. After driving the tractor and tanker a few feet forward into the field around the tank, he emptied the contents of the tanker. The water that Pat said he had sucked out of the tank, the one he thought would be one-third to two-thirds full, came to about a hundred litres as it was poured out on to the ground in an adjacent field – just under one-tenth full.

Tony Chearnley, a retired local garda who had been contacted by Sergeant Godfrey and asked if he could get a digger to help in the retrieval of a body, arrived with a small, 360 excavator shortly before 7 p.m. In preparation for the removal of the tank's roof, Detective Superintendent Hayes used a shovel to scrape off some of the clay lying on top of it, during which a metal gate was placed across the opening to prevent debris falling into the tank below. While the team from the fire services changed into their chemical suits and attached breathing apparatus, the arm of the digger was carefully brought into position over the tank.

As the digger pulled away the concrete, the lid broke where there had been a pre-existing crack and several small pieces of debris fell into the tank below. Finally, the roof now off, the fire services had room to enter the tank with the body.

Detective Inspector O'Callaghan put in a call to Michelle Ryan. It was important that the family was notified of the situation before they heard it via the media, or indeed social media. So he rang her mobile to tell her that human remains had been found where her father was last seen alive.

Michelle was in the car when the phone rang, on her way to pick up her son from school. As soon as she answered, O'Callaghan asked her where she was and if she was sitting down. He explained to her that a body had been found on

Mary Lowry's land, that there was a possibility it was her father, but that there was no confirmation yet. It was the call the Ryan family had been waiting for and dreading.

Michelle immediately called her brother, Robert, and they made their way to Fawnagowan. They were met by crime scene tape at the end of the lane, where they were asked to stand and proceed no further. There, the Ryan children waited.

Assisted by sub-officer Eddie Leahy, O'Brien placed a short extension ladder down into the tank and used a rod to measure the depth. Leahy measured six to nine inches of liquid in the bottom of the tank.

Patrick Meagher, wearing a yellow biohazard suit, carefully made his way down the ladder and into the tank below. His colleague, Andy Kavanagh, also in protective gear, had descended the ladder and disappeared into the gloom just ahead of him. The suits were bulky and in the confined and cramped space where the men found themselves, manoeuvring was difficult. As they reached the end of the ladder and stepped on to the bottom of the tank, their knee-high boots became submerged in what turned out to be about twelve inches of a dark, slimy substance.

Once in the tank, Kavanagh and Meagher positioned themselves at either end of the body.

'We could see clearly that it was a body,' Kavanagh said. 'The ribs were clearly showing.'

They assessed the scene in front of them. The gardaí had asked them to keep the body intact as much as possible, but that was going to be challenging in such a narrow space. The plan was to slide a tarpaulin sheet under the body, and then carefully lift it out of the tank.

As they began to try to slip the tarpaulin sheet under the

body, they encountered a difficulty. Meagher noticed a 'slight problem with his right arm and shoulder' when he tried to push the sheet under the right side of the body: 'It appeared that his right hand was slightly underneath him. I asked Kavanagh if he could come up and get the ground sheet up further. We managed that.'

It took about ten minutes to get the tarpaulin sheet fully under the body. Once it was in place, the two men gripped the corners and attempted to lift it across to the opening, where the ladder was. But there was another problem. Sludge from the body had gathered in the sheet, adding extra weight to the load they were trying to lift. The two men decided to tilt the body slightly, releasing some of the sludge and lightening the load. That worked.

They resumed their slow approach towards the opening, carefully, carefully lifting the body up towards the light. Their colleagues were ready, arms stretched out, waiting to receive the sheet with its tragic load. The sheet emerged into the open air and was transferred gingerly to the ground beside the tank. The operation was complete.

Bobby Ryan was above ground, and no longer a missing person.

The murmurs flew through the assembled officers and onlookers that the body had been safely retrieved. The long wait was over. This was the moment when everything would change, when the story of Bobby Ryan would be picked up again and pushed towards its conclusion. While the various crews and teams petered away, a local priest arrived to say prayers over the body. It was a solemn scene as darkness fell at Fawnagowan and the first steps towards a dignified burial were set in motion for Bobby Ryan.

Huddled together on the main road, behind the blue-and-white tape, Michelle and Robert Ryan watched as a hearse from Devitt's Funeral Directors in Cashel slowly emerged from the farmyard and inched its way down the driveway towards the entrance to Fawnagowan. Michelle caught a glimpse of the body bag, carrying the flat and depressed shape of what remained of a corpse, and she gripped her brother tightly.

The official confirmation would take time, but Michelle and Robert knew in their hearts that they were witnessing the final journey of their father, Bobby Ryan.

12. 'My name is destroyed in this town'

Dr Khalid Jaber, the Assistant State Pathologist, dressed in a green plastic apron and matching gloves, slowly ran a hose across Bobby Ryan's badly decomposed body. The remains, depressed and brittle, were covered in a dark, algae-like substance. In order to carry out a detailed post-mortem, Dr Jaber had to wash off as much as he could. The body had been wrapped in a plastic sheet and placed in a body bag at the scene and now, as it lay on the stainless-steel post-mortem table, its pungent odour enveloped the room. Dead bodies always carry a strong odour, but this smell was so strong, it carried outside the building.

It was shortly after 11 a.m. on 1 May 2013 inside the mortuary room of University Hospital Waterford, where the team from the GTB, Detective Inspector O'Callaghan and Detective Garda Kieran Keane were all gathered to observe the post-mortem.

Dr Jaber had decided against travelling to the scene the day before, but now he was carefully examining the corpse on the table to determine the cause of death. As he carried out his examination, he handed Detective Garda Sharon Langan, from the GTB, samples he removed from the body: a sample of deep tissue muscle; a gold watch; a sample of bone marrow; a strand of hair from the head; a maggot; a tooth. One by one, as Dr Jaber handed her each item, Detective Garda Langan placed them in a clear, tamper-proof evidence bag. She labelled the bags SL1 to SL6, signed and dated them, and gave the exhibits to the exhibits officer, Detective Garda Keane, who would later deliver them to the forensic scientists for forensic examination.

As Dr Jaber worked his way over Bobby's remains, he made oral observations about what he could see. Detective Inspector O'Callaghan carefully recorded his findings, noting down every item mentioned. He was now heading up a major murder investigation and knew the value of keeping meticulous notes, which have evidential value in a court of law. He had assumed the role of acting SIO in the case due to the imminent departure of his colleague, Detective Inspector William Leahy, who had been promoted to the rank of superintendent the day before the body was found and would shortly take up a post at Listowel garda station, down in County Kerry.

Detective Inspector O'Callaghan was a seasoned detective and SIO. He had been posted to Tipperary town garda station in 2010, following a sixteen-year stint in Limerick. While there, he had worked across the city during the violent gangland feuds involving the McCarthy-Dundon and Ryan gangs. He was involved in the investigation of numerous high-profile murders, including the murders of Brian Fitzgerald and Frankie Ryan. More importantly, he was a local, from Tipperary town itself, and familiar with both the Quirke and Lowry families. His chief suspect, Pat Quirke, had been two years above him in school.

O'Callaghan listened attentively as Dr Jaber concluded that the cause of death was blunt force trauma, mainly to the face and side of the head. The victim had sustained multiple fractures to the skull in the region of the forehead, eye sockets, right and left sides of the face and the cheek bones. There were several rib fractures, six to the right of the torso and three to the left, as well as a fracture of the right femur (thighbone), the strongest bone in the human body. The injuries were fatal and Dr Jaber told the investigators that the victim would have died within minutes.

O'Callaghan noted it all down, including Dr Jaber's conclusion that the injuries could be the result of an 'accident/traffic collision or serious assault'. He discussed the findings with the crime scene manager, Detective Sergeant Grant, who was also present. O'Callaghan was of the opinion that, due to the naked state of the body, there was a possibility death had occurred inside the house. After consultation with Detective Superintendent Hayes, a decision was made to examine Mary's house, as well as the farm sheds, for blood spatter evidence. At this stage, the gardaí were considering every possibility. Every person was a suspect, and every location around the farm was a possible murder scene.

That evening, Detective Inspector O'Callaghan travelled back to Tipperary town garda station, where an incident room had been set up. The incident room would be the central hub of the investigation, taking in, collating and sifting through every single lead and piece of evidence. The officers there already had much to do, and O'Callaghan now brought in the findings of the post-mortem, which led them to believe they were dealing with a murder case.

O'Callaghan had arranged to meet with Michelle and Robert Ryan at the station, to update them. He told them what was known so far, although advising them that the remains had not yet been identified as their father's. To that end, he would require a DNA sample from each of them in order to formally identify the body.

At this point, Detective Inspector O'Callaghan produced

SL2, to see if they recognized it. As he held it up in front of them and her father's gold watch slid down the inside of the evidence bag, Michelle broke down in tears. Her worst fears had now been realized. Her father had been murdered, and they had spent almost two years chasing his ghost.

In the days that followed, Mary Lowry's house and farm, including all the outhouses and sheds, were searched forensically. The working theory was that the number of injuries Bobby had suffered would have resulted in large amounts of blood spill at the scene. Accordingly, the ceilings, walls and skirting boards inside the house all underwent luminol testing, a spray that gives off a blue fluorescence when it comes in contact with a substance that may be blood.

Several items were taken away for further testing, including a light fitting in the living room, three pieces of carpet from the bedroom and the kickboard of the wardrobe. Nothing of evidential value was found.

As the media attention around the story grew, reporters started calling to Eddie's house in Newport, to try to speak with Mary Lowry, the woman at the centre of the investigation. Mary moved on, staying with her sister in Thurles to escape the glare. When the glare followed her there too, she later rented a house for herself and the boys in nearby Dundrum, about eleven miles from Fawnagowan. Her world had been turned upside-down, and this was only the start of it.

Pat knew he was a person of interest to the investigation, and he was busy thinking about his mobile phone, the one he had handed over to the gardaí on 30 April. He knew they would check who he had been in contact with and, in anticipation of whatever questions they might put to him, he wanted to make sure his story matched his phone activity.

On 9 May, he logged on to his computer and sent a request to Vodafone customer support, asking for help with getting hold of 'details relating to my account'. On 11 May, he requested an invoice for June 2011. Two days later, he asked for a log of all incoming calls and texts to his phone from 2 June to 5 June 2011. Like the investigators, he was working the angles, covering all bases, making his case watertight.

Two weeks after the discovery of the body, the gardaí were able to finally confirm that the remains found on Mary's property belonged to Bobby Ryan. The identification was completed with the aid of a DNA sample taken from one of Bobby's teeth, which was matched with DNA samples taken from Michelle and Robert. Dr Jaber's post-mortem had concluded that the level of decomposition was consistent with death 'some time' earlier and it was 'entirely plausible that Bobby died on or about 3 June 2011' – the date he went missing.

Now that the gardaí had a formal ID on the body, the incident room could drill down into Bobby Ryan's life and try to figure out who might have wanted to kill him. The first step was to interview Pat Quirke again. On 16 May, Detective Sergeant John Keane called to Breansha to invite Pat into the station for a voluntary cautioned interview. Pat agreed to call to Tipperary town garda station at 8 p.m.

Later that evening, the interview was carried out by Detective Sergeant Keane and Detective Garda Buckley and started at 8.08 p.m. After some general questions about his movements the night before Bobby disappeared, the gardaí turned to events leading up to his discovery of the body on 30 April 2013. They began by asking Pat if he had ever emptied the slurry from the slatted tank prior to April 2013. He said that he had and that it could be 'awkward to mix' because it was so thick.

They asked him if the slatted tank was full, and he said it was. He told them that he became concerned about the amount of slurry in the tank towards the end of March, that it might be full or overfull.

'Where do you normally draw the water to agitate the slurry?' they asked him.

He said he would normally get water from the open tank or else the contractor would bring a load.

'So, knowing the tank was full, why didn't you bring water with you?'

He said he had brought his tanker and tractor over on the Monday and emptied the open tank. Imelda had collected him so that he could pick up the contractor's tractor and bring it to Fawnagowan.

'Why not bring the tractor and vacuum home and bring water back on the thirtieth?' they asked him.

Pat said he knew there would be water in the run-off tank because of the leak and that it would be enough to get the 'slatted tank started'.

Did he check to see if there was enough water in there?

'Not until I went to suck it out,' he replied. He told them that it was in the back of his mind that there had been two days' worth of water flowing into the tank because of the leak in the milking parlour.

'Would logic not tell you to check the tank on the twenty-ninth?'

'I thought it would've been enough water there,' he said.

He conceded that when he'd opened the tank, he 'thought there would have been more'.

When he opened the tank, how much did he see?

'Maybe half full, maybe two-thirds.' He wasn't sure.

The gardaí asked him if he'd ever opened the tank before. He said he had, when a calf got its leg stuck in one of the slabs covering the tank.

'I freed the leg and looked into the tank. I considered it to be empty.' He had closed the gap with the slabs and called the vet to treat the calf.

'So, how many times previously have you drawn water from this tank?' asked the gardaí.

'I haven't,' he replied.

He told them that Mary's brothers-in-law, Jimmy and Johnny, knew about the tank. Mary knew about it too, he added.

This, of course, completely contradicted Mary's reaction when she learned of the discovery earlier that day. She clearly had no idea about the tank and was surprised to learn of its existence.

They moved on to the process of agitating the slurry in the slatted tank.

Pat said the slatted tank had already been mixed and emptied in January, so he 'didn't think it would be tough to get going'.

'I take it you tried to agitate before you added water?' asked the gardaí.

Pat said he had started the machine and 'just stirred it' on the Monday evening, just to see if it was 'stirring okay'.

'On Tuesday my plan was to start it,' he said, 'but it was too thick and I was afraid I would overheat the bearing.' He said he worked it for about 'five or ten minutes' on the Monday, but he 'wasn't having much luck' because it was too thick.

'Would you not have thought to look into the tank to see if there was enough water?'

'What difference would it have made?' replied Pat. 'Normally you'd get lucky. Worst-case scenario, I'd bring over water. I considered there was enough in the tank. Maybe there was, maybe there wasn't.'

He told the gardaí that on 30 April, the day the body was discovered, he went to Fawnagowan in his jeep with a shovel to prise open the tank so that he could put in the hose and 'suck out the contents'.

'After I stopped the agitator, I drove my tractor with vacuum over to the tank, got my shovel, prised it open, put in my pipe, saw how much water was in there first and, you were right, I was disappointed. I wasn't sure of the depth of the tank so I said, "I'll take what's here." I hitched on my hose and started sucking the water. I thought the hose was stuck to the ground, so I moved the tractor forward about a foot, went back to the tank and sucked again. This time I was watching closer. The water level was lower, that's when I saw the body.'

After that, Pat said, he shut off the tank.

'What then?' asked the gardaí.

'I turned, I pulled off the other flagstone to get a better look and I saw for sure what I was looking at – a body, head facing down, facing towards me. That's it.'

They asked him what position he was in when he first saw the body. He told them he was looking through the hole 'wide enough to take the pipe'.

'The pipe from the tank was in the hole?'

'Yes,' replied Pat.

What did he see when he initially looked in?

'Initially what I saw when looking into the hole, before I

pulled back the second flagstone, was a foreign object,' said Pat. 'I suppose it looked more like carpet than plastic. I don't think I gave too long looking at it. I think I just pulled back the second flagstone.'

Again, they asked him what he saw before he pulled back the second stone.

'I couldn't see far enough with my line of sight,' he told them. 'I couldn't see how long it was, I couldn't see the end of it.'

'How long did it look to you?' they asked.

'I couldn't see the end of it.'

Pat, by this stage, knew the detectives were zoning in on what he said he could see before the second slab was removed. Based on his interview on 30 April, he had told them what he had seen when the second slab was removed. (Gardaí believed he said, 'it was down through the hole the pipe was in. I had the other lid off' in that interview.) Now that story had changed.

He couldn't be sure if he thought it was a body at that stage, he told them, so he 'turned the other stone upside down'.

'How did you do that?' they asked.

'I caught it by my hands, lifted it up and put it back against the bank.'

They asked him what he could see after the second slab had been removed.

'I could see very clearly it was a body,' he said.

'Can you describe it?'

'Graphically,' said Pat. 'Every time I close my eyes . . . Body lying facedown. I could see ribs, that was kind of confusing. I thought the body was up and face down. I thought I saw the head, but Imelda said it was a skull. Pelvic area, what I thought looked like his private area, legs together, arms I couldn't see but I thought by his side. Feet, I couldn't make out. Naked, no sign of clothes, no sign of ribbons of clothes. Lying in parallel position to the length of tank, dead centre, that's it.'

He said that he didn't stay long looking at the body before he rang Imelda.

Why did he not call the gardaí when he saw the body, they wanted to know.

'I didn't think of anything logical,' he said. 'I just thought of ringing Imelda.'

Why ask her to come up and look into the tank, though?

'I suppose to confirm what I saw,' replied Pat.

'I suppose if it was me,' said one of the Garda interviewers, 'I'd prefer my wife not to know there was a body in the tank.'

'That possibly crossed my mind when I saw her looking in,' said Pat. 'I know what Imelda is like in a crisis. I knew she'd know what to do.'

He told the gardaí that his first instinct was that the body in the tank was Bobby Ryan.

If that was the case, they pointed out, why did he not alert Mary Lowry, whose land the tank is on?

Pat said he didn't think she was there and added that he was afraid what she might say. He wasn't 'thinking straight or acting straight'. He was concerned that the body was naked and when the gardaí pressed him on that he said: 'My first concern was that the man didn't walk out of the house.' He added: 'I just didn't want to meet her [Mary Lowry], I just wanted to meet one person [Imelda].'

He had a theory in his head at the time, he said, about the body being naked, but he later had a conversation with someone who told him that a professional killer would remove the clothes to destroy forensic evidence. He was afraid of Mary Lowry, he said, adding: 'The whole thing frightened me.'

When asked why he was afraid of Mary, he said that he was 'always afraid of her. She is vicious.' He said that she had abused him the previous day, when he met her on the farm. 'She let fly verbal abuse,' he said, after she was 'caught snooping and didn't like to be caught'.

He said he avoided her at all costs but that she wasn't violent, just verbally abusive. He accepted that he was probably verbally abusive towards her as well.

The gardaí asked him why he instinctively thought the body was that of Bobby Ryan and he replied: 'Who else would it be?'

He said he didn't believe Bobby had gone to Spain to start a new life, as some had claimed, and had always thought something sinister had happened to him. Pat said he was curious by nature and couldn't 'go with the flow' or accept what other people were saying. He didn't believe Bobby committed suicide or hitched a lift to Rosslare and took a ferry to France.

'People who commit suicide want to be found,' he told the gardaí.

When asked about his relationship with Bobby, he said he didn't know him well enough to like him, that they had nothing in common and so probably weren't going to be friends. While he wasn't happy with how his relationship with Mary had ended, her being with Bobby didn't bother him.

He said that he had spent his life in Tipperary and now his name was 'destroyed' in the town.

'I had an affair with this woman, but this is my only crime. I hate to say that I need to clear my name, but my name is mud.'

After almost five hours of questioning, the interview ended at around 1 a.m.

As Pat made his way home to Breansha, tired after an interview that had taken most of the night, he had no idea that a raid was due to take place in his home the following morning. Three days before, Detective Sergeant Keane had been to the District Court to obtain a warrant to search Pat's house. Gardaí were looking for any evidence that would connect him to Bobby's murder. The search, which would include the house and the farm, had been planned days in advance. The team of roughly ten gardaí, including Detective Sergeant Keane, Detective Garda Steed and Garda John Walsh, had carefully picked the date and time. The fact that Pat had two young children had been taken into account and a decision taken to land at the house after they had gone to school.

Although the murder investigation was still at an early stage, the team had already built up a very accurate profile of their chief suspect. They knew they were dealing with a very cunning individual, someone who had planned and calculated every move to date, a man who saw himself as something of an intellectual and a cut above the rest. As he briefed the team in the station kitchen that morning, Detective Inspector O'Callaghan gave a specific direction to seize any computers found in the house. He had a gut feeling that in advance of opening the tank Pat would have researched material to do with the decomposition of bodies. It was a very specific hunch, one that would later both intrigue and baffle the state prosecutor, but ultimately it was a hunch that proved to be spot-on.

The knock came to Pat's front door at around 10.45 a.m. on Friday, 17 May. As a team of gardaí descended on the farm, Detective Sergeant Keane, the man who had questioned Pat the night before, held up his Garda badge and identified himself. After cautioning Pat, he handed him a warrant that listed the items being searched for: Bobby Ryan's clothing, footwear, jewellery, keys and the weapon used to kill him.

Pat held the document in his hand, reading his way down the page, then he looked up at Detective Sergeant Keane and said, 'The media were wrong when they said clothes and a wallet were found in the tank with the body.' He asked the Detective Sergeant how Bobby Ryan had died, and Keane replied that he couldn't tell him.

A search of the house and lands began. The team, wearing latex gloves and carrying large, transparent evidence bags, worked slowly and methodically through each room in the main house, including the home office, a small room with a grey filing cabinet and computer station. It was here that Garda Walsh came across a series of notes on a lined A4 sheet of paper. As he carefully lifted it with his gloved hands, he could clearly make out a list of handwritten questions:

Mary last one to see him?

Body naked, either murdered and clothes taken off or never left the house?

Why did she find his van so quickly? Why did she look for him in a place where she knew he would not have needed to go? Very strange, token search?

Why wouldn't she act on leads by travelling salesman?

Why did she give varying accounts of how long he was in yard before he left for work? Two mins? 10 mins?

Why was she so adamant of no activity took place in yard eg second car? How would she hear? Wasn't always possible.

Why did she rip down photos of Bobby after Ryan family put them up?

Why was she relieved after Crime Call, it was a rubbish programme and no help to jog anyone's memory.

nearby interview room by Detective Garda Buckley and Detective Garda Kevin O'Keefe.

Further to the two interviews he had already given, the gardaí told Pat that they wanted to progress further with their inquiries, asking him first to confirm who minded his two sons while he and Imelda went to the Heritage Hotel for her birthday the weekend Bobby went missing. He told them that Imelda's sister Catherine had collected them from school and looked after them until they returned.

Next, they probed Pat's relationship with Mary Lowry. He told them that Martin Lowry was his best friend and best man at his wedding. After Martin's death in 2007, he had rented the land at Fawnagowan from Mary for €12,600 per year. The affair started in January 2008, he said, recalling that he told Mary that they should 'pull back' because he was falling in love with her. He said that she had replied: 'Me too.'

They usually met at Fawnagowan for their trysts, although he stayed overnight only once or twice. He said he occasionally discussed the future with Mary, but not very seriously. He told Imelda about the affair in March 2012. He said he needed to know that their marriage could survive and added, 'I needed to be honest.' He told them that Imelda didn't take it well and had not spoken to Mary since. Previously they had got on well, he said, having known one another for twenty-five years.

Pat said his conversations with Mary during the affair would be about her children, her upbringing and day-to-day stuff. He also detailed to the gardaí his financial dealings with her. They had shared investments totalling tens of thousands of euros and she had also loaned him €20,000 to pay off a bank loan. He said he also presented her with a bill for cattle that had died due to an infection from the herd he'd inherited from her husband. He said she had agreed that he could keep the €20,000 loan as compensation.

He found out that she was seeing Bobby Ryan in December 2010, but he didn't think they were physically intimate at that time. She told him she wasn't interested in a relationship with Bobby and Pat agreed that she could still meet Bobby, 'as long as we don't fall out'. She asked Pat what he would do in that event and he told her: 'I still have Imelda.'

Around 15 December 2010 he became aware that Mary had lied to him about where she was the night before, and the following week he saw text exchanges on her phone with Bobby Ryan. He took her phone and texted Bobby, 'pointing out she hadn't been honest [with him] and was seeing me for the last three years'.

He was angry and Mary was angry, he told the gardaí. They had a 'heated' argument in which Pat accused her of lying and she told him they were finished. He described Mary as 'fiery' with a 'heated temper', but that the argument was not physical. The next time they met she was still angry because Bobby didn't want anything to do with her, but she later made up with him and seemed happier then. Pat added: 'I was angry because she was happy and she didn't care if I was happy, sad or indifferent.' He said he was 'disgusted' with Mary's 'whole attitude', which he found difficult to justify. He said he spent a lot of time and effort sorting her out after her husband's death and that 'was all forgotten about'.

Following the argument over the phone, Bobby arranged to meet Pat at Hayes Hotel in Thurles. They talked about the break-up of Bobby's marriage and Pat apologized for the incident with the phone. He was impressed with Bobby Ryan, he said, and happy with the meeting because 'he didn't perceive me as a person who was going to kill him'. He denied trying to warn Bobby off and said that he had wished the couple well. He said that at this time he realized that he hadn't properly grieved at his best friend Martin's death and had entered into counselling to help him with this and with the breakdown of the affair.

He was not jealous of Bobby and Mary because he was getting on with his own life, and with his wife. In August 2011, following Bobby's disappearance, he said he got back with Mary a few times, but it wasn't the same. He told the gardaí they went to the Cliff House Hotel in Ardmore, County Waterford, in September 2011 and to Fitzpatrick's Hotel in Killiney, south Dublin, in January 2012. They talked about Bobby's disappearance, he said, telling the gardaí: 'I'm inquisitive, I'm curious.' He said he wanted to know what happened and had theories. He said Mary had no theories and added: 'It didn't bother her. She was quite indifferent about it.'

He put an end to the affair this time, he said, after he found out she was again seeing someone else. When the gardaí asked him if he was in love with Mary up to the time when they split he responded: 'Yes.' He said she had filled a void left when his best friend died. He was angry at how she had treated him but added that he was never going to leave his wife.

He concluded the statement by saying that he had never threatened Bobby Ryan 'in any way and I challenge anyone to show that I did. I did not kill Bobby Ryan. There's somebody out there who did do it and he is laughing at the moment because you are looking at me.'

As the handwritten notes of the interview were read back to him, Pat asked to correct the record. He asked for the line 'he didn't perceive me as a person who was going to kill him' to be changed to 'he didn't perceive me as a person who had it in for him'.

*

While Pat was being interviewed at Tipperary garda station, RTÉ's *Crimecall* was on air and again featuring the murder of Bobby Ryan. Michelle appeared in person on the programme and made a renewed plea for information about her father's disappearance and death.

'He loved life,' she said. 'He loved his job of getting up every morning and going driving trucks around here and there and having the laugh with the lads. He was constantly at his DJing, which he loved as well. He would always be messing and blackguarding.'

Detective Inspector O'Callaghan appeared on the programme as well, asking for information from anyone who had spotted Bobby's silver van between Thursday, 2 June, and Friday, 3 June 2011. The gardaí were also keen to speak to anyone who had seen a silver van with a person sitting in the front seat at around 6.45 a.m. on the morning of Bobby's disappearance, as well as anyone who had spotted any comings and goings at the Lowry farmhouse that same day.

Behind the scenes, as gardaí studied Pat's initial interviews, there were a number of lines of inquiry that needed to be followed up. They were particularly interested in the claims he had made about a leak in the milking parlour, so they arranged for a plumber to investigate.

Stephen O'Sullivan went to the Lowry farm on 22 May with Detective Garda Kevin O'Keefe. He was asked to examine the old dairy and the milking parlour for any evidence of a leak. He looked at the pipework and found several pipes that had been repaired over the years. The repair work was shabbily done, he would later say, and it was obvious that it had not been carried out by a professional.

He was asked by Detective Garda O'Keefe to disconnect the pipes, to see if water went from the building to the milking parlour and from the milking parlour into the run-off tank. He did so and found that it did.

Stephen O'Sullivan had corroborated Pat's story about a leak occurring, but he wasn't able to say when it had occurred. The fact of its occurrence was one thing, the cause was quite another. Gardaí strongly suspected that Pat Quirke had caused the leak himself.

Meanwhile, in a deliberate attempt to deflect suspicion, Pat started to fabricate and spread a series of malicious lies about Bobby Ryan. He told his farming student, Gary Cunningham, that he had heard a rumour that Polish people were involved in the murder. He told another person that Bobby had got the girlfriend of a Polish farm worker pregnant and he had been murdered as a result.

During one conversation with a former friend, he told him that he had heard Bobby had gone to meet drug dealers in Bansha Wood on the day he disappeared. Pat told the friend that a relation of Bobby's owed them money and that he had gone to settle the debt. He told the same friend that the gardaí were coming under pressure from the Ryan family in relation to arresting someone for Bobby's murder, and that's why they had been questioning him.

'Pat often said to me that he wanted to help the gardaí,' said this friend. 'He was presenting himself as something of an "intelligentsia" who could help the poor gardaí. He said he would like justice for the Ryan family, that he was doing his best to help them.'

One by one, Pat started to subtly apply pressure to the people he would need to corroborate his alibi. During one of many conversations about the murder he had with Breda O'Dwyer, the artificial-insemination technician, he told her that gardaí had taken his mobile phone and examined the data on it. He warned her that they would be contacting her as a result. In an attempt to coach her on what to say, he asked her whether she remembered that Sean Dillon was with him on the morning of Friday, 3 June 2011. When the case came to court, Breda would say that she hadn't seen Sean at all that day.

Pat also called various members of the syndicate he was part of and asked them if they had spoken to the gardaí about the investors' meeting in the Horse & Jockey.

His main strategy, however, was to shift the cloud of suspicion on to his former lover. He had drawn Mary Lowry into his police interviews and deliberately painted her in the worst possible light. Moreover, in the note seized from his house, he had put pen to paper and presented his own detective work to find the killer, so the gardaí wouldn't have to figure it out. It was all there, in black and white, for them to read and follow up on.

For all his foresight and planning, Pat had underestimated just how thoroughly the document would be investigated. In that very same note, gardaí were about to discover hidden clues that would point the finger of suspicion right back at him.

13. Good old-fashioned detective work

While Pat Quirke was busy covering his bases and trying to stay one step ahead of the gardaí, the truth was that the team inside the incident room in Tipperary town garda station had been studying him for some time. By now, September 2013, he had given three interviews about discovering the body at Fawnagowan, detailing his actions, what he saw and what he did. He had talked about the affair with his wife's sister-in-law, about his interactions with Bobby Ryan and about his movements on the morning Bobby disappeared. He had, however, made one major and interesting omission: he hadn't told them that he was being forced off the land.

Thanks to statements made by Mary and the solicitors' letters found in Pat's house during the search in May 2013, the gardaí were aware of the eviction notice Mary Lowry had handed to Pat Quirke, which meant they knew he had a potential motive for murder – to keep Bobby out of the picture so he could continue his affair with Mary and keep control of the land. They knew he was in a very small club of people who knew about the tank and had the opportunity to use it. They also knew that they were dealing with a very calculating individual, a man who, time after time during interviews, demonstrated an air of impenetrable confidence. What they didn't have was hard evidence – no murder weapon, no crime scene, no forensic trail. They had the end-point, but none of the steps that led to it.

In this scenario, it was clear they would have to build a

case based on circumstantial evidence. There is a view among the general population that circumstantial evidence is 'lesser' and more tenuous, but this isn't the case in law. Circumstantial evidence does not directly link a person to a crime, but rather is a particular fact or collection of facts from which guilt may be safely inferred. Generally, circumstantial evidence can be admitted in court, but the courts are careful when the only evidence in a case is circumstantial.

Circumstantial evidence must be examined closely and must be looked at in conjunction with other evidence. A court would be very slow to convict a defendant based on one piece of evidence – for example, if the defendant's fingerprints were found at the scene of a crime, but there was no other evidence, that wouldn't be seen as adequate circumstantial evidence. If there are a number of different pieces of circumstantial evidence, however, they have more weight when taken together as a collection of evidence. For example, in a burglary case, if the defendant was seen in the area at the time of the theft, their fingerprints were found at the scene and they were found with a large sum of money they could not explain, the court would be more likely to convict.

Gathering circumstantial evidence that will stand up in a court of law requires a layered approach, bringing in expert analysis, opinion and testimony across a wide range of disciplines. Detective Superintendent Dominic Hayes, the man overseeing the Ryan murder investigation, had spent his detective years in Dublin and was one of the investigators in the murder of Rachel O'Reilly, which successfully prosecuted her husband for the crime. Under his direction, the team worked methodically to cover every possible angle. They called in computer analysts, fingerprint experts, pathologists, a forensic anthropologist, an engineer and an entomologist. It was an intricate network of people who could each supply one piece of the puzzle.

But ultimately, as the months wore on, the task of sorting all these pieces into a solid case against Pat Quirke came down to a very small team of locally based gardaí. It started at the top, with Detective Inspector Paddy O'Callaghan, the SIO in charge of the day-to-day management of the investigation. If anything went wrong, it was on him. His right-hand man was Detective Sergeant John Keane, the man who had interviewed Pat and carried out the searches of the farm at Breansha. Garda Mick Fitzgerald, the incident room co-ordinator, was charged with making sure all lines of investigation were explored as well as co-ordinating and retaining all material of value. The exhibits officer was Detective Garda Kieran Keane, who was responsible for safeguarding and cataloguing all items of evidential value. Garda Tony O'Brien, the telephonic liaison officer, was tasked with examining mobile phones and CCTV footage, which was a mammoth job that required patience and perseverance in equal measure.

On the wall in the incident room were several maps, including one of the farm at Fawnagowan and one of the wider Tipperary area. A missing-person poster for Bobby, his face smiling out at the room, was pinned close by, a reminder of the man at the centre of all their work. Murder cases take a long time to work, so it's important to have a daily reminder of the reason for the intense activity: the fact that an innocent person has lost his life, and all the ripples of grief that span out from that loss.

The modus operandi was simple but painstaking: they started at the beginning, on 30 April 2013, the day the body was discovered, and worked backwards. Strand by strand, layer by layer, they peeled back every event, every interaction, every moment possible in order to leave only one person standing: the killer.

Due to restrictions on budgets and cutbacks across the force, a lot of the work on the investigation was done during the team's own time, sitting at home in the evenings and at weekends, poring over statements. They read them over and over, line by line, highlighting anything that didn't match and going back to the person who gave the statement to speak to them again. It was old-fashioned detective work, assembling the clues and pounding the pavement to hunt down every morsel of fact that pointed towards the truth. The team was well aware that if they were to present this case to a judge and jury, it would require every element to be perfectly in place to get it over the line.

To this end, they took nothing at face value. An investigator must interrogate every piece of evidence. Detective Inspector O'Callaghan was interested in the note found during the search of Pat's house. It was a lined sheet of A4 paper, with the notes Pat had made about Mary handwritten in black ink. The notes appeared carefully written and were neatly arranged one after the other on the page. It was routine practice to have all handwritten notes that had been seized as evidence tested for further clues. The detective inspector ordered this note to be sent to the Documents & Handwriting Examination Section of the Garda Technical Bureau at HQ in Phoenix Park. There, Detective Garda Jeremiah Moloney used a machine called an electrostatic detection apparatus (ESDA) to forensically examine the note. He discovered a number of indentations.

In general terms, indentations are imprints left on a page by handwriting marks from another page that was above it. In some cases, depending on the pressure applied when writing, the indentations can come from a page that was two to three pages above the one being examined. Some indentations are visible to the naked eye, but in the main they are invisible. An ESDA is used to detect these indentations because it can see what the human eye cannot.

The page found in Pat's home office was on its own, but it may have been torn from an A4 notepad, where writing from the pages above had left indentations on the single page now in the hands of gardaí. On one side of the page, indentations revealed that someone had written: 'What the gardaí will know.'

Two lines below that were the words: 'Murdered poss in house.'

Four lines below that was the word 'location?'

Further down the page: 'Mary walk kids to school?' and the word 'yes' with a circle around it.

On line 16 of the page were found the words: 'dispose of clothes phone any other evidence'.

On line 25, it read: 'Mary had to see him, be with him.'

The document also noted: 'Mary' followed by something illegible and then: 'Needle in haystack.'

And finally: 'Bobby stayed in yard, ie two mins ten mins.'

On the other side of the page Detective Garda Moloney found the words: 'Agitate need water', 'Get load of ... following', 'Tuesday' and a person's name towards the bottom of the page.

The traces of notes found on the A4 page were uncannily similar to what Pat had stated during interviews with gardaí about Mary and about Bobby's disappearance. It raised the question: had he made those notes before the 'discovery' on 30 April and, if so, why would he be preparing for Garda interviews unless he knew he was going to discover Bobby Ryan's body?

As another Christmas without Bobby approached, the first since his body had been discovered, his heartbroken family took the opportunity to thank everyone involved in the efforts to bring him home to them. On 12 December, the day after what would have been his fifty-fifth birthday, a lengthy birthday remembrance appeared in the *Tipperary Nationalist*. The family thanked 'all those who sympathized and supported us in our tragic loss'. In particular, they paid tribute to Bobby's friends and work colleagues, as well as the 'people who didn't even know Bobby', for all their countless hours of searching while he was missing. To all the search-and-rescue agencies involved they said thank you, 'from the bottom of our hearts for all the searching and driving you did over the two years for Bobby while he was missing'. They also thanked the local gardaí in Tipperary town garda station and the local priest in Cashel, Fr Bernie Maloney.

Meanwhile, gardaí had been talking at length to Mary Lowry. They were now building a very clear picture of the depth of Pat's obsession with her. They had details about him pressuring her for money, arguments over muck being left on the driveway and the gate being left open, her passport going missing, alleged break-ins at her home and several heated exchanges between her and Pat. Mary had given gardaí a major statement, taken over a series of interviews, and from this Detective Garda David Buckley had identified thirty-two different incidents that, taken together, came under the umbrella of harassment. Under Section 10 of the Non-Fatal Offences Against the Person Act, any person who, without lawful authority or reasonable excuse, by any means, including by use of the telephone, harasses another by persistently following, watching, pestering, upsetting or communicating with him or her, shall be guilty of harassment.

That definition most certainly applied to Pat's behaviour over the previous years.

To arrest Pat on suspicion of murder at that point would have given them twenty-four hours to talk to him. Instead, they had enough to arrest him on suspicion of harassment and use the relevant detention time to question him, under caution, about matters that could later be used as evidence against him for murder. Then, when the time came to arrest him on suspicion of murder, they could use the time they would have to talk to him to question him on other matters.

After being arrested at the farm in Breansha on 20 January 2014, Pat was taken to Tipperary garda station for interview under caution. In a series of interviews on 20 and 21 January 2014, Detective Garda Buckley and Detective Garda Steed questioned him in relation to a number of suspected offences. The first interview began at 10.45 a.m. on 21 January. Pat was cautioned and his rights were explained in full before questioning commenced.

'Mary Lowry had an affair with you?' asked the gardaí.

'That's correct, yes,' replied Pat. He said that the affair had lasted three years and had begun four months after the death of Martin Lowry.

'When Martin died, what happened to his cows?'

Pat said they were sold and that he took some into his own herd. He said he paid Mary Lowry for these when he later sold them. In October 2010 he discovered that his herd had been infected with bovine venereal diarrhoea (BVD), which had come from Martin Lowry's herd. He estimated that he had by then lost twelve cows to the disease and he discussed this with Mary.

'Can you tell me how those talks went?' asked the gardaí.

'She was anxious to compensate me,' he told them.

The gardaí told him that Mary alleged he became violent towards her during the discussion about compensation. She told gardaí that Pat had 'lashed out' with both hands and caused her to fall over in the kitchen. Pat denied the allegation.

'Absolutely not,' he said. 'I never raised a hand to her or anyone else.'

'Would you be a forceful man, Pat? If you believed you were entitled to it?' asked the gardaí.

'No,' replied Pat.

He denied being forceful with his demands or that he pestered and hounded Mary for compensation. According to Pat, Mary was 'anxious' to compensate him. She asked him to suggest an appropriate figure, but he was reluctant to supply one 'because I didn't want to be seen as extorting money from her'.

The detectives asked him about Martin Lowry's investments, which Pat said he 'managed' for Mary and which involved shares, CFDs (contracts for difference) and property worth about €200,000. The gardaí wanted to know if he had profited from these investments.

'No,' he replied.

Was he ever paid money from these investments?

'No, and I didn't ask for it.'

Wasn't it the case that he was to receive 50 per cent of the profits?

That was 'a separate arrangement', Pat said. He said that Mary gave him €80,000 to invest in CFDs. Their agreement was that he would manage the CFD investment and they would split the profits 50/50. He did so and the CFDs accrued €80,000 in eighteen months, he said.

'You were in a win–win situation,' the detective noted.

Mary had put up the money so he 'was not going to lose' either way.

'But I had to manage it,' Pat insisted.

The detectives asked what he used the money for – the €40,000 that was his half of the earnings.

'Nothing, I just put it into my farm account,' he said. He later added that he bought a jeep and a cattle trailer with the proceeds. Imelda was aware of this he said, and 'she was happy'.

'Pat, I have to say this is another example of you having control over a vulnerable woman,' said the gardaí.

'I cannot accept that,' he replied.

The gardaí put it to him that he could 'see Mary Lowry had considerable cash flow and you were into the CFDs and you guided her towards them' and received a profit of €40,000 from her €80,000 investment.

Pat replied: 'I had put work into it. Would you go without wages for a year and a half?'

He was asked about the Single Farm Payment to Fawnagowan, which was worth €11,000 per annum. He said he leased the land from Mary for €12,600 per annum, but also took control of the Payment.

'So, the lease of Fawnagowan is costing you €1,600?'

'Okay, if you want to use those figures,' Pat replied.

'So you get the sixty acres off Mary for €1,600?'

'Yes, it was beneficial to me.'

When the gardaí suggested this was further evidence that he 'used Mary Lowry in every way', he replied: 'The gain was a two-way street.'

He was asked what financial assistance he had received from Mary since Martin's death in 2007.

Pat said he was under pressure to repay a €20,000 bank

loan. 'I told her I would have to sell shares at a loss to repay them and she said she would lend me the money. She told me she didn't want it back until the lads were in college.'

So it was not the case that he put pressure on her and told her he would be financially ruined if he didn't get the loan?

'No,' he said.

The gardaí suggested to him that he had demanded this money. He replied that he didn't demand it, that if he was able to get €20,000 by demanding it, he would have asked for €200,000. He denied that he was trying to 'take Mary Lowry to the cleaners'. He further denied their suggestion that he was 'getting cash on demand and sex on demand' from Mary.

It was Pat's contention that Mary had allowed him to keep the loan of €20,000 when his herd was infected with BVD.

'She asked me did I wish to be compensated,' he insisted.

'She asked you?'

'"Should I compensate you?" were her words,' he said. 'I said, yes, I believed I deserved to be compensated.'

The gardaí put it to him that he had pressured Mary Lowry into giving him a cheque for €50,000. He said that was a 'downright lie' and challenged them to prove it. A cheque would leave a paper trail, Pat told them, and they would find no evidence of a payment to him of €50,000 from Mary Lowry.

Mary would later say in court that she had mistakenly thought she had made out a cheque to Pat for €50,000, when in fact the cheque was for €20,000. She corrected the amount in a statement to gardaí in 2018.

In an interview later that day, Detective Garda Steed asked Pat about his interest in financial matters.

'Would you agree with me that money matters do not frighten you?'

'It would be part of my business,' Pat said.

The detective talked about the death of Martin Lowry and how it had left three young boys without a father. Pat said he was close to Martin, who was best man at his wedding. He was personally affected, he said, as was his wife, Imelda, Martin's sister.

He was then asked about his relationship with Mary in 2008.

'You were married.'

'That's right,' said Pat.

'Were you unhappy at home?'

'No,' he said.

Asked then why he had the affair, Pat said: 'It's a good question that I've asked myself.'

Did he see anything wrong in it?

'Yes, and I bitterly regret it.' He said his relationship with Mary was 'a combination of companionship, intimacy, trust, honesty'.

'Honesty?'

'There was honesty between Mary and myself,' Pat stated.

Would he agree that Mary was vulnerable?

'No.'

So, he believed that a woman who had lost her husband and had three young boys wasn't vulnerable?

'I believe she knew what she was doing,' he said.

'In going to bed with you?'

'Yes.'

'You loved Imelda but were in love with Mary?'

'Yes,' said Pat.

Life was 'normal' for a time, he said, but then in December 2010 that all changed: 'I found out she was seeing Bobby Ryan and had deceived me.'

He told them how he had a suspicion that Mary was not

being honest with him, so when they were lying in her bed he took her phone from under her pillow. He saw 'lots of texts' with Bobby. He accepted that he had no 'authority' to take the phone and that this might have been an invasion of privacy, but he was angry at being deceived. She objected, but he did not give back the phone.

He used her phone to send a text to Bobby, telling him that Mary wasn't being honest with him and had been in a relationship with him, Pat, for the past three years. Bobby called back immediately. Pat answered and told him: 'I'm the other man. I'm sorry you had to find out this way.'

He left the house with her phone, 'in a rage'. Mary had to plead with him to get the phone back. The gardaí suggested his behaviour had the hallmarks of jealousy.

'It was anger,' he said. 'The jealousy came later.'

At that time he thought their relationship could survive the argument, but it broke them up. He agreed that he was sad and depressed and that the break-up was a blow to him. He denied ever telling Mary that he was considering self-harm or had suicidal tendencies, saying that was a misunderstanding on her part.

He said he met Bobby Ryan on a couple of occasions and denied telling Mary that he didn't like Mr Ryan or that he 'smells'. When the gardaí asked if he was jealous he said: 'I wouldn't say I was ever jealous. Angry, sad, but not jealous.' This contradicted what he'd said earlier about jealousy setting in later, but both statements were made during the course of his interviews.

He was asked if he had contacted social workers regarding a claim that Mary was neglecting her children, and Pat agreed that he had done so.

'Was that not a giant step to take?' they asked him.

He feared for her three boys, he said, after an incident when Mary left them alone and when one of them woke up and was distraught to find his mother wasn't there. He said he knew of this because Rita Lowry, the boy's paternal grandmother, had told him about it.

'I thought Mary had lost her way a little bit,' he told the gardaí. 'I think she was in a situation where she was party to the neglect to her children. It's very obvious she was neglecting her children and left them on their own.'

'Did you have any concern for Mary's children when you were out with her for the night?' they asked him.

Mary had a babysitter in place on those occasions, he said.

The gardaí put to him that, having been so close to Mary and in love with her, it 'might have been more appropriate to talk to her rather than bring a government department down on top of her'.

Pat replied that this had been 'the last straw'.

When Mary asked him about it, he denied reporting her to the social work department He told the gardaí he was 'afraid of what she would say or do to me'. He denied that he was afraid she would expose the affair, telling the gardaí that he was afraid of how angry she would be.

'Sure, she's only a woman,' said a detective. 'All women get angry.'

'I wanted to avoid that,' said Pat.

He said that he and Mary had exchanged words at an eighteenth-birthday party for a member of the Lowry family the following week after the social worker's visit, in February 2011.

'She said she wasn't going to the party,' said Pat. 'I don't believe she was getting on with any of the Lowrys at that point so people were happy she wasn't going to turn up.'

In the end, she did go to the party, and with Bobby.

'Did you say to her, "I thought I told you not to come here?"'

Pat said he couldn't recall, but that the Lowry family were 'disgusted' when she appeared.

Detectives asked about a night away in Killiney some months after Bobby disappeared. Mary had described that trip, saying she was uncomfortable, got drunk and fell asleep. What was Pat's version of it?

Pat said they had 'intercourse when we got to the room straight away'. They had a meal, went to a show and back at the hotel he was 'fairly sure we had intercourse again'. He said they had a 'good time', but he got the feeling she was regretful on the way home in the car the next day. He said there were 'doubts on his part too' and that he had seen a 'different side to her' over the previous fifteen months. Their relationship was 'not the same, deep down. I had a trust issue. She probably had a guilt issue.'

Had they ever discussed having a no-strings-attached sex arrangement?

'No. Mary wasn't that kind of woman,' he said.

'I'd say you were not that kind of man.'

'I'm a man who'd done something stupid and woke up to it.'

His affair with Mary ended 'abruptly' in March 2012 when she told him she had met someone.

'Florence, I can't think of his surname,' he said. 'I wasn't hurt because a leopard doesn't change its spots. I was more disgusted at being made a fool of twice.'

Two weeks later, he told Imelda about the affair.

'Did you tell Mary you were going to tell her?'

'Yes. Because it was on my mind for a while and Mary had always warned me away from doing it any time I broached the subject.'

Had he told Imelda before Mary sent her a card saying 'Sorry'?

Before, he said. Mary had 'figured out quickly that Imelda knew. She sensed it. She confronted me over it at the farm.'

'Are you sure you told her *before* Mary's card [arrived]?' asked the gardaí.

'I'm sure if Mel got a card with "Sorry" on it, it would have prompted questions, but I had already told her. Mel was furious with the card and tore it up.'

A third interview began at 9.48 p.m. on 20 January 2014. Pat was asked about an incident when Mary found him inside her porch. Mary said that in late January 2011 she had come home after being out for a walk to find Pat standing behind the door in the porch. She had locked the front door before she left, but he claimed the door was open. She believed he had used a key to get into her house while she was gone. He denied it ever happened and said Mary had been 'out to get him' for the past three years.

He said that following Alan's funeral he told Mary that he was unhappy with how she had conducted herself at the funeral and with her lack of support. They had a 'heated exchange'. He agreed that he could have said to her: 'Not a text or a phone call from you and all I did for you.'

'Did you say, "What did I do to deserve that?"' asked the gardaí.

'I'm not going to confirm or deny that,' replied Pat.

He told the gardaí that she was cutting cabbage at the time of the conversation and had a knife in her hand.

'Were you in a rage at the time?'

'I was possibly angry, yes,' Pat replied.

He denied stealing her passport to prevent her from going

on a family holiday in September 2012 and denied ever entering her property when she was not there.

'Were you still angry with Mary at that stage?'

'I was quite indifferent with Mary at that stage. I decided to have nothing to do with her.'

He said she confronted him about the passport and he told her that he 'sold it and made money on it'. But that was just him being sarcastic.

'Why would you say such a comment?'

'I explained why,' replied Pat.

The gardaí suggested he had a motive, that he wanted to ruin Mary's holiday.

'No, I didn't.'

In December 2012, Pat said he realized he had a key for her front door. He had had the key for about six months at that stage, but only realized what it was for when he tried it in the door.

At this stage, there was a break in the interview to allow Pat to have the requisite hours of rest. He was placed in a cell and kept there overnight on 20 January 2014.

The following day, Detective Garda Steed interviewed him again. Under the terms of Section 4 of the Criminal Justice Act 1984, Pat could be held and questioned for an initial six hours before a charge had to be brought or he had to be released. The interviewing gardaí had applied to have this extended by a further twelve hours. This gave them time to interview Pat further on 21 January. With Pat refreshed after a night behind bars, detectives took him back into the interview room to go through his relationship with Mary and the charge of harassment.

As Pat settled into the seat, the questions started up again.

'When you were leasing the farm at Fawnagowan, how did you gain access to the property?'

'Up and down the passage,' replied Pat.

'Do you mean the main entrance?'

'Yes,' said Pat.

'Did you leave excessive muck on the driveway?' they asked. This was a reference to Mary's contention that Pat deliberately left the private road in a mess to rile her.

'I left muck from the tractor, yes,' said Pat.

'Were you spoken to about this by Mary Lowry?'

'Yes.'

He accused her of taking his tools from the yard and hiding them and he texted her about this. He said he told her he couldn't help the amount of muck he was bringing across the drive.

The gardaí asked if Mary had instructed him not to use the tractor at Fawnagowan.

'No, she took the keys out of it,' he said.

'How did you discover the keys out of it?'

'When I went to use it,' he said.

They asked him about the leak in the milking parlour, and he said he had discovered it in March the previous year, 2013. He said he had mended it using supplies from the Co-op in town if he didn't have the necessary fittings at home. Relations between himself and Mary were not good at this time.

So why, they asked, did he bother returning the key?

'I thought it was the best thing to do,' he said. 'I hadn't realized it was the key to the front door.'

He told the gardaí he did this on 4 December 2012, the day after the alarm went off and he was captured on CCTV. They put it to him that, given 'all the surrounding circumstances', the key wasn't the ideal thing to have in his possession.

'Yes,' he replied.

'So the person who had this key had means to gain access to Mary Lowry's house?'

'Yes,' replied Pat.

That may have explained why he was uncomfortable or frightened giving back the key, they suggested.

Frightened was the wrong word, he replied, he was annoyed with himself when he realized he had the key.

The gardaí asked him about his letter to the *Sunday Independent*'s agony aunt and if Mary had discussed it with him. He said she had.

'And you accepted to Mary you had written it?'

'Yes,' he replied. 'It was obvious to her.'

'Would it be true to say you were heartbroken at that stage?'

'I was very sad, yes.'

Pat was then shown several CCTV clips of his car in Mary's yard the day before Bobby's body was found.

'Who's that?' they asked him

'It's me,' he said.

'And you're running back into the yard. You weren't driving?'

'No,' replied Pat. 'I think Imelda was driving.'

Pat was then shown footage of him getting into the car, followed by an image of Mary entering the scene.

'Why did you go into the yard after Mary?'

He said he didn't go after her, that he had left Pat O'Donnell's tractor in the farmyard and he ran back in to get the key, which he'd left in the ignition.

'In actual fact, she harassed me in that clip you showed,' he said.

'In what way?'

'She shouted obscenities at me and said she'd have to tell Mary Dillon to watch her clothes line.'

'It was to tell Mary Dillon to watch her knickers?'

'Yes,' said Pat.

'Which was referring to the incident you had with Mary's knickers?'

'Yes.'

As a result of these interviews, on 21 January 2014, Pat was charged with assault causing harm to Mary Lowry at Fawnagowan, Tipperary town, between 1 and 31 August 2012. He was also charged with burglary and handling stolen goods (the key to Mary's house) at Fawnagowan on 3 December 2011.

In tandem with the wider investigation into Pat Quirke and his actions with regard to Mary Lowry, the Bobby Ryan murder investigation also continued to gather pace. Gardaí were still poring over Pat's interviews about the discovery of the body, focusing specifically on his claim that he had opened the tank to draw water for slurry spreading on the basis that the tank had filled up with water from the leak in the milking parlour. In order to test his story, they needed to find out everything they could about the construction of the tank, namely if it was capable of holding the amount of water he would have needed.

In February 2014, an engineer, Michael Reilly, tested the tank, pumping more than 21,000 litres into a tank that held at its maximum 4,212 litres. Over the following two days it lost more than 17,000 litres because, he told gardaí, the tank was too porous to hold water. Days later, he found the water level in the tank had dropped back to the same level it had been before the tests began, at 250 mm. Once it reached a certain level, the water went out of the tank as quickly as it was put in. This was an important finding as the gardaí could use it to show that the tank couldn't possibly have contained the amount of water Pat claimed it did.

In May 2014, Pat appeared in court in relation to the charges against him for burglary and assault. During a brief appearance at Tipperary District Court before Judge Elizabeth McGrath, the court heard that the Director of Public Prosecutions (DPP) had directed that all three charges be withdrawn, although the reasons for this were never made public. Sergeant Cathal Godfrey told the court that the case file had been submitted to the DPP in late March. Following the withdrawal of charges, the sergeant said that gardaí would now make preparations for the return to Mr Quirke of any personal possessions held as part of their investigation.

As the third anniversary of Bobby's disappearance came and went, the Ryans were now focused on bringing his killer to justice. They had long suspected Pat Quirke was responsible for Bobby's death and as they patiently waited for charges to be brought, life carried on.

They were in regular contact with gardaí in Tipperary town, and although they were kept abreast of developments, they had little knowledge of just how much evidence was being amassed against Bobby's killer.

The next point of focus for the investigation were Pat's claims about what he had seen when he had first looked into the tank upon opening it. The investigating team took the view that he couldn't have seen what he said he saw. In order to prove this, they decided to stage a reconstruction of the scene.

On 11 June 2014, Detective Inspector O'Callaghan visited Mary Lowry's home in Dundrum to inform her that the reconstruction would be taking place the next day. He then went to the local hardware store and bought some insulated slabs and heavy-duty plastic. At around 7.30 a.m. the following morning, the detective inspector met with a team of gardaí, organized by Sergeant Deborah Marsh, at the Lowry farm.

The area around the tank was overgrown and half of the roof was still in place. This was removed to carry out the reconstruction. It was a sunny day and the sun was high in the sky, just as it would have been on the day of the discovery. At 10.45 a.m. Detective Sergeant John Grant, the scene of crime manager who had attended the scene on 30 April 2013, arrived with Garda John Kavanagh, the original crime scene photographer. As Detective Inspector O'Callaghan supervised the reconstruction, Garda Kavanagh took photos and several short videos of the process.

The insulated slabs were placed on top of the tank, mirroring the concrete slabs that had lain on it the day the body was found. A life-size training dummy, provided by the fire service, was dressed in a crime scene protective suit and placed in the same location as Bobby Ryan's remains were when recovered. The team pulled back the nearest lid and put a pipe down, similar to the pipe Pat had used on that day. When Detective Inspector O'Callaghan looked down into the tank, through the gap where the pipe was, he could see absolutely nothing. The pipe had disappeared into the darkness and he could see nothing else. After the second slab was lifted, he noted that he could see the 'head of the dummy and light trace of remainder'.

The team finished up the exercise at 1 p.m., the time after which the gardaí had started arriving at the scene on the day of the recovery.

The reconstruction had confirmed what they already

knew. There was no way Pat could have seen what he said he saw when he'd first looked into the tank. Bobby's remains were badly decomposed, having lain in the disused underground tank for twenty-two months. Even with the second flagstone pulled back, gardaí didn't believe it was possible to tell that the body was naked, as Pat had said in his statement. The only way Pat could have known that detail was if he had placed the naked body in the tank himself.

It had been twelve long months of meticulous work, but the disparate pieces were finally starting to come together in a compelling and convincing picture of a coldly calculating murderer at work. Bobby Ryan was three years disappeared, three years dead, but the time was coming when the team would be able to point the finger at his killer, confident in the knowledge that they could disprove Pat Quirke's version of events. The net was closing in ever tighter on their target, while he continued to believe that he had done enough to outsmart everyone.

14. A fly in the ointment

Modern police investigations often have a powerful ally in crime-solving: the digital witness. In many cases, a successful conviction hinges on technological evidence procured from the defendant's mobile phone or laptop. The inanimate objects in our lives can be a rich source of information, and it was no different for the team investigating Pat Quirke. An important member of the team was Detective Garda Paul Fitzpatrick from the Garda National Cyber Crime Unit at HQ in the Phoenix Park in Dublin. He was the man tasked with analysing the hard drive taken from Pat's house during the search in May 2013. It was a highly technical and onerous task, given the time period involved and the millions of records viewed, but this methodical work would prove to be a key facet of the case against Pat Quirke.

In order to help Detective Garda Fitzpatrick conduct the analysis efficiently, Detective Inspector O'Callaghan and the incident room team came up with a number of keywords for him to search for on Pat's browser history. They would sit together in groups, putting themselves in Pat's shoes and trying to come up with words and phrases that could be relevant to the case. Those words, like 'Bobby Ryan' and 'murder' and 'decomposition', were passed to Detective Garda Fitzpatrick to examine whether or not they correlated to material on Pat's computer.

It was an ongoing process. If something new came up in one of Pat's interviews, they sent the information back to

Detective Garda Fitzpatrick and he used it to carry out a search of the hard drive and maybe get a hit. Aside from the very specific direction to look for searches about human decomposition, Detective Inspector O'Callaghan asked him to find out who Pat had emailed, what websites he had visited and what he did in his spare time. It was this kind of intelligence-gathering that would give them an insight into the real Patrick Quirke.

The computer evidence came back to the team in waves. It was a significant moment in the investigation when they received the report telling them that Pat had researched decomposition – repeatedly. Pat had studied body decomposition closely, a pursuit that included reading articles on the limits of DNA evidence and videos illustrating the process of decay of human flesh. Even after Bobby Ryan's body was raised from the tank, it was clear that Pat had tried to stay one step ahead of the game. He had requested his phone bills from Vodafone, in anticipation of anything the gardaí might ask him, and he had kept abreast of any developments in the case, reading up on news articles as often as he could. All of this was evident from his computer records.

When confirmation came through that Pat had been searching for material on decomposition, it was a major coup for the investigation. Moreover, the dates when the searches were carried out fitted with the theory that Pat Quirke had carefully planned and researched every move he made well in advance. Detective Inspector O'Callaghan and his team knew they needed a timeline to fit with the murder and the discovery of the body. If they only had evidence of searches for 'decomposition' after the body was discovered, it could be of no evidential value to the investigation. When Detective Garda Fitzpatrick provided them with the report on the frenetic burst of activity on 3 December 2012, they knew they were on to something solid.

That was the morning Pat had set off the alarm at Mary Lowry's house. He had then returned home to Breansha and started a grisly research session that focused solely on rotting human corpses. Shortly after 3.30 p.m., he typed the words *human body decomposition timeline* into a search engine. From the options, he read an article called 'The five stages of decomposition', viewed images of a corpse in various stages of decomposition and read an article called 'How a body decomposes after death'. He also viewed videos that discussed 'human remains, skin slippage and DNA analysis'.

Less than half an hour after the last of this activity, Pat sent an email from his personal account to another man in relation to shares. This put Pat in front of the computer at the critical time. Garda Fitzpatrick discovered that a new operating system, Windows 7 Home Premium 6.1, was installed on the computer on 11 September 2012. This would have overwritten most of the data stored on the computer prior to that date. However, using internet interrogation software, he was able to find evidence of searches that had been carried out when the old operating system was in place on the computer.

Internet cache records of the URLs visited by the user showed evidence that a search for the term *body decomposition* had been carried out on 25 July 2012. There was also evidence that a search for the *limitations of DNA evidence* had been carried out when the old operating system was in use; no specific date or time could be found for this search, but it did occur prior to 11 September 2012, when the new operating system was installed.

In 2014, the Cyber Crime Unit updated its equipment and

Detective Garda Fitzpatrick examined the computer again. The team in Tipperary were working towards making an arrest and he wanted to see if he could glean any additional information from the computer. This time he found references to searches for slurry tankers. Websites including Abbey Retail, a farm machinery website, and the trading website DoneDeal were visited in September 2012. There was also an email from pquirke@eircom.net to Seamus Buckley that contained images of a slurry tanker.

The evidence that had been gathered was discussed at a detailed case conference attended by Detective Superintendent Hayes and chaired by Detective Inspector O'Callaghan. The investigating team had established that someone with access to the computer in Pat's house had been researching human decomposition. Furthermore, they were able to place Pat at the computer, sending an email, within thirty minutes of the relevant activity. After discussing what they had at great length, O'Callaghan gave the order to arrest Pat on suspicion of murder. It was time to turn up the heat.

For a short time, the local feeding frenzy around the case died down. But that all changed on 18 June 2014. Early that day, Imelda Quirke was arrested for questioning, and the gossips went into overdrive. When the Garda Press Office announced that a 45-year-old woman had been arrested, many thought it was Mary Lowry, only to be proven wrong when word got out that Imelda had been taken from her home at Breansha by gardaí. She was taken to Tipperary town garda station, under the provisions of Section 30 of the Offences Against the State Act, with regard to withholding information. The arrest allowed officers to hold her without charge for up to seventy-two hours.

Imelda wasn't considered a suspect in the Bobby Ryan

case, but she had been interviewed previously in relation to the case. This time, detectives interviewed her several times under caution, but she said very little in response to questions.

A day later, on 19 June, her shocking arrest was overshadowed when Pat was arrested on suspicion of murder. This was a huge step up from the alleged assault of Mary Lowry, and it laid the investigation team's cards on the table, confirming that Pat was their prime suspect. He was at home in Breansha when Detective Sergeant James White came to arrest him that evening. Pat was brought to Tipperary town garda station and detained under the provisions of Section 4 of the Criminal Justice Act 1984. Imelda was still in custody at the same station, so a decision was taken to move her to Cahir garda station, away from her husband, so that detectives could continue their interviews with her.

After a night spent in custody, on 20 June Pat was served breakfast inside his cell in Tipperary town garda station. Shortly after 8 a.m., after consulting with his solicitor, he was taken into a nearby interview room, where he was met by Detectives Larry Bergin and Dan Quinlan. They were based in Clonmel garda station and had been brought in to conduct the interview because of their high level of expertise. They had been briefed in full about the evidence that had been gathered and had prepared a detailed set of questions in advance.

This particular set of interviews was aimed at putting to Pat the various parts of the case against him for the record – in particular, what had been found on his computer.

During the first interview, which began at 8.21 a.m., the detectives pressed him about the amount of water he drew from the tank on the day he discovered the body.

'How much water was in the slurry tanker?'

'I don't know. I didn't measure it,' Pat replied.

They told Pat that they had carried out an assessment of the tank and that Michael Reilly's 'comprehensive report' had concluded that the tank was incapable of holding any significant amount of water. It was like a 'colander' they told him.

'It leaks out after a few days?' asked Pat.

'No, it leaks out as quickly as it flows in.'

Pat said he hadn't realized that the tank was porous.

Using a number of photos that were taken of the scene at the tank on the day the body was found, the gardaí asked Pat about what he saw as he was attempting to draw water.

'How did you find the body of Bobby Ryan?'

Pat pointed to one of the slabs covering the tank and told them: 'I had seen it before I took off that corner . . . I had seen something that warranted further investigation.'

'How far down was the pipe at that stage?'

Initially, he replied, it was against the floor of the tank. He had to move the tractor forward, and when he looked into the tank he was surprised there was so little water. He saw what he thought was a 'roll of carpet'.

'Would that have been through down where the pipe was?'

Pat said he couldn't remember.

As the interview ended, Pat was handed a copy of the interview notes, which he signed, and was allowed a rest period before again consulting with his solicitor.

The first interview had deliberately not mentioned any of the intelligence that had been gleaned from the computer. The carefully selected questions were designed to make Pat think the engineer's report on the tank was all they had to go on.

Later that afternoon, at 12.38 p.m., a second interview got underway. The detectives told Pat that, this time, they wanted to focus on one particular item: exhibit number KKPPQ1, a computer hard drive with no make or model number that was taken from his house.

'We have an exhibit we are going to produce to you,' they told him.

Pat said that he was under the impression that everything that had been taken from his house was in the process of being returned to him.

'Can I take it from that you're taking ownership of the exhibit we are talking about?'

'I haven't seen it so I can't comment,' replied Pat.

He said he wasn't aware of what exactly had been taken during the searches because he couldn't be in 'two places at the one time'.

'Would you like us to produce it?'

'There's no need,' replied Pat.

As the exhibits officer, Detective Garda Keane, produced the black hard drive, Pat was asked if it was the same computer that was taken from his home.

'It looks like it,' he replied.

They asked him if he recognized the sticker on the front: 'Computer Solutions For You'.

'I've dealt with that crowd before, yes.'

'How long have you had that computer, can you recall?'

'I can't,' replied Pat.

'Okay, fair enough.' They asked him who owned the external hard drive and the memory stick. He said he wasn't sure, but that Imelda would know.

'What would be your level of computer knowledge, Pat?'

'I've never done a course, but I can manage to navigate a computer.'

The gardaí explained to him that Detective Garda

Fitzpatrick had made a copy of the hard drive without inter-fering with the original. He was able to use this mirror image to examine what was inside. He had compiled a report of his findings, which they were going to show to him now.

They explained to Pat that the report would refer to 'cook-ies', which they explained as the 'internet leaving a fingerprint inside your computer' of a person's actions on that computer. Cookies, they told him, gathered analytic data of what was looked at and retained that data. 'Do you have a good com-prehension of what these cookies are?'

'Yes,' Pat replied.

'Are you aware of the term backup?'

'I am, yeah,' replied Pat.

'Can you explain that to me so we're on same hymn sheet,' asked one of the detectives.

'It's where the computer has backed up the info,' said Pat.

Using Detective Garda Fitzpatrick's report, they drew Pat's attention to what had been found on his computer. They showed him that they had found a record of a website called howstuffworks.com, which contained information on DNA evidence and its limitations. They further told him that the site was visited prior to 11 September 2012. This was the date that a new operating system had been installed on the computer.

The gardaí put it to him that on 3 December 2012 he per-formed a search for *human body decomposition timeline*. They said the search yielded a number of results and that he clicked on a website address for forensics4fiction.com. They asked him if he could eliminate his wife and children as the people who carried out those searches.

'I don't understand what you mean,' said Pat.

He also said he was not familiar with 'in private browsing' when asked if he had activated a private browsing session when carrying out the searches. Detectives told him they had evidence that he had visited suite101.com on the same date and had read an article on how a human body decomposes after death. They showed him an exhibit, PF30, that was a visit to forensics4fiction and the viewing of an article entitled 'The five stages of decomposition'.

The detectives tried to appeal to him.

'For the sake of the two boys and Imelda, you've to be fair to them, Pat, is there anything you'd like to get off your chest?'

'My son had recently died. That's all I'm saying,' replied Pat.

While Pat knew he could explain his belief that the tank held water, the computer evidence was different. He had no logical explanation for his dark fascination with body decomposition. When cornered, he attempted to use his son's death to cover his tracks.

The detectives sympathized with him over Alan's death, telling him they couldn't imagine what that was like. The last number of years must have been torturous, they said, and they weren't trying to be insensitive.

'Look, you guys don't believe a word I say,' Pat replied.

He told them the gardaí were 'all under the one umbrella' and had charged him with an assault on Mary Lowry that had never happened. They replied that those charges had been brought by Tipperary town gardaí and that they, his current interviewers, had nothing to do with that.

They asked him why he had looked at an article on the *limitations of DNA evidence*, but he said, 'I don't recall.' The gardaí then put it to him that he was searching over a prolonged period and on a number of occasions for terms relating to decomposition because he knew where Bobby's body was and was trying to establish what condition it would be in if disturbed.

'Why would I need to know what condition the body would be in?' asked Pat.

'You tell me.'

'Sure you're saying that's what I was doing,' said Pat.

They said that they believed he was looking it up online, trying to establish what state the body was in and perhaps planning to 'dispose of him further'.

'If I knew where Bobby Ryan was and I wanted to view his decomposition, surely all I would have to do was open the lid of the tank and look in,' he said.

The gardaí suggested that his 'hand was being forced' in relation to discovering the body because the lease on the farm was coming to an end.

He had elected to leave the farm, he told them, and he could have stayed on if he'd wanted to. What they were suggesting 'didn't make sense'.

They asked why it didn't make sense to him.

'Because I could have got a load of earth and covered in the tank, couldn't I?'

'There was a million and one things you could have done, Pat,' they replied.

'That was the obvious one,' Pat said.

The detectives said that it all went back to his need for control.

'I decided to give the body back? What a load of crap. Why would I invite that into my life? There is enough intelligence in the guards to answer that,' he retorted.

They put it to him that he had staged the discovery of the body, but he rejected that suggestion.

'You thought if I discovered the body, I'm removing suspicions from myself?' Pat said. 'Would I not have thought of the nightmare that would unfold?' he said, pointing out that his relationship with Mary Lowry would be forced out into the open as a consequence. 'If I knew I could check on the condition of the decomposition of the body myself at any time, why would I need to go looking at websites?' he demanded.

'The simple answer is, Pat, you were taking a chance someone would see you.'

He dismissed that because it wasn't like the tank was 'down a main street'.

They pointed out that he was under scrutiny because he had been caught already on CCTV and he was having 'hassle' with Mary. They suggested that someone might have seen him and asked questions, but Pat argued that it didn't make sense and that, given the remote location, he could have checked it when nobody was around.

He told the detectives that they weren't taking on board anything he was saying and added, 'What I say does stand up and make sense and you say, "No, no, no, it wasn't like that Pat."'

The detectives turned again to KKPPQ1. They told him that evidence gleaned from it included a link to a YouTube video entitled 'The Body Farm'.

'It's a couple of minutes long. I'd invite you to look at the laptop,' they said.

The short clip showed the work carried out at a facility called the 'Body Farm', an open-air laboratory of decay in Tennessee, USA, where researchers observe bodies in varying states of decay, all in the name of science.

'Pat, do you remember viewing that online?'

'I don't.' He insisted he had no recollection of ever watching another YouTube video 'The Body Farm and Beyond', which was also found embedded in one of the links to websites he had visited.

They then turned the conversation to his son, Alan, asking Pat when he had died.

'The eighth of August 2012,' he told them.

The detectives had Pat where they wanted him. They had evidence that at least some of the searches pre-dated Alan's death. They moved to challenge him again on it.

'In fairness now you offered us an answer but now we've established it's not true because you'd already looked it up online.'

'Well, that's not fair to say,' he replied.

'Why?'

'You can't say the answer isn't true,' he said. 'Maybe it doesn't cover every search, but you're specifically referring to a date in December at that point.'

The gardaí told him they had reviewed the evidence and found a search for *body decomposition* on 25 July 2012.

'That was before what happened at home, so it completely blows out of the water what you've told us.'

Pat knew where this line of questioning was going. What's more, he knew he was in trouble. He'd said his explanation wouldn't account for every search. He'd said the previous search didn't 'blow out of the water' his explanation for the searches on 3 December 2012.

'What I said was that it wouldn't cover every search,' he said.

'Can you explain that to me?'

'It won't account for every search,' said Pat.

The gardaí put it to him that he was trying to establish the condition Bobby Ryan's body was in and not Alan's. Again, Pat said that didn't make any sense, that he could have viewed the body at any time if he had known where it was. He'd had unlimited access to the remote location where it lay.

'That would be too risky,' they said.

'I don't accept that,' he replied.

'You are an articulate and intelligent guy,' they said, adding that this was the forum to discuss the evidence they had and whether or not he thought it was correct.

Pat disagreed. 'Well, to my mind this isn't the forum for it.' He took the line that the interview suite had been the forum 'the last time' and they had still charged him, referring to the burglary and assault charges in relation to Mary Lowry.

This was a 'different ballgame', they told him, as this time the consequences for him and for his family were a lot more serious.

'Absolutely,' agreed Pat.

The detectives went on a charm offensive then, telling Pat that there was 'no hiding' with the CCTV cameras, that they weren't trying to manipulate him or manufacture evidence. They understood why he wouldn't want to engage, because of what had happened before, but they didn't want him to adopt the same stance this time because it was so serious.

'If you have something to tell us to help us progress the investigation, now is the time to tell us.'

At the end of the day, he was still in control, they reminded him. Eventually, they asked him straight out to come clean, but Pat wouldn't be drawn.

'Can you tell us what happened?'

'I've given numerous statements,' said Pat.

'Okay, we'll park them. I appreciate you made yourself available to lads here in the town and you were helpful.'

'And where did that get me?' said Pat.

'You're an inherently decent man who may have made a mistake,' they said.

Pat replied: 'There's a connection between losing my son

and I wanting to do the decent thing – is that what you're saying?'

'And closure,' they replied.

When it was again put to him that he was a decent man and that he should do the 'decent thing', Pat stood his ground.

'Why would I murder a man, then ponder over it later and say, I'll show people where it is and try and manipulate that?' he asked. He told them that he could not understand why they could think he would bring that on himself in April, 'one of the busiest times in the farming calendar', asking them, 'Why didn't I do it in January?'

The interviewers changed the subject. Now they wanted to introduce the evidence that showed Pat had been shopping for a vacuum tanker. They knew he had an umbilical application system on his own farm, which is a sophisticated method of slurry spreading that means farmers don't have to use heavy tankers. It invited the question: why was he prepared to spend money on a vacuum tanker to use at Fawnagowan knowing that he was shortly being evicted?

'Your own farm at home, correct me if I'm saying it wrong, Breanshamore, isn't it?'

'Yes,' replied Pat.

'What slurry-spreading system do you use?'

'That knowledge is all out there,' replied Pat.

He told them that he'd had a vacuum tanker for twenty-five years and always needed it during the year. They then asked him about the searches on the DoneDeal website and if he remembered looking up second-hand slurry tanks.

'I've already made it clear,' said Pat. 'I had an existing slurry vacuum tanker, okay, so that's all you need to know.'

'Sorry, Pat.'

'I've already said I had an existing vacuum tanker,' Pat

continued. 'It's not as if I was trying to arrange to acquire one. There is no crime in trying to upgrade a slurry tanker.'

They asked him again about his plans to spread slurry that day in April.

'It's all well documented,' he said.

The detectives put it to him that it would have been unusual for him to be buying a bigger vacuum tanker, and even more unusual for him to be spreading slurry at Mary Lowry's farm.

'Perhaps discuss it with me again,' said one of the detectives.

'Why?' asked Pat.

They told him that they were led to believe the system he had at Breanshamore didn't require a tanker.

'The system I have at home is only suitable for at home,' he replied.

'I appreciate that, but would you personally spread slurry at Fawnagowan?'

'No,' replied Pat.

'So why was it necessary to buy the tanker and do it at Fawnagowan?'

'Because I had the means to do it. I had bought a new tractor.'

'Can you remember when you last spread slurry at Fawnagowan?'

'No.'

Their interviewee was becoming frustrated, that much was plain. But he was now under arrest on suspicion of murder, so there was nowhere to hide. If Pat had the information or alibi that would save his skin, now was his chance to produce it. But as the questions wore on, his answers seemed to circle back in on themselves, rather than leading to any evidence that would convince the detectives he had nothing to do with Bobby Ryan's murder.

While Pat continued to be interviewed on suspicion of murder, members of the investigation team spent days questioning Imelda. She was held for the full seventy-two-hour detention period and interviewed several times. After three days, she was released without charge. After one day in custody, Pat was also released without charge, free to return home to his wife and family.

The Quirkes could now be in no doubt that the focus of the investigation was very much on them.

Overall, Bobby Ryan's killer had done well in covering up any forensic trail that might link him to the murder. He had thought of all the obvious things, removing Bobby's clothes, disposing of his phone and keys and making sure not to leave any fingerprints on his van. It was unlikely that he knew he had left behind one tiny clue that had piqued the interest of the investigating detectives.

Exhibit SL5 was a single insect larva removed from Bobby Ryan's body at the post-mortem. It had been sent to a UK-based forensic entomologist, Dr John Manlove, earlier in the year. Gardaí wanted to understand more about the insect, how and when it had got there and if it bore any significance to the case.

Forensic entomology is the study of the insects associated with a human corpse and is often used to determine the time elapsed after death and before discovery. Insect evidence may also show that the body was moved to a second site after death, or that the body was disturbed at some time, often by the killer returning to the scene of the crime. Calliphoridae, better known as blowflies, can detect death from as much as ten miles away and are often the first to find a dead body. In the UK and Ireland, they include among their number the common bluebottle and greenbottle. These are the forensic entomologist's raw material.

Underpinning the science is the helpful fact that flies go through four main and identifiable developmental stages, from egg (which will generally hatch within twenty-four hours), to larva (which will feed on the corpse for about five days, then spend another couple of days preparing to pupate), to pupa (equivalent to a butterfly's chrysalis and taking up another seven days), and onwards to adult fly. The maggot stage can be further subdivided into three distinct phases, known as instars.

The exact rate at which a fly develops through these stages can vary significantly according to a number of factors, notably the temperature at the scene, the size of the body, whether it is in the open air or in a sealed room, and whether it is naked or clothed. The forensic entomologist's job is to collect and measure the insect life on and around a dead body, factor in all the variables and come up with an approximate time for when the first flies arrived on the scene.

In this case, Dr Manlove was asked by the investigating team to establish when insect infestation had commenced. Specifically, he was requested to determine whether this had happened in 2011 or 2013.

In September 2014, Dr Manlove flew over from England and spent two days liaising with investigators and visiting the scene at Fawnagowan to examine the run-off tank. In the report he compiled on his findings, using the single fly larva removed from the body and photographs of the body after it was removed from the tank, he was able to estimate its age and stage in the life cycle. He identified the common blowfly of the Calliphoridae family. The insect that was retrieved from the body was a third-stage larva, as were the larvae he had identified in post-mortem photographs. He concluded that the infestation was 'at least 11 days' old and quite possibly more'.

Dr Manlove had been shown Michael O'Reilly's report, which stated that the tank would have been tightly sealed by the two concrete slabs that Pat Quirke said he had removed on the day he found the body. The report stated that once muck and cow waste were placed over the slabs, this would create a 'perfect seal', making it impossible for flies to get in or out.

On this basis, Dr Manlove concluded that the first time the tank was opened was not on 30 April 2013, the date when Pat said he had prised it open, but some weeks before that. Otherwise, he said, 'flies could not have gained entry'. The fly infestation did not happen on the day the body was found, nor was it a longer-term infestation, because that would have led to a greater level of decomposition. He found that the small number of larvae and lack of other insects indicated that the body hadn't been exposed for a long period. This, he would later say in court, suggested that the tank had been sealed until March or early April 2013.

The entomology evidence confirmed what the gardaí already suspected. They believed Pat had secretly opened the tank to check on the remains several weeks before the staged discovery. In doing so, he had inadvertently allowed flies into the tank, giving them SL5 to use in the case against him.

In the months that followed, the painstaking process of gathering evidence continued. The pressure was now on to prepare a file for the DPP, and the investigating team were working to ensure that all bases were covered. They knew they had only one shot at securing a prosecution and that their circumstantial case had to be watertight.

While they carried on in their efforts, life for those involved in the case got back to some semblance of normality. Mary, while still helping with the Garda inquiries, was trying to move on. Pat was now off the farm, having surrendered the lease in July 2013, but relations between her and her in-laws were now strained and she had not returned to live in Fawnagowan.

Everyone had been drawn into the Garda probe into Bobby's death. Her brothers- and sisters-in-law had been asked to give statements, as well as her ailing mother-in-law, all for an investigation that was focusing on sending Rita's daughter's husband to prison. By now, Mary had moved to Bansha, a small village that was about a five-minute drive from Fawnagowan. Martin had owned a plot of land there and her brother Eddie had helped her build a new four-bedroom home for herself and the boys. She had talked to Bobby about some day building a house there and his disappearance had been the catalyst for action. Rita remained in the granny flat at the farm, while the main house and the farm were rented out.

It wasn't just the Lowrys who were feeling the strain. The local people in Tipperary were waiting and watching, wondering when Pat was going to be charged with murder. He had already been arrested on suspicion of it, so why, they wondered, weren't the gardaí moving in and taking a suspected killer off their streets?

'Pat was going about like nothing had happened,' said one local. 'He was driving around in a 2015 Kia Sportage and people were all the time waiting for gardaí to charge him with murder. It was like a two fingers up to everyone, "Look at me, I have nothing to worry about." People were really annoyed about that.'

It may have looked like inexplicable procrastination from the outside, but inside the incident room the team were as busy as ever and working hard towards an arrest. By June 2015, Detective Superintendent Hayes was meeting with the team in Tipperary every three to four weeks. They were putting together a case that would go down in history as one of the most complex the State had ever seen. By the end, the Bobby Ryan murder investigation was the biggest ever undertaken in County Tipperary. Some 300 witness state-ments were taken and 700 lines of inquiry were followed up – a remarkable number given the rural location in which the crime occurred. The endpoint was in sight, but they weren't quite there yet.

As preparations for the file to be served to the DPP were in their final stages, the decision was taken to arrest Pat on suspicion of murder again. Almost a year to the date of his last arrest, he was arrested at home in Breansha on the morn-ing of 17 June 2015.

Gardaí had by now located a copy of the 'Dear Patricia' letter in the National Archives and were able to produce it to him in full. On this occasion, Pat was interviewed several times but refused to answer questions, replying, 'No com-ment', to almost every one put to him. He had consulted his lawyer, who had briefed him about his rights and advised him in full. The gardaí weren't perturbed by this. The interview was, in Garda terms, a mop-up. The officers were putting various questions to him in case they became pertinent in months to come when the case came before the courts.

By early January 2016, the file on the investigation into the murder of Bobby Ryan had been completed and sent to the

DPP for consideration. The sheer volume of the document (the Summary alone ran to 140 pages) was a reflection of both the mammoth effort that went into compiling it and the level of detail that had to be included. In the three and a half years since the body had been discovered, gardaí were confident that they had built a wall of strong circumstantial evidence to support a charge of murder against Pat Quirke. Ultimately, however, the decision to prosecute or not lay with the DPP and would involve months of scrutinizing every single block in that wall.

The DPP had never come across a case quite like it. This was a farming case, one littered with references to agricultural terminology and processes that many in the Office of the Director of Public Prosecutions in Dublin city had never heard of before. For the investigators, this meant schooling some of the greatest legal minds in the country on some of the more technical aspects of farming life in rural Ireland.

Every detail, from the simple difference between a bull and a heifer to the scientific explanation for the formation of crust on slurry, had to be explored and explained in full. It was crucial, for example, that those considering the case had an understanding of the slurry-spreading process, in particular the process of adding water or agitating the slurry. There were other subtleties to the case that were particular to the farm environment – like the clothes Pat was wearing when he was in the process of agitating and the fact that he was spotlessly clean when gardaí arrived on the scene. At the most basic level, the murder of Bobby Ryan was a puzzle with a network of intricate pieces. If one piece was lost along the way, the case against Pat Quirke would come to nothing.

It took months for the DPP's office to reach a decision on the case. During that time, as well as submitting the detailed file on the investigation, gardaí presented a forty-page slide show on the evidence. The team knew they had a massive task in convincing the DPP to run with the case, but after throwing all they had at it, all they could do was wait.

The file, like all those compiled outside Dublin, had gone through the local State solicitor, who in this case was Paul Fitzpatrick, the State solicitor in Clonmel, County Tipperary. Detective Inspector Paddy O'Callaghan had been in constant contact with Mr Fitzpatrick at that stage, answering queries and clarifying matters as well as checking on the status of the file. All the while, the team waited. The incident room was emptied and Bobby's picture filed away, and the various investigating team members tried to focus on other matters. It was like they were all in suspended animation, waiting for the jolt that would waken them to action.

It finally came on Monday, 20 March 2017. O'Callaghan got the word, via telephone, that a direction from the DPP to charge Pat Quirke with murder was on its way. A formal document with the direction for the charge would arrive at Tipperary town garda station the following day.

Under the terms of Section 8 of the An Garda Síochána Act 2005, which allows the DPP to give general or specific directions to the gardaí in relation to the institution and conduct of prosecutions, the DPP issued a direction to charge Patrick Quirke with the murder of Bobby Ryan.

The investigating team greeted the news with a sense of quiet satisfaction. After years of work, they had jumped the first hurdle. The case was very much back on again.

*

The preparations to arrest and charge Pat got underway immediately. He would have to be brought before a court to be formally charged, so after confirming that the District Court in Tipperary town was sitting on Wednesday, the decision was made to arrest Pat the following day, Tuesday, 21 March.

Although it had taken many years to get to this point, there was little drama or fanfare as the small party of detectives made their way out to Breanshamore to let Pat know the game was up. They knew he would put up little resistance to the arrest and, having dealt with him before, that there would be no need for a heavy-handed approach.

It was just another evening on the farm for Pat, as he busied himself in the milking parlour, getting ready for the evening milking. As Detective Inspector O'Callaghan, Detective Garda Kevin O'Keefe and Detective Garda Martin Steed drove along the narrow road that leads up to Pat's house, they knew to turn right and drive past the family home and head straight for the farmyard.

It was shortly after 5 p.m. when Detective Inspector O'Callaghan made his way into the milking parlour alone, leaving his two colleagues waiting nearby at the car. Pat was in his green overalls when the detective walked in, and he stopped whatever he was doing as his eyes met his visitor's. The two men knew each other, so there was no need for an introduction.

It had taken years to come to this moment, a moment when two men who had grown up together in Tipperary town found themselves on opposing sides of the law. Finally, after years of battle, their duelling was coming to an end.

'Patrick Quirke, I am arresting you on suspicion of the murder of Bobby Ryan on a date between June the third,

2011 and April the thirtieth, 2013. Do you understand the reason for your arrest? You are not obliged to say anything unless you wish to do so but whatever you say will be taken down in writing and may be given in evidence.'

O'Callaghan then told Pat that the arrest was for the purpose of charging him with murder.

The colour drained from Pat's cheeks. He bore the look of a man who knew the curtain was about to fall on his freedom.

Ashen-faced, he remained silent as he removed his overalls. Detective Inspector O'Callaghan handcuffed him and led him out of the milking parlour and into the back of the nearby patrol car.

They arrived at the station at 5.20 p.m., where Pat was formally detained by Garda Samalita Meehan. A custody record, which becomes a live record of every single occurrence in relation to the person arrested, was opened. It would detail what Pat said and did in custody, when he used the toilet, what he ate and drank and anything else of note.

Pat was asked for his name, address and date of birth, and if he had consumed any alcohol, among other things. Garda Meehan contacted Pat's solicitor, Aoife Corridan, on his behalf and he was read his rights. A draft charge had been written up on the PULSE system, and after Pat was searched it was read and handed over to him. He was cautioned again and asked if he had any reply in relation to the charge.

'I don't agree with the charge,' he said.

He was brought to a holding cell until the next morning, when he would be formally charged before a judge. As his hour of reckoning approached and Pat pondered his fate, Imelda visited him in the station, where she learned that he would face court in the morning.

The following morning, at around 10 a.m., Detective Inspector O'Callaghan and several other members of the investigation team took Pat from the station to the nearby Tipperary Excel Theatre, the venue where the Tipperary District Court sat for hearings. He reached the building at around 10.10 a.m. and stepped out of the car, flanked by detectives.

He never looked around to see who was present, but the Ryan family had been notified about his arrest and were there, watching as the first official step towards justice for their father was taken.

Inside the building, the hearing lasted no more than five minutes and Pat was treated like any other common criminal. Detective Inspector Patrick O'Callaghan informed the court that Pat had been formally charged in the station at 6.30 p.m. the day before and had replied, 'I don't agree with the charge.'

His solicitor told the judge that she would be making an application for bail to the High Court, which is the only court with the authority to grant bail in cases involving murder charges. When the District Court procedure ended, Pat was remanded to Limerick Prison until his bail application was heard.

A week later, the bail application was heard at the High Court in Dublin. It was successful. Pat paid the €20,000 bond himself and a separate independent surety of €20,000 was provided by one of his sisters. Under the terms of his release by the High Court, he was required to surrender his passport and instructed to report twice a week to his local garda station. He was forbidden to contact anyone connected to the case.

For Pat, watching the public reaction to his appearance in

court on a charge of murder was both humiliating and infuriating. His entire personality was built on notions of respectability and standing within the community, and now his cherished reputation was in tatters. When he was released on bail, he soon discovered that few people wanted to know him. His neighbours avoided him. Local people crossed the road when they saw him coming. Farm workers declined offers of employment on his farm. He hadn't yet been convicted for murder, but in the eyes of the community in Tipperary, he was no innocent man.

Pat, however, was as incredulous as ever. When two members of the farming discussion group he was part of politely asked him to step down from the group, he whipped out a notebook to take notes of all that was being said and threatened to sue. He was already telling everyone he was going to sue the gardaí, for wrongful arrest and harassment. Everyone, it seemed, had it in for Pat. And, one by one, he would make sure they were brought to book.

Of course, one person in particular had crossed him most grievously. She was about to learn that, even from the dock, he would try to control and manipulate her in any way that benefited him. Pat had one more roll of the dice with Mary Lowry. The stakes were very high: this time it was his liberty on the line. As his trial for the murder of Mr Moonlight approached, the gloves were well and truly off.

15. Too many coincidences

'Mary Lowry, please.'

A flutter of excitement raced through the public benches. Eyes darted towards the back of the room. Heads turned to get a better view. As the crowds blocking the wooden doorway of Court 13 stepped aside and parted, the woman everyone had been waiting for slowly emerged from the scrum. She was dressed smartly in a striped top embellished with pink flowers along the hem and sleeves, navy jeans and a short navy woollen jacket. She wore her hair in a short bob. She strode briskly towards the witness box that was next to the judge's chair, taking a route along the side wall, which meant she passed behind, rather than in front of, the man in the dock, her former lover.

Onlookers nudged each other and exchanged knowing glances as she quietly settled into the black leather swivel chair. They had all come to see Mary Lowry. The middle-aged housewives. The amateur sleuths. The retired farmers. Pat Quirke was on trial for murder, but in the titillating soap opera playing out in the courtroom, it was the mistress who captured the prurient attention of the public. There was an uneasy air of theatre about it all, with queues to get seats and sweets being passed around the pews; to the feverish audience, it was a spectacle to be relished.

'Tickets, get your tickets. Popcorn, anyone for popcorn?' remarked a veteran clerk one morning as he observed the crowds waiting to get into Court 13 for the Quirke trial while passing on his way to his own courtroom. In the macabre world of the court watchers, where the Mr Moonlight trial was seen by some as entertainment, Mary Lowry had box office appeal. The trial opened in the fourth week of January 2019 and Mary Lowry was called on Tuesday, 29 January. She would spend four days in the witness box and in the process become a household name across the country.

The 'Love Rival' trial, as it was dubbed in those opening days, was allocated to court number 13, on the fourth floor of the Central Criminal Court in Dublin. It was one of the bigger courtrooms in the building, often used for trials that were expected to draw large crowds to the public gallery. The last time it hosted a high-profile case was during the 2015 trial of Graham Dwyer for the murder of Elaine O'Hara. Elaine, like Bobby, was initially a missing person. Gardaí believed she had taken her own life before her body was discovered in Killakee Woods in the Dublin mountains.

The room itself was modern and spacious, with wood-panelled walls and matching seating. The judge's seat was positioned in the centre of the room, on a raised area along the back wall that was partly glazed. On particularly sunny days, when blinding sunrays streamed through the glass, the blinds were drawn over the windows. As Mary took her seat on the stand on that cold January day, the blinds were open. The sky outside was clouded white, masking the sun's light as the room settled into silence.

Michael Bowman gently led her through the evidence, starting with a few questions on her early life, when she was born, where she was born, the jobs she had worked. She spoke softly and clearly, but when it came to the moment she met her husband, her voice quivered with emotion.

'I met him in a nightclub,' she said, 'where lots of people

met in those days.' She said she was 'completely lost' and 'vulnerable' after he died.

She spent a day giving her evidence for the prosecution, detailing the affair, the aftermath and all that had happened before and after Bobby disappeared. It was an astonishing tale, told in detail by the person who knew it best.

As she left court that day to return home, she probably knew that it was also a story that would be scrutinized to its fullest extent.

Mary Lowry's cross-examination began the next day, 30 January. Pat Quirke's defence barrister, Bernard Condon, was adept at cross-examination and he was ready to tackle Mary Lowry. She was on the stand, alone, her face set in steely determination to withstand the barrage of questions about to be aimed at her. At one point she said defiantly to Condon, 'I'm not on trial. Mr Quirke is on trial. Mary Lowry is not on trial.' She was right, Mary Lowry was not on trial, but at every opportunity her ex-lover sought to place her front and centre of the trial, exploiting the age-old trope of the lustful and immoral woman to cast doubt on her testimony. He would drag her name through the mud in court, brazenly watching on from the sidelines as his legal team labelled her 'devious', 'manipulative' and a person who told 'out and out lies'.

In a series of tetchy exchanges during her three days of cross-examination, she reminded Mr Condon over a dozen times that she was telling the truth.

'You want to rewrite history,' suggested Mr Condon.

'I want to solve this murder mystery as best I can,' she shot back.

Her demeanour, scrutinized and picked over by the fascinated observers, was at times combative, maybe even confrontational. She came across as a fiery woman who wouldn't be walked over, no one's doormat. But Mary Lowry had every reason to defend herself. Patrick Quirke had attacked her in every way possible. She was accused of having a selective memory, of rewriting history to suit her own agenda, of being an unreliable witness.

In truth, she could remember it all.

'From the time my husband died, Mr Quirke manipulated me,' she told the court. 'I've suffered under the hands of Patrick Quirke, I can remember everything he did to me.'

It was time for Mary Lowry to set the record straight.

Pat Quirke had hired the best criminal-defence team he could find. In what was interpreted as a pre-emptive strike to avoid losing his fifty-acre farm if convicted, he registered his farm business as a limited company, Breansha Farms Ltd, on 26 March 2014. This move had the added benefit of making him eligible for free legal representation at trial. Pat listed himself as an employee of the firm, ensuring that his earnings of between €10,000 and €15,000 per year were less than the minimum wage. Pat was a man of considerable means, however. He had property interests in Poland and Tipperary, understood to be in the region of between €2 million and €3 million, as well as stocks and shares in various schemes. In preparation for his legal-aid hearing, gardaí forensically accounted his finances, but put up little fight against his application. It was in their interests to ensure that he had the best counsel available in order to limit his grounds for appeal.

Accordingly, Pat ended up with three barristers defending his case: two senior counsels, Bernard Condon SC and Lorcan Staines SC, and one junior counsel, Edward Doocey BL. They were instructed by one of the best-known criminal-defence legal firms in the country, Michael Staines & Co., where Pat's solicitor, Aoife Corridan, was a partner. This sort of trial would normally feature just one SC, but Pat had two, although Staines only 'took silk' in late 2018. It was said that Pat had specifically asked for senior counsel Bernard Condon, who, famously, had defended the former chairman of Anglo Irish Bank Sean FitzPatrick during Mr FitzPatrick's 2017 trial for allegedly misleading the bank's auditors about millions of euros in loans made to him.

It was Mr Condon who cross-examined Mary, skilfully dissecting her evidence and slowly, ever so slowly, trying to debase her credibility as the prosecution's star witness. His style as a defence barrister is to pick through the finer details of a case, homing in on anything that could be questioned or probed for inconsistency. Well-spoken and articulate, he is schooled in the well-crafted art of drawing a witness in, making it seem like he is going along with their version, before a delicate skewering that casts everything they have just said in a pall of doubt. Many witnesses fall foul of his intimidatory style, but in Mary he found an able sparring partner. In a piercing cross-examination that lasted three days, Mr Condon tested her accuracy and reliability as a witness. Her motives were questioned repeatedly, her every action scrutinized and the most intimate details of her personal life were microscopically examined. It was suggested that her evidence was not consistent with what she had previously told gardaí and that she had added details to spread poison about Pat.

When she said she couldn't remember exactly what she had done seven years ago, Mr Condon put it to her that this was a 'devious lie' and that she was out to trash his client.

'You made that up. I imply that is a lie and you made it up as part of your agenda,' he said.

'Pat Quirke has managed to trash himself, not me,' she replied.

By the time she finished her gruelling stint in the box, on Friday, 1 February, the media was enthralled by the story of Mr Moonlight.

Mary, the star witness in the prosecution case, had set the scene for a trial that had all the elements of a gripping story. Watching her give her evidence and parry the blows rained on her by Condon gave a tantalizing insight into her personality and how she might have interacted with Pat during the many years of intimidation and sinister happenings that had brought her to this point. While some might have crumbled at the thought of spending four days in a witness box, poring over the innermost secrets of their private life, Mary held her resolve throughout. It was clear that she had been waiting for this moment for a long time. There were many in the room who instantly took to her, finding her feisty demeanour both impressive and likeable. If nothing else, she certainly left her mark.

Pat never looked at her once. For four days straight, as she detailed their sordid affair and everything he had done to her since, he stared ahead, unflinching.

The defence had an uphill climb. They hadn't managed to break Mary Lowry and they still had to counter all those pieces of the puzzle that the gardaí had put together over six years. The outcome was far from certain.

Seated at the desk opposite Bernard Condon and his colleagues, the prosecution team were headed up by Michael Bowman, SC, one of the most renowned barristers in the country. Although he was now working for the other side, he had an established reputation in legal circles as the most in-demand defence barrister in Ireland. As junior counsel he had acted for Sharon Collins, the 45-year-old Clare woman who was convicted in 2008 of hiring a Las Vegas poker dealer to kill her partner and his two sons. Since then he had acted in dozens of murder and rape trials.

In keeping with the practice of selecting a junior from the district where the alleged crime took place, the Thurles-based David Humphries, BL, was called upon to assist. He was joined by Tessa White, BL, a Dublin-based barrister whose areas of expertise included white-collar crime. She had worked with Staines and with Condon before as part of the defence team that represented another former Anglo Irish Bank CEO, David Drumm, in 2018, who was jailed for six years after being convicted for his role in the €7.2 billion fraud perpetrated at the peak of the banking crisis in 2008.

So ranged on both sides were six barristers. They sat on the first row of benches positioned just below the judge, the prosecution on the right, next to the jury, and the defence on the left, next to the accused.

They arrived on the fourth floor every morning, their long black gowns billowing around them as they swept along the marble floors leading to Court 13. The juniors would normally enter the room first, armed with heavy files and documents that they would carefully lay out on the wooden bench. The senior teams would come next, settling into their positions on opposite sides and studying their notes in quiet concentration. They were ready to do battle.

For the State, the task of convicting Patrick Quirke would involve telling that very complex story without losing a single detail along the way. In Mr Bowman, the debonair legal eagle with the curly, swept-back hair, they had a master storyteller. He was articulate and highly intelligent, but he was also a man with the common touch. He had the unique ability to engage and hold a jury's attention, but, more importantly, he also had the skill and charisma to prove his case.

The case against Patrick Quirke was that he had an affair with Mary Lowry, the widow of his wife's late brother. She ended it when she met Bobby Ryan, a DJ known as Mr Moonlight. Pat, the jilted lover, murdered Bobby and dumped him in a hidden run-off tank on Mary's farm. Mr Bowman referred to the tank as 'a concrete sarcophagus' – a disused waste tank that had once been used to collect mud, milk, cow faeces and chemicals washed through an underground pipe from an old dairy farm across the yard. Having removed his love rival from the equation, Pat thought he could resume his role as Mary's secret partner – both in bed and in controlling her financial affairs to his own benefit. But Mary had no desire to rekindle the romance. Moreover, she wanted him off her land and instructed her solicitor to terminate the lease. This left Pat with two options: leave the body where it was and run the risk of the next farmer discovering it; or keep control of the situation by unearthing the body himself in what the prosecution described as a 'staged discovery'.

As Bowman began to outline the State's case against Patrick Quirke, it was immediately apparent that this was a murder trial guaranteed to attract the attention of the nation. It would end up running for seventy-one days and over those fifteen weeks, from January to May, rarely a day went by when the trial didn't make the front page of at least one national newspaper. This was a story of lust, land, jealous obsession and murder. It was a story about ordinary people, in ordinary Ireland, and what happens when they do the unthinkable. As such, it was utterly compelling and the nation watched the drama unfolding with bated breath, hooked on the revelations laid bare in Court 13.

Imelda Quirke's evening routine had always included a leisurely stroll with her three little Jack Russell dogs. She walked at lightning speed, said her neighbours, alone with her thoughts and the company of her beloved pets. As the trial of her husband for the murder of Bobby Ryan got underway, there was a change to the routine. Pat, a man rarely seen off his farm, was now out pounding the pavements beside her each evening.

The pair, who took the train to Dublin every morning for each day of the fifteen-week trial, made the two-hour journey home, returning to the farm in Breansha for a short time before taking to the roads for their evening circuit. Word among locals was that Pat was on a PR offensive, parading his wife around the place while his trial was going on, letting everyone know that he was a happily married, innocent man. As he had told gardaí during interviews, his name was 'destroyed' in his home town and he 'needed to clear it'. So off he went, parading along Main Street, the busiest thoroughfare in the town, with his ever-loyal wife marching alongside.

For her part, Imelda appeared to be a willing participant in her husband's desperate bid to salvage his reputation. By all accounts, going by her steadfast support during his trial for murder, she was standing by her man. Day in, day out, for over three months, she accompanied her husband as he faced a blitzkrieg of cameras on the way into the court building. Dressed in a navy or blue suit, a light hunting jacket and his trademark flat cap, Pat led the charge, with Imelda often trailing behind. Hollow-cheeked and wide-eyed, she always seemed to have the same perpetually startled expression as they sped up the steps and into the foyer. After a short consultation with his legal team upstairs on the fourth floor, they would speed-walk towards Court 13, Imelda always first to enter the room. Pat became known for gallantly opening the door to let female journalists into court; Imelda had to fend for herself.

Once inside, Pat would head to his seat on the bench for the accused, carefully placing his black laptop bag beside him. The bench was on the opposite side of the room to where the jury were seated. He sat alone there, cut off in his ambiguous status of not innocent and not guilty. He wore a look of indifferent detachment, always facing blankly ahead, his rheumy eyes continuously blinking.

The Ryan group, a large contingent of close family and friends who often took up a whole bench in the public gallery, would normally already be seated when the Quirkes arrived. Imelda would take her seat on the end of the public bench behind them, a solitary figure amid the dense crowds.

From here, three rows back from the bench for the accused, where her husband sat, she watched the proceedings and took copious notes, tending to her husband when needed. Whenever he signalled for her attention with a commanding flick of the head, she would scurry to his side. His hand would hold out a plastic cup, which she would carefully fill to the brim from a bottle of Tipperary still water. During downtimes, when proceedings had paused for one reason or another, if Imelda wasn't summoned for water, it was to bring his phone or for a quiet word in her ear.

They had a well-established lunchtime routine. They avoided the lift, which was often crammed with rubberneckers and journalists, opting instead to take the stairs and exit at the second floor. They never dined in the canteen, choosing instead to sit outside courts numbers 8 or 10 on the cold, hard marble seating in the outer atrium. Imelda would go to the canteen and get the hot drinks, dutifully carrying them back on a tray for her husband, who would sit on his own, away from prying eyes.

They shared a packed lunch she had prepared and drank their drinks, and then Imelda would return to the canteen with the tray. As the days and weeks passed by, this well-worn path, one she traipsed back and forth on every day, became a barometer for the obvious strain she was coming under. She always held her head high, striding with purpose, but her face bore the look of a woman far older than her years. And as Easter approached, marking her third month pacing back and forth to the canteen for Pat, she had become painfully and notably thinner, her face hollow and gaunt. Pictures of her taken in happier times show a fresh-faced, smiling woman, still slight and petite but without the veil of sadness that seemed to shield Imelda Quirke as her life, with all its shocking twists and turns, was laid bare to strangers.

Inevitably, comparisons were drawn to Mary Lowry. Both women were slender, dark and fine-featured, their physical resemblance close enough to be remarked on by several onlookers during the trial. People were fascinated by Mary, but they were intrigued by Imelda, maddened with wondering what she was thinking and feeling. What did she think of her sister-in-law, Mary? How could she stand by Pat? Why did she not leave him? The questions were endless. In a story with so many leading characters, everyone was mesmerized by the quiet, obedient wife.

By all accounts, life had dealt Imelda some cruel cards. After losing her brother Martin to cancer in 2007, she was then told that her husband was having an affair with his widow, an affair that had gone on under her nose for almost three years. In 2012 her little boy, Alan, was tragically killed in an accident involving his father, and now her husband was on trial for the murder of Mary Lowry's other lover. It was a dreadful litany of sorrow and hurt and there was nobody in the court who did not have sympathy for her. Sitting amid the daily gathering of unaffected onlookers, Imelda Quirke listened as details of her husband's 'seedy' affair with her sister-in-law were described in upsetting detail. There were weekends away to luxury hotels, midweek trysts in the house she had grown up in at Fawnagowan and the 'Dear Patricia' letter in which he said he 'loved her [his wife], but wasn't in love with her'. Through all of this, Imelda Quirke sat, alone with her thoughts, never flinching. The perfect wife.

For fifteen long and stressful weeks the routine was the same.

At 4.30 a.m., Michelle Ryan woke and quietly crept out of bed and into the shower. As her four children slept, ranging in age from thirteen years to thirteen months old, she carefully prepared their school lunches and neatly laid their uniforms on their beds. Then, she was collected by her mother, Mary, who lived ten minutes away in Meelin village, County Cork. The two women went to the train station, where they boarded the train to Dublin.

As the clock ticked towards 5 a.m., forty-three miles away in Kilcrea, County Cork, her brother was setting off to catch the 7 a.m. train to Dublin. It fell to his partner, Leanne, to ferry him to the station, along with two sleepy children the couple had to drag from their beds for the thirty-minute journey to drop him off. After Robert boarded the train alone in Cork, his sister and mother began their journey on the 8.40 a.m. train from Mallow to Dublin. Their journeys would converge at Court 13 in the Central Criminal Court on Parkgate Street.

Like her children's routine, Mary Ryan's began early every

morning, usually by frying sausages to bring with her to make sure they had something to eat.

'I would meet Michelle over at her house,' Mary said. 'I made sandwiches to take on the train, the journey was about two hours. We would buy the papers and read them just to put in the time. There was no switching off really.'

Making the same journey to Dublin's Heuston Station, on the same early-morning train, was Patrick Quirke.

'He always got on with his wife in Limerick Junction,' said Mary. 'Michelle and I would have been on since Mallow, so we were already in our seats. One morning they sat straight across from us. They looked at the two of us and sat down. We just did what we do every morning and we just sat there and said nothing. When they saw us they could have moved on, but they didn't.'

Michelle remembers the incident well: 'He [Pat Quirke] looked down at us and he sat in the seat across from us. It was very intimidating. We knew he was brazen and we knew we had to be strong and not react.'

Robert, travelling alone on the Cork train, would also come across the man who was accused of killing his father on his way to court. He described how, 'If we had to be in court early, they would be on my train. I would be on my own, with my headphones on, and if I saw them coming, I would just look out the window. Sometimes I would peep out to have a look and he would be staring back.'

Others spotted Pat on the train too. During one particular journey, he noticed a fellow passenger stealing an inquiring gaze. He looked straight at her and addressed her curiosity directly.

'Do you want me to put my hat on?' he snarled.

Once in Court 13, the Ryans had to listen to the evidence,

which was often distressing. Robert and Michelle were visibly shaken at times. On one occasion, a photograph of their father's remains, freshly taken from the tank and blackened by the filth it had lain in for twenty-two months, was accidentally displayed on the court monitors. Michelle and her mother left the room, sobbing.

They later said that they found the medical evidence particularly difficult, especially when CT scans were shown to illustrate the fatal fractures to Bobby's skull.

'That was him,' Michelle said later. 'When I was looking at those scans, it was the first time I felt that.'

While the Ryans fought back tears as they stared at the X-ray image of their father's skull, the moment provided an interesting glimpse into the mind of Pat Quirke. He was staring at the image too, so much so that he seemed to forget himself momentarily, smiling slightly as he watched on.

'Did you see that?' reporters whispered to each other on the press bench.

'Chilling,' was the unanimous conclusion.

It was a rare insight into the mind of someone who seemed devoid of any human emotion. He was impassive through evidence that reduced the Ryans to tears. That moment, that smile, was a moment when the mask slipped. The only other time that happened was when Jack Lowry took the stand. With Pat watching him intently, Jack's voice quivered and stammered as he began to take the oath. Flame-haired and with a distinctive jawline, he bore a remarkable resemblance to his mother. He was the middle-born of Mary Lowry's three boys, a baby-faced nineteen-year-old who was the youngest witness in the trial. Taking a deep breath, he exhaled loudly into the microphone, sending a crackling wheeze through the courtroom speakers.

'I was eight years old when my father passed away,' he said softly.

He'd had a happy childhood, from what he could remember. During those happy years, when he was 'younger', he got on well with Pat Quirke, he told the court.

'I had nothing against him,' he added.

Jack 'got on well' with all of the Quirke boys, Pat's three sons, he explained to the court. He was particularly close to Alan.

'Do you remember Alan's passing?' asked Lorcan Staines, SC, for the defence.

'Very well,' he answered quietly.

Sitting on the bench for the accused, his lips trembling, Patrick Quirke was visibly fighting back tears.

Jack Lowry had gone back in time, to a period before Alan's death, when he and his cousin played in the fields at Fawnagowan. Alan was a year younger than him and he came to the farm most days with his father. After Martin Lowry's death, Pat Quirke began renting land on the farm, Jack told the court.

'He went around the farm as if he kind of owned the place,' he said.

He described Pat as being 'in control most of the time, grumpy most of the time'.

On the day Bobby went missing, Jack remembered coming home from school and seeing his Uncle Eddie, which was 'strange'. He said he couldn't remember who told him Bobby was missing and he didn't know about the tank where he was found.

It was painfully clear from Jack Lowry's evidence that he too had been traumatized by all of this. Not only had his childhood been scarred because of Pat's murderous obsession, but he was now caught up in his trial. Jack had only recently been called to give evidence and agreed with Lorcan Staines that the trial was a very difficult time for his mother and brothers.

'Very difficult, yes,' he said. 'I did not want to be here.'

It was a trial that was less about twists and turns and more about revelations and slow-burning intrigue. In what would become one of the enduring mysteries of the case, it was Bernard Condon who raised the question of the Cliff House Hotel in Ardmore, County Waterford, and a romantic break that Mary Lowry swore under oath she couldn't remember happening. Even when he produced Mary's bank statement, showing that the payment for the hotel stay had come from her account, she never lost her composure or wavered in her testimony.

The barrister pointed out that the village of Ardmore was particularly picturesque and that a stay in its five-star luxury bolthole was unlikely to be something anyone could forget. Mary, however, had no memory of the trip, which was alleged to have taken place on 16 September 2011. Was she suggesting, then, that Pat went on holidays to the Cliff House and somehow put it on her account?

'Well, I don't remember doing it,' she said. 'Stranger things have happened.'

Mary readily admitted to rekindling her affair with Pat during a trip to Killiney in Dublin after Bobby disappeared, but she was adamant that she never went to Ardmore with him.

The truth would never be discovered. Long after the trial had ended, the mystery of who had actually spent time at the five-star Cliff House would remain unsolved. Even though Siobhán Phillips, the manager of the hotel, confirmed that the booking had been taken up and that someone had indeed dined in the Michelin-starred restaurant during the stay, the hotel's

CCTV system had been upgraded after 2011 and there was no footage to reveal the identity of the mystery guest or guests.

In February, another Mary caused a stir in court. Dressed in a black lace cardigan and a leopard-print dress with a large gold cross draped around her neck, Bobby's ex-girlfriend, Mary Glasheen, gave evidence in a subdued tone, smiling occasionally as she responded to the questions put to her.

She and Bobby had remained friends after they parted ways romantically and would 'still go to lunch on Sunday if he wasn't working', she told the court. Sometime after their break-up, a friend told her that Bobby was seeing Mary Lowry.

'I was delighted that he met someone,' she said when asked how she felt about that. 'That he would be happy hopefully,' she added wistfully.

After his disappearance, the two Marys continued to run into each other on the dancing circuit.

'I met Mary Lowry at different dances after Bobby went missing,' Mary Glasheen said in a statement given to gardaí. 'She would look at me but wouldn't salute.'

As the weeks wore on in court, the narrative routinely switched from the salacious to the mundane.

The jury had visited Fawnagowan in the opening week of the trial, viewing all the relevant locations on the Lowry farm and the surrounding area. With each new witness in court, they learned about the everyday chores on the farm, milking and feeding cattle, how slurry is mixed and spread on the land. From Breda O'Dwyer, they learned about the artificial insemination of cows.

After she took to the witness stand in the first week of March, Michael Bowman asked Breda to describe her work.

'Do you want me to go through the AI process?' she replied, incredulous. Mr Bowman said that he did.

Breda O'Dwyer proceeded to describe her job, how it entailed 'me driving round with a tank full of frozen bull semen'.

The witness, an AI technician for twenty years, drew muted laughter from the gallery on a number of occasions during her evidence. She herself giggled when Bowman asked her: 'This may sound like an obvious question, but what's a heifer?'

'It's a cow that hasn't had a calf yet,' she replied.

Later on, the interaction drew smiles from several jurors.

'If there are no cows [that need insemination], do you call [to farms]?' asked Bowman.

'No,' she said, followed by 'Silly question' muttered under her breath.

After the morning texts came in from the farmers requesting AI, she wrote them into a book and set off. If a farmer called after she had started her round, it was a case of 'Feck them. I would leave them,' she said amid laughter in the court.

Given the effect of a testimony like that of Breda O'Dwyer, which placed a question mark over Pat's version of events, the defence team had to drill down into any doubt that could be generated. This came to seem like a relentless focus on the same key issues. In particular, they zoned in on the idea that Bobby could have died as a result of a collision with a vehicle rather than as a result of being beaten with a blunt object. They questioned numerous witnesses about a Toyota Corolla in a shed that was used by Mary Lowry's teenage son Tommy as a 'field car', asking why gardaí had not taken it away for forensic examination. They asked Jack Lowry, who was eleven years old when Bobby Ryan went missing, whether he ever drove the field car. He had to insist more than once that at age eleven he had no idea how to drive, did not know how to start a car and could not reach the pedals.

There were also repeated references to the fact that the concrete slab covering the tank had broken during the recovery process. Parts of the lid fell into the tank as a result and the defence implied that this could have caused injury to the body below. At least half a dozen Garda witnesses were asked about it, as well as the experts who gave evidence on the pathology. Staines argued that the breaking of the slab must have been a 'significant event', yet in the Book of Evidence, which was more than 1,000 pages long, it was not mentioned once. Paddy O'Callaghan said 'the most significant event on the day was the discovery of the body' and that when the slab broke, the gardaí present just got on with their jobs.

The defence continued to draw Mary Lowry into the narrative again and again. They focused on the fact that her house was not properly searched when Bobby Ryan went missing in 2011. Gardaí did search the Lowry house in 2013 following the discovery of Bobby Ryan's body. While on the stand, the defence questioned Detective Garda John Grant about discovering suspected blood stains in Mary Lowry's bedroom and living room. The following day, dramatic headlines screamed that blood was found in Mary Lowry's home.

The very next day, an expert from Forensic Science Ireland revealed that the samples were not blood at all. Dr Martina McBride said one sample on a light fitting and ceiling that gave a 'presumptive positive' result for blood was probably fly faeces, which can be mistaken for blood by equipment routinely used by gardaí. The finger of suspicion had wrongly been pointed at Mary. Again.

Within the public gallery, and even beyond Court 13, there was much intrigue at this approach. Although the defence never directly implicated Mary Lowry in the murder, inferences about her knowledge or involvement drew the curiosity of those following the case. Anywhere that the case was discussed, all anyone wanted to talk about was Mary. What did she know? What wasn't she saying? What didn't we know about her?

All of it was scurrilous fantasy.

As the weeks wore on and the evidence mounted, it became clear that Mary, as much as Bobby, had been a victim of Pat Quirke. The detail in his Garda interviews showed that, from the start, he had tried to pin the blame for Bobby's death on Mary. If Pat had had his way, it would have been her, and not him, who was sitting in the dock.

For all the stunning evidence, the shocking revelations and scandalous headlines, there were many days of what seemed like interminable legal argument. It was a gruelling trial for Bobby Ryan's family and friends, stretching past the original estimate of six weeks as barristers niggled at the minute details and crossed swords. Much of the proceedings took place in the absence of the jury as the legal teams argued over the admissibility of various pieces of evidence. As is usual in these cases, it was generally the defence causing the interruption. Each time Bernard Condon, SC, rose to his feet, there was clearly frustration in the public gallery. More often than not, he had 'an issue'. There were the countless challenges over the evidence – the warrants for the searches of the farm, the tank reconstruction carried out by gardaí, arguments over whether Pat Quirke had said the word 'had' or 'hadn't' in a Garda interview. It was a piecemeal attempt to unravel the work of the gardaí and thereby the case against Pat Quirke.

The most urgent wrangling over evidence was the days spent trying to stop the contents of Quirke's computer going before the jury. Many in the courtroom – the media, the public gallery – knew about the now infamous Google searches months before they came into evidence. Moreover, locals in Tipperary who never ventured near the trial knew all about it too. The fact that Pat had searched repeatedly for material relating to human decomposition was a solid plank in the prosecution's case. Accordingly, the defence was determined to have it declared inadmissible. In the end the judge, Ms Justice Eileen Creedon, allowed it and it was entered into evidence on 21 March.

It seemed to be a watershed moment for the jury – and for observers everywhere – when it was later revealed in Garda interviews that Pat's explanation for those searches was the death of his son. This was a step too far.

The sense of distaste in the room was palpable. After the interview was read in full, several jurors exchanged glances, their widened eyes belying their sense of shock. The following day, newspaper headlines hinted at Pat's unravelling: '"MY SON HAD RECENTLY DIED ... THAT'S ALL I'M SAYING." MURDER ACCUSED QUIRKE ASKED TO EXPLAIN SEARCHES'.

The defence had lost that particular battle, but there was another card to play that could prove decisive. Staines suggested that the DPP was trying to hide evidence by refusing to call Acting State Pathologist Dr Michael Curtis.

Dr Curtis and several of his colleagues had carried out a peer review of Dr Jaber's post-mortem of Bobby Ryan in 2015. Dr Jaber had left his post by that stage and had returned to live in Saudi Arabia. When a more complete report on the post-mortem was required, the Office of the State Pathologist recommended Professor Jack Crane, the former State Pathologist for Northern Ireland. The two eminent pathologists agreed with the cause of death in relation to Bobby, but had differing opinions on the mechanism of death, or how he had come to sustain his injuries.

It was Dr Curtis's expert opinion that Bobby Ryan's injuries could have been caused by a vehicle, but this was at odds with the prosecution pathologist, Professor Crane, whose expert testimony was that the injuries were most likely to have been caused by a blunt object.

The prosecution refused to call Curtis, leaving the defence to call him themselves. They did so in March and on the 30th Dr Michael Curtis took the stand. His testimony was that the most likely mechanism for Bobby's injuries was 'vehicular impact trauma, that is, a person being struck by a moving vehicle'.

The effect of the witness being 'interposed' by the defence during the prosecution case was that the DPP's team were able to cross-examine the pathologist, something they could not have done had he been their own witness. Bowman used the opportunity to spectacular effect. He suggested that the removal of Bobby's clothes and personal effects suggested that the person responsible knew something about the limitations of forensic evidence. Dr Curtis agreed.

Mr Bowman put it to him that 'an individual could be lured into an environment of the choosing of another individual – maybe an environment more easy to clean or wash up.' Again, Dr Curtis agreed.

Dr Curtis further agreed that any vehicle which had caused those injuries to Mr Ryan would have suffered 'significant damage', most likely to the windscreen or the roof. This scotched the theory that the field car was used because it was spotted during the search of the farm and gardaí hadn't noted any damage.

By the time he had finished cross-examining Curtis, Bowman had effectively turned the defence's only witness into an ally for the State.

*

'She's had the hair done,' whispered one of the women sitting on the public benches.

It was 28 March 2019 and Mary Lowry, dressed in a purple coat and matching purple leopard-print scarf, was settling into the witness box, oblivious to the stir her reappearance had caused. Word of her return to the Central Criminal Court had trickled through to the press benches earlier, when photographers stationed at the steps of the court had spotted her marching up the steps to the entrance.

Mary's back! was the text that was quickly relayed to various newsdesks.

The press wasn't the only contingent that had got wind of her imminent return to Court 13. Somehow the regulars in the public gallery knew about it too. They descended en masse into the public benches and quickly there was standing room only. The crowds, including several women armed with fold-up chairs, swarmed in from early morning, vying for prime position in an already packed room.

Imelda watched intently, seated in her place at the end of the bench just down from the witness box, as her former rival swept into the room. Her face betrayed no hint of emotion. Mary Lowry had last appeared in January, giving evidence over four days as icy weather took hold outside. When she returned in late March, the blazing spring sun was piercing through the windows on the fourth floor of the Central Criminal Court. The seasons had changed, but the trial of her ex-lover for the murder of her boyfriend was still not over.

Mary Lowry had been required to return in order to confirm that it was her voice on an audio recording Pat had secretly made of her and her then boyfriend, Flor Cantillon. Gardaí had discovered it on a hard drive taken from Pat's house during the search in 2013.

'You are familiar with Detective Sergeant John Keane?' asked Michael Bowman.

'Correct,' she replied softly.

'You met on the eleventh of January 2019 in Tipperary town garda station and he had an audio disc?' continued Mr Bowman.

'That's correct, yes.'

After confirming that she had identified her own voice and that of Flor Cantillon on the tape, the audio began to play for the jury.

As the hearty laugh of a female boomed out of the speakers all around the courtroom, Mary Lowry sat with her head tilted towards the floor, unflinching. Her light-brown hair, neatly parted to one side, fell over one side of her face as the jury looked on. The recording, largely inaudible due to the poor sound quality, also featured a male voice, that of Flor Cantillon.

'You are only having me on, ya fecker, ya,' said Mary as the eight-minute tape continued to play.

The couple, who the court heard had met in Killarney in 2012, could be heard joking about the problem pages in one of the national newspapers.

'He's a cross-dresser,' Mary could be heard saying as she read out a particular letter, naturally making everyone present think of the 'Dear Patricia' letter she had discovered one Sunday in 2011, detailing Pat Quirke's lovesickness for her.

'Ach, stop,' she said as the conversation continued, followed by the sound of her high-pitched laughter echoing around the courtroom.

'Read the top one,' she could be heard saying, before Flor began to speak.

'I can't hear anything,' she said to Flor.

There were long pauses in the audio, pauses filled with a crackling sound and muffled movement. As the court clock ticked by in seconds, the entire room was silent, waiting for the next section of dialogue.

Mr Cantillon was sitting on a bench at the back of the courtroom. He had finished giving his own evidence just a short time earlier. A wiry man, with thick white hair and a thin face, he had told the court how he had met Mary Lowry at a dance in Killarney on St Patrick's weekend in 2012. He spoke gently in a thick, often indecipherable Cork accent. He said he had 'danced with her a couple of times previous' and he had stayed talking to her afterwards. Their relationship lasted two years. 'We were in a relationship for a good while,' he said.

While they were going out, he had stayed with her on occasion at her home in Fawnagowan. He liked to buy the 'small papers', like the *Sunday World*. He followed the racing while she liked the problem pages, the court heard. Gardaí contacted him for the first time in January 2019 and played him the recording they had found on the hard drive taken from Pat's home. Mr Cantillon said he recognized Ms Lowry's voice very clearly, reading the problem page of a newspaper, and he recognized his own voice from a word that he had used. He told the court that he didn't know he was being recorded and had not given his permission for it.

The tape played on. The sound of Mary's laughter and witty chat ricocheted around the room, bringing a blast of warmth to the grim proceedings and the austere surroundings

'After a business trip I saw him in frilly knickers,' she recited.

Mary Lowry listened, her head to one side. Eventually, the voices stopped, replaced by what sounded like the beeping rhythm of a dial tone ringing out. Seconds later, the recording ended.

'You didn't record this, or give anyone permission to record it?' Michael Bowman asked her.

'That's correct,' she replied.

How the recording came to be made, and how it came to be in Pat Quirke's home, was never explained.

'We cannot say how it came to happen,' Mr Bowman would say about the tapes.

Despite not knowing how they came into existence, the gardaí believed that Pat had been recording Mary for some time. The tapes added another layer to his sinister obsession and playing them to the jury allowed them to infer that Pat was involved in their creation.

Later that day, Flor and Mary, the former lovers, were spotted in a nearby bakery having lunch. Despite it all, they were clearly still friends.

As the trial wore on, week after week, the many layers of circumstantial evidence began to slowly coalesce, forming a picture of guilt in the minds of those on the press benches. But beyond the doors of the Central Criminal Court, the court of public opinion wasn't convinced. It seemed like everyone in the country had an opinion. In every pub, from the swanky surrounds of the Saddle Room bar in Dublin's Shelbourne Hotel to the Black Sheep Inn on Tipperary's Main Street, punters dissected and debated the case, all of them focusing on whether or not Pat Quirke would be found guilty. In the main, the feeling was that the dairy farmer was going to walk. There's no evidence against him, said the taxi drivers, he probably did it, but sure they have nothing on him.

In rural Ireland, however, the consensus was very different. The case had generated huge interest among the farming fraternity. In the minds of those who knew the ins and outs of Pat's world, the evidence on the discovery of the body was enough to convince them of his guilt.

'Once we heard about the staging of the scene, it was all over,' said one. 'The clean clothes, the crusted slurry tank, going to the run-off tank for water. It was all out of kilter.'

Others found it peculiar that Pat, the very man who wanted Bobby out of the way, had unwittingly found himself discovering his body in a tank that only a few people knew about. That simply didn't ring true.

On the press benches inside the courtroom, everyone believed Pat was the killer. There was no other person who had the motive and opportunity, and all the evidence was pointing in one direction. Whether or not the jury was on the same page was another issue. Everyone was aware that this was a circumstantial case, one that had to meet the threshold of proof, and one that could hinge on the doubts of just a few people.

When the prosecution case closed, the defence asked the judge, for the second time, to take the fate of their client out of the jurors' hands and direct them to acquit. The only evidence against Pat was speculative, they argued, and at most might arouse suspicion, but it fell far short of proof beyond reasonable doubt. A conviction on such evidence would therefore be unsafe.

On a previous occasion the defence had asked for a direction to the jury to acquit over the late disclosure of evidence and alleged flaws in the Garda investigation. This request was rejected by the judge.

As before, Ms Justice Eileen Creedon disagreed with the defence's position. She left Pat Quirke's fate to the six men and six women on the jury.

In his closing argument, the prosecution counsel, Michael Bowman, SC, spoke directly to the jury about the lack of forensic evidence.

'This was a forensically barren case,' he said dramatically. There was 'no weapon, location or time of death'. However, he asked the jurors to approach the evidence before them with a critical mind, since 'There are only so many coincidences the human condition can take before you say, that's not coincidence, that's planned.' He said he would lead them through the evidence of the case but warned that, 'In truth, I don't believe there's a huge amount of it.' Nonetheless, a combination of circumstantial evidence pointed to the 'inevitable conclusion' that Pat had murdered the man who had replaced him in the affections of his sister-in-law, the widow Mary Lowry.

'Maybe it's the case that whoever did this planned it,' he said. 'Maybe the person or persons responsible took the opportunity to plan and execute this in a way that would afford them the comfort and belief they had evaded justice and gotten away with murder. Someone took the time to make sure no forensic trace was left behind.'

He urged the jurors not to lose sight of the reason why they were all gathered in the courtroom.

'I want to recalibrate the case,' he said, with his foot on the bench beside him, his reading glasses in one hand. 'It may well be we have lost somebody in this trial. It may be we have lost focus in terms of what we are doing here.' Fundamentally, this case was about a man who was 'living a quiet and peaceful and content life in a small village, a man who loved his job, a man who loved music, a man who loved to dance, who loved his girlfriend and who very dearly loved his two children. It is about a man who loved life, about a man who was universally loved and liked. This case is about the fact that Bobby Ryan's life was taken. Who would want to take the life of such a man? To strip him naked of his worldly possessions and his dignity and leave his body to decompose in a sealed chamber on a farm in Fawnagowan?'

Pat's defence counsel jumped to his feet within seconds of his prosecution counterpart resuming his seat. The first thing Bernard Condon told the jury was that this was a case based only on theory. Wearing the black robes of a senior counsel, he stood squarely facing them, speaking mostly without the aid of notes. Slowly and deliberately, he told them: 'There is no hard evidence.'

Mr Condon told the jurors that they were about to 'take a journey in something forensically equivalent to a train'. They would start the journey at a station called 'Innocence' and prosecution counsel Michael Bowman would bring them to the last station on the line, called 'Guilty'. Mr Bowman's fuel for this train journey was evidence – and he didn't have enough of it.

Condon then launched into a savage attack on Mary Lowry, labelling her evidence unreliable, uncorroborated and 'devious'. In a stinging summation of her four-day testimony as the main witness in the trial, he said she was 'not capable of telling the truth' and that she had 'fabricated evidence' to suit the narrative. He spent several tedious hours going through Mary's evidence in detail, alleging that she had the 'capacity to say whatever suited her' and that she had tried to 'do down' her ex-lover in court. Condon said that behind the prosecution case was a 'crumbling edifice of almost nothing'.

He questioned how, at 6.30 a.m. on a June morning in the countryside, nobody heard anything at a time when the prosecution alleged a murder was taking place. Rita Lowry and her daughter-in-law both had their bedroom windows open, and yet not a sound permeated into the house.

The fact was, Condon stated, 'We don't know anything about what happened in Fawnagowan or anything that happened to Bobby Ryan.'

After these dramatic speeches to the jury, both sides laid their cases to rest. The judge directed the jury to retire to the jury room to consider their verdict. The twelve men and women filed out quietly into the adjacent jury room to begin the toughest task. In the courtroom the various parties slowly trickled out, the Ryans to the downstairs canteen, the gardaí out to the hall to talk among themselves, the press to prepare copy in advance of a verdict. Imelda and Pat left together, briskly taking off down the stairs, away from everyone else. There was no more anyone could do. Pat Quirke's future lay in the hands of twelve strangers, who had fifteen weeks' worth of evidence to ponder. It was anyone's guess what the outcome might be.

After the jury were sent out to begin their deliberations on 23 April, tensions began to rise as each day passed without a result. Even though there was no evidence to hear, every morning the jury had to gather in court for a roll call, before they were sent to the jury room. They would file in again at lunchtime to be sent off for a break and then return around 2 p.m. to be sent to deliberate once again. At around 4 p.m. every day they were brought into the courtroom again and released to go home.

Pat may have been impassive in the courtroom, but his tightly guarded emotions boiled over into anger on the third morning of the deliberations when he became involved in a scuffle with a press photographer. Pat was making his way into court when the photographer allegedly got in his way. Pat pushed his camera and the two men brushed up against each other. Pat's legal team raised concerns that members of the jury might have seen what had occurred and the judge ordered the media to give Pat space.

As the days dragged by, there were few clues as to which direction the jurors were leaning. Unusually, they did not come back with any questions regarding the law. Their only request came a short time into their deliberations, when the jury sought all Pat's interviews with gardaí as well as phone records, which were handed in.

Eventually, after a total of twenty hours and thirty-nine minutes over the course of seven days, a verdict in the longest-running murder trial in the history of the State was returned. On Wednesday, 1 May 2019, the word flew around the court building: the jury were coming back in, they had a verdict.

Less than two hours earlier, Pat had headed off for lunch with his wife, chatting animatedly as he skipped down the stairs, giving no inkling that his fate lay in the balance. At that stage, unable to reach a unanimous verdict, the jury had been offered a majority, but had still not returned. To all watching on, Pat Quirke seemed remarkably confident. He and Imelda whiled away the hours on the second floor of the courthouse. From the floors above, Pat could be seen sitting beside his wife, bent over, with his arms resting on his knees. As the lunch hour came and went, the couple retreated to the outdoor veranda next to the canteen.

Upstairs on the fourth floor, if the customary knock on the door from the jury ever came, few connected with the case heard it. While the jury were deliberating, another case got underway, *in camera*, and Court 13 was cleared to make way for it. Evicted from a courtroom they had spent over three months in, the Ryan family retreated to a nearby room for some quiet and privacy. Meanwhile, the gardaí, the legal teams, the swarms of journalists and the assembled viewing public waited outside.

Just before 2.30 p.m., as the various parties connected with the *in camera* case exited, Court 13 was handed back to the Mr Moonlight case. Outside, in the marble atrium that circles the fourth floor, detectives, gardaí and members of the press were milling around aimlessly and pacing the floor. As word filtered through that the jury were on their way back in, there was an undignified surge towards the door. Within minutes, the courtroom was jammed. A couple of minutes later Pat strode in, dressed in one of the grey suits he often wore and a bright-red tie. He settled back on to the black cushion he had brought with him, his coat and laptop bag beside him.

He sat as he always did, hands clasped and his head slightly bowed, staring intently at a spot in front of him. Breathing slowly and deeply, he waited. After struggling to make their way through the hordes of people gathered in the courtroom, the Ryan family took their seats, their faces showing the strain and tension they were feeling. Around them the courtroom fell into a respectful silence, broken only by occasional whispers and the rustling of the pages of reporters' notebooks.

There was an air of nervous anticipation. People strained to see how Patrick Quirke was coping with the fact that in a very short time he would learn his fate. The Ryan family gathered close together, their faces grim, their anxiety plain for all to see.

'All rise,' the tipstaff called.

Ms Justice Eileen Creedon returned to the bench and took her seat. Minutes later, at around 2.37 p.m., the jury minder led the jury back into the courtroom. The quiet chatter immediately died down and everybody stared at them. Pat remained motionless, his seeming calmness betrayed only by his darting eyes. The foreman passed the issue paper, the page on which the verdict must be written, to the registrar. For a room so packed, there was an eerie silence you could feel pressing against your skin.

The senior registrar, Mr Michael Neary, glanced down at the issue paper and read it silently. Then he asked the jury if they had reached a verdict.

'Yes,' the jury foreman replied.

Had a majority of ten agreed a verdict?

'Yes.'

Ever so quietly, the word 'Guilty' was pronounced. It was a muted denouement to what had been a dramatic trial. As the ramifications of the decision were digested, an extraordinary calm fell over the room. A collective exhaling of breath was all that was heard from the row where the Ryan family were sitting.

The Ryan family had waited longer than anyone for this moment. Longer than Pat, awaiting his fate. Longer than the jury, waiting to return to their jobs and families. Longer than the gardaí, waiting to go back on the beat in Tipperary. The Ryan family, Mr Moonlight's son, Robert, his daughter, Michelle, and his former wife, Mary, had waited every single day since 3 June 2011 to hear if justice would finally be done for Bobby Ryan. When the verdict was given, they struggled to comprehend what had just happened. As the registrar took the issue paper from the jury foreman and confirmed that a guilty verdict had been reached, the Ryan family looked puzzled. In the end, it fell to a journalist sitting close by to confirm what they had just heard. Guilty.

That's when the tears came. The rigid composure that had seen the family through the darkest days of their lives deserted them and with shoulders heaving they huddled together and sobbed. Wrapping their arms around each other, Bobby Ryan's two children cradled their mother. They rocked in gentle unison, crying and crying.

In the end, there was nothing from the man at the centre of all this heartache. No knowing glance towards his wife, no tear-filled eyes, no obvious sign that it was over. Nothing. Pat Quirke didn't flinch as the jury returned its guilty verdict. His pursed lips and his slightly sullen expression never changed for a moment, not even when the Ryan family threw themselves into each other's arms, unleashing cries of relief and heartbreak that were audible throughout the courtroom.

Behind the Ryans, sitting at the end of the bench, was Pat's ever loyal wife, Imelda Quirke, her gaze fixed on the floor. She sat motionless and impassive, not lifting her head, even when the various members of the public sitting next to her began to gently pat her arm and offer words of comfort. Imelda, the woman who had shown such remarkable stoicism and steadfast loyalty through the weeks of her husband's murder trial, didn't even glance in his direction.

Her husband's sister was sitting beside her, visibly rattled by the news of her brother's fate as it sunk in. She reached for her phone, her hands shaking, and frantically sent a text as the room came alive with activity.

As Pat was led from the bench for the accused by two prison guards, his deflated legal team scurried behind. Suddenly, and without uttering a word to each other, his wife and sister briskly rose to their feet and exited the courtroom minutes later. Once outside in the circular corridor, Imelda bolted out the front door, her head held high and her face scornful. That was the last time she would walk through the doors of Court 13. Her husband's defence team had asked gardaí if she could be shepherded out through the back entrance, in a bid to avoid the waiting cameras. While the request for compassion was granted, the plea for her to be ferried away in a Garda patrol car was not.

While Imelda walked away from Court 13 never to return, her husband was brought back into the courtroom fifteen minutes later to listen to the victim impact statement and to receive his mandatory life sentence. For this part of the process he returned a noticeably different man. Gone was his bright-red tie, the one that had been tightly bound around his neck. Gone was his wife, the one who had never left his side during his ordeal. Gone was his pale complexion. Pat Quirke, the convicted murderer, returned to court with a face mottled pink and red, an open-necked shirt and not a friend in the room.

After stepping outside to gather her thoughts and steady herself, Michelle Ryan returned to Court 13. It was time to read the victim impact statement she and her family had so carefully prepared.

On the 3rd of June 2011, our lives and world as we knew it was torn apart.

I can't find the words to describe how it feels emotionally. It's a torment that's constantly with us, a black hole that we carry every day, the mental anguish every day wondering was Daddy calling out for help, was he calling our names to help him.

We close our eyes every night and picture Daddy with fear in his eyes. We wake up every night with the nightmares. This is something we will never ever come to terms with. God didn't decide to take Daddy from us and knowing how his life was taken and where he was found, rips us apart every day. We are completely destroyed beyond repair because of the trauma of how our father was brutally taken away from us.

We don't have a life to live anymore just an existence for us to drag ourselves through every day. Daddy was also a Grandfather whose grandchildren love him dearly. 'You know he was their Grandad Bob' and the ones who do remember him struggle every day to try come to terms how Grandad Bob was here one minute and gone the next and the other little ones just have a picture of him that they carry every day. Grandad Bob will always be a part of their lives because we talk about Daddy every day and tell them stories of their Grandad Bob. They laugh and smile remembering Grandad Bob and the little ones wondering what kind of Grandad he was and our torment growing bigger knowing someday we will have to sit them down and try explain how Grandad Bob was taken away from us and visioning the light burn out in their eyes and hearts as well. Our lives will never be the same again, we know we have to carry this cross for the rest of our lives and we know our children will have to bear it as well. We will never be doubtful of just how much Daddy loves us, I can't put into words how much we love him, we will continue to love and cherish what precious memories we have of Daddy. That is something no one will ever take from us, this has consumed our lives completely. We will live through this heartache for the rest of our lives. While we hope that Daddy will now rest in peace, it's a peace that we will never know until we meet him again.

Daddy, I described you as "Wow" when I was asked because that's what you are, such a wonderful, caring Father and Grandfather. We will carry you in our hearts everyday in everything we do for the rest of our lives. So, until we meet again Moonlight, just know how much you are loved and sorely missed by us everyday. So spread your beautiful wings and fly high with the angels. You are gone but will never be forgotten.

And, with that, Michelle Ryan limped out of the witness box, holding her stomach as she passed the man who murdered her father, and went back into the arms of her brother and mother. Michelle deliberately didn't mention Pat's name in the statement. After an excruciating trial that had been all about the man in the dock, the Ryan family had decided to leave him out of this part of the story. They gave Bobby Ryan a voice and let it be heard.

The focus in the courtroom then turned to the judge. As Ms Justice Creedon prepared to address the court, Pat cut a solemn figure in the dock. He nervously bit down on his bottom lip. The next part was over in minutes.

Ms Justice Creedon told Pat Quirke that he would serve a life sentence in prison for the murder of Bobby Ryan. Pat didn't even flinch. In a country where the average life sentence served in prison is eighteen years, this meant that he would see out his later years behind bars.

Pat rose to his feet, seemingly unfazed, and was escorted from the dock into custody. As predicted, he never took the stand during his lengthy trial for murder. Instead, his defence team were instructed to employ the age-old tactic of blaming the gardaí – castigating members for not taking notes, berating detectives over their style of questioning and alleging, time after time, that they hadn't done their job properly. In truth, Detective Inspector O'Callaghan and his small team of detectives and gardaí from Tipperary town had worked tirelessly for years to nail Pat Quirke. The heavy lifting had been done long before the case ever made it to court. To even get a case like this in front of the DPP, let alone secure a murder charge, was testament to the level of work that went into catching a clever killer. Hours of work, often at weekends and outside clocked Garda time, hundreds and hundreds of statements taken, every avenue explored, checked and rechecked. There was no murder weapon, no murder scene, no forensics, Pat Quirke had made sure of that. It was a circumstantial case, the hardest kind to prove, but, in an era of cutbacks and stifled resources, a small band of gardaí did it.

Outside, in the marbled atrium, the speculative chatter had stopped. The day-trippers, the people who had diligently followed the trial since it began, said their final farewells and left. Hours after the verdict had been passed, Detective Inspector O'Callaghan and his team quietly slipped past the Ryan family, and headed off back to Tipperary town garda station, to resume their unending police work.

For the last time, Bobby Ryan's children walked out through the glass doors of the Central Criminal Court. Hordes of cameras clicked as they emerged into the warm May air, holding between them a framed photograph of their father. As they walked off, the siblings held each other close, still clutching their father to them as they headed home to piece together the threads of a family torn apart on the day their darling father disappeared.

Somewhere, away from the celebrations and the media, there was another family experiencing different feelings. She had stood by her husband throughout the seventy-one-day trial, behaving with dignity at all times, and now Imelda Quirke was on her way home to what was left of her family. She had two boys to think of and a lifetime to ponder over everything that was now lost.

The members of the jury slipped away, unnoticed. Twelve strangers plucked off the street to do the most difficult job imaginable. The judge thanked them and excused them from ever going through the rigours of a trial again. Their work was done.

Back in Bansha, in her new home, a home she never wanted, Mary Lowry was grateful to them.

Epilogue
After the end

It was always the same routine. He would come in just before lunchtime, dressed smartly in a pair of slacks and a neat hunting jacket. He wore a flat cap, of the tweed variety that the older gentleman would wear. He loitered at the magazine section, flicking through the pages of the farming magazines, usually admiring tractors or other farming machinery. He never bought anything or spoke to anyone. His face always wore the same cold stare.

It was his baby-like face that caught the attention of the person who regularly saw him in Hanley's newsagents in Fermoy, County Cork. He thought it odd that he dressed like a man of a certain vintage but had the facial features of someone much younger. He only realized the visitor was Patrick Quirke some time after the visits had stopped. By then, he had seen the same person on the front pages of the newspapers and made the connection when he spotted the trademark flat cap.

Unbeknownst to the person who regularly noticed Pat in the newsagents, someone else made frequent trips to Fermoy. Music-loving Bobby Ryan made a habit of driving to the town to drop into the Tom Baylor Music Centre, a famous music shop on Newmarket Street. There he would spend 'ages' testing lights and speakers and trying out the vast selection of guitars. According to his son, Robert, Bobby was making trips to the shop right up until his disappearance. Hanley's newsagents, where Pat Quirke was killing time buying nothing, is a one-minute walk across the road and to the right, in a nearby side-street.

Maybe it was just coincidence that Pat was lurking around the music store that his love rival liked to visit. Or maybe, as the prosecution barrister Michael Bowman put it, 'There are so many coincidences the human condition can take before you say, that's not coincidence, that's planned.'

Whatever the case, it was just one of several chilling stories that came to light during the research for this book. It was also just one more example of how much we might never know about the man in the dock.

As is so often the case in murder trials, there was much evidence that could not be brought before the jury because it was ruled inadmissible. But once the conviction was secured, this information could be made public. As Pat himself so well knew, once your reputation is destroyed, there's very little you can keep hidden.

Immediately after the verdict was pronounced, as news outlets rushed to reveal the suppressed evidence that the jury didn't hear during the trial, it became clear that Pat Quirke had an even more sinister and perverted side to his character. In one of the most explosive revelations, it emerged that he had made more recordings than the one of Mary and Flor Cantillon talking. It transpired that the gardaí had uncovered a number of audio sex tapes he had recorded of himself and Mary, as well as one with his wife, Imelda. In total, twelve deleted audio recordings were recovered from the hard drive found in Pat's home office. The prosecution had sought to include a further two, described as 'intimate recordings' made of Pat and Mary without her knowledge, but the judge deemed them inadmissible. The prosecutor said the recordings spoke 'of an obsession which will not let go'.

In arguing to throw the tapes out of the case, Bernard Condon for the defence said they were 'inflammatory pieces of evidence'. He dismissed their usefulness in court: 'Most of it is not spoken. There's audible breathing and occasional inaudible speech.'

After listening to them in private, Ms Justice Eileen Creedon ruled that they were more prejudicial than revealing, so they were not put before the jury.

There was huge interest in the source of the recordings. Had Pat used his mobile phone, or had he installed some kind of device in the Lowry home? Certainly, some of the recordings were made on a Nokia mobile phone, but Garda sources later said they believed Pat had planted a secret voice-activated recording device in Mary's bedroom.

Like the murder weapon and Bobby Ryan's belongings, the device was never found.

It sounds extreme, but then, taken altogether, Pat's actions present a picture of a man given to extreme behaviour. His obsession with Mary Lowry and his need to retain her affections – and thereby her money – were a dark and pressing urge. It's easy to understand why the gardaí believed him capable of installing a device to check up on her movements and monitor her relationship with Bobby Ryan, and later with Flor Cantillon.

Apart from the audio recordings, the jury were also not allowed to know that Pat had researched articles on notorious Irish murderers, including Joe O'Reilly. The page Pat accessed in relation to the Rachel O'Reilly case appeared on an Irishcrimereporter.com blog in an article entitled, 'Why Joe O'Reilly thought he had committed the perfect murder'. He also conducted searches on a missing woman, Jo Jo Dullard, who disappeared in 1995 and is believed murdered. The title of that article was: 'I have to live with knowing who killed JoJo – sister'. He also made searches in relation to Siobhán Kearney, a Dublin woman who was murdered by her husband in 2006.

While news of the verdict sank in, commentators and pundits filled thousands of column inches with their deep psychological analyses of what prompted Pat to murder in cold blood. Was it rooted in his own background and formative years? What made him so lustful for land and cash? Was he a sociopath? Most pertinently of all, what was it all for? We will never know. Pat may not know himself.

Many mysteries remain when a murderer doesn't confess his or her guilt. Getting justice for a crime is one thing, but getting the truth is something different. For years to come, the mystery of what exactly happened at Fawnagowan on that hot summer's morning in June 2011 will endure. Months after Pat had been sent to prison, people who knew him were sitting in pubs in Tipperary town, mulling over one question: how did he do it?

Gardaí believe the 'how' of the murder was planned well in advance. The 'when' came when the opportunity arose. After that, it was just 'pure anger'.

In the theory put forward by those involved in the investigation, Pat went to the Horse & Jockey the night of Thursday, 2 June 2011, as the evidence showed. If, as the gardaí believe, he was secretly recording Mary in her home, he would have known Bobby was staying over that night. In the absence of the covert surveillance, he would have gone over to Fawnagowan to check for the Mr Moonlight van.

He returned early the following morning and parked his jeep close to the road, but out of sight, and walked up to the farm. While some investigators believe he called Bobby over to the tank under the guise of helping him with something and struck him at the tank, others believe he may have lured him into the milking parlour and struck him from behind in there. In both scenarios it is believed that Pat placed Bobby's body in the tank there and then.

Afterwards, he jumped into the Mr Moonlight van and made his way to the woods. After parking the van, he made his way through the forested landscape of Bansha Wood, down through Cordangan, and across several other hidden fields, before exiting at a point close to where he had parked his car. He later returned to Fawnagowan, where Mary observed him looking 'hot, sweaty and bothered'.

Bobby Ryan stood in the way of something Pat wanted badly – Mary, her land and her cash. With Bobby out of the picture, Pat arrogantly believed he could seize back control. He had committed the almost perfect murder, but his relentless pursuit of Mary would be his ultimate undoing.

There was no denying the intense public interest in the entire affair. What gave the case a special piquancy is that a saga of sex, land and money was played out against the hinterland of rural Irish life. The key players were middle-aged farming folk, normal and ordinary and familiar. So when the extraordinary occurred, it was even more shocking and compelling. The nation was gripped by the trial for over three months and it has no doubt secured its place in the list of famous Irish murders. For those directly involved, it was a nightmare scenario. They are still living with the aftermath, and perhaps always will.

Pat Quirke has settled in well to his new life behind bars. Officially known as prisoner 107243, he spent his first night in detention at the Mountjoy Prison complex in Dublin, where all new prisoners are kept during the first twenty-four hours of their incarceration.

In line with procedures for new prisoners, he was checked on as often as every fifteen minutes. This is routine practice for any criminal sentenced to life, in case they try to kill themselves. His cell in the basement had in-cell sanitation, a television and a kettle. For breakfast he dined on cornflakes and bread along with a pint of milk and a bag with tea and sugar to take back to his eight foot by twelve foot cell.

The following day he was transferred to a cell on a wing of the prison. A week or so later, he was moved to Limerick Prison, where he was closer to his family for visits. Upon his arrival at Limerick jail, the killer was greeted by his new fellow inmates with a raucous chorus of the hit song 'Dancing in the Moonlight', by the band Toploader. In Limerick Prison, where he is neighbour to some of the most notorious gangland killers in Ireland, he has secured a job in the kitchens and is housed in a cell on his own because of his high profile. He is believed to get on well with prison officers and most of the inmates, although he has told friends that he doesn't like being among hardened criminals and 'undesirables'. Imelda visits him twice a week and Pat is believed to use their time together to direct her on how to manage the farm.

He continues to protest his innocence and is in the process of lodging an appeal. It is not known what the grounds for the appeal will be, or when it will be heard.

In July 2019, more than two months after his imprisonment, it emerged that Bobby's two children, Robert and Michelle, are pursuing him in the civil courts over the death of their father. The exact details of the case are as yet unknown.

*

Back in Breansha, Imelda took to the roads again, her fragile frame dragged along the lonely country roads by the three dogs she held on individual leads. Locals say her relationship with her family is strained by her loyalty to Pat, which remains as steadfast as ever, regardless of his conviction.

As he did with Mary Lowry, Pat manipulated Imelda for his own selfish ends. Right throughout the terrible events that transpired around the murder and the discovery of Bobby's remains, Pat relied heavily and unfairly on his wife's personal strength of character and ability to 'cope'. He used her birthday as an excuse to flee the scene after the murder in June 2011, booking a weekend away to the Heritage Hotel in Portlaoise, which was unusual for them. Imelda was the first person he called after 'discovering' the remains of Bobby Ryan. A garda later put it to him that if it had been *his* wife, he would not have liked her to have seen the body in the tank. Pat's reply was that Imelda would know what to do. It was she who alerted the authorities to the gruesome find – in a panicked fifty-five-second phone call to Garda Tom Neville, known to her through her sons' GAA training. Pat calculatedly used his wife's innocence to deflect from his own guilt in a most despicable way. And yet there she was, almost a week after her husband's conviction, visiting for the first time in Mountjoy, where she was photographed making her way towards the prison with one of her sons.

The Quirke boys too have had their lives set on a different path by the actions of their father. A few weeks after Pat's incarceration, his eldest son, Liam, was made a director of the farm business as his father stepped aside. He had been studying at UCD but is now back at home, manning the farm. The sad irony of this is not lost on those once close to

Pat, who say he 'never wanted his sons to end up like him, forced into a life on the farm'.

Mary Lowry survived the intense public interest in her private life and moved on quickly. Long before the trial got underway, she was in a new relationship, happily coupled up with a farmer from a nearby town. She made no secret about her new boyfriend and was regularly spotted with him in Nellie's, her local pub in Bansha. The tight-knit village community there, where she is involved in the Tidy Towns committee as well as the local set-dancing group, had been a sanctuary to her over the years.

Despite the shocking event that led to her leaving Fawnagowan, those close to her say she is happier in her new village life, where she can walk to the local shop and pub and where she feels part of the community. Life on the farm, on the isolated hill overlooking the mountains, left her lonely and lacking interaction.

Speaking briefly to Nicola Byrne, a reporter from the *Irish Mail on Sunday*, several days after the verdict, Mary said the trial had taken its toll: 'There are no winners here . . . this isn't about winning. It's going to take a long time [to get on with life]. I have three boys and their father died of cancer. I just want to get on with my life and in the way I would have wanted to with Bobby Ryan.'

Rita Lowry, who was in her early nineties when the trial began, remains at Fawnagowan, the place where she has lived for over sixty years. She resides in the granny flat and Mary's part of the house is rented out. The farm, Martin Lowry's pride and joy, is being leased by a local farmer. Mary's three boys have moved on with their lives, concentrating on school and college, and have no plans to take on the family tradition of farming. For now, the fate of Fawnagowan lies in Mary's hands.

They say that when the person you love is no longer with you, you cling to the possessions they treasured most. Robert still has his father's 'Mr Moonlight' van, the same silver Citroën that was found abandoned in Bansha Wood all those years ago when his father disappeared. Michelle has his 'disco kit'.

A fortnight after the verdict, I sat down with the Ryan family and talked about everything that had happened since their husband, father and grandfather disappeared. They pored over hundreds of photos of 'Mr Moonlight' – pictures of him with his guitar in Doolin, in his truck with one of his granddaughters at the steering wheel, behind his disco kit, smiling. This was their Mr Moonlight, always smiling. They proudly talked of how much he did for them. Robert talked about how his daddy took him to Rosegreen Raceway every Sunday to watch car racing, taught him how to drive and encouraged him to enjoy life. Michelle reminisced about how he taught her to DJ and called her every day, without fail. Mary, Bobby's ex-wife, chuckled about how bad he was at waltzing and jiving, but later improved to become a pretty nimble dancer.

Mary Lowry was right. When the verdict was finally handed down, there were no winners, least of all among Bobby's family. There is no bringing Bobby back. The Ryan family know it. And so they talk about Mr Moonlight. They talk about him as much as they can. They talk about him in a desperate bid to fill the devastating void he has left in their lives. A void created at the hands of someone he barely knew.

During the fifteen-week trial, the twelve-person jury heard the full horror of what had happened to Bobby Ryan on that hot June day in 2011. He became the absent victim, often lost in the sheer volume of evidence built around his murder.

For those who knew him best, Bobby Ryan was so much more. He was much more than Mary Lowry's boyfriend, much more than Patrick Quirke's love rival and, to them, much more than the body found in the tank.

'Wow,' was the simple word used by Michelle to best describe him on the stand when she was giving evidence.

'Happy ... always a bit of craic,' is how Robert sums him up.

To his former wife, he had remained a friend, despite the breakdown of their marriage. Likewise, he had remained a friend to his former partner Mary Glasheen after the end of their three-month relationship. Even his boss at Killough Quarry, Niall Quinn, recalled him as a punctual and 'perfect' employee.

While the salacious details of their father's case ensured huge public interest, at the heart of it all was their searing loss. Bobby enjoyed the simple pleasures in life. He enjoyed having a few drinks and seeing other people having a good time. As the prosecution barrister Michael Bowman, SC, put it, he brought a smile to the face of everyone called to give evidence about him. Even in death he could light up a room.

After the verdict they came together that evening in Michelle's house, with her mother's extended family, and reminisced about the Moonlight days. Robert, however, retreated to the living room, alone with his thoughts. They talked about the many difficult years that had passed since Bobby went missing. When he first disappeared in June 2011, the Ryan family spent every waking hour searching for him. But after a while Michelle and Robert found it too difficult to remain in Tipperary, relocating to Cork to be closer to their mother. As time passed, with no sign or word of their father, life carried on. New grandchildren were born without him, something that is a source of huge pain for Robert.

'I found that hard,' he said. 'When Leanne found out she was pregnant it was very hard, very bittersweet. The thought of Daddy missing that was just so painful.'

As his eyes glazed over, a grief-filled silence filled the room, until Mary spoke.

'When you think about it,' she said, 'Bobby would have loved being around his grandchildren. He would have gotten such a kick out of it.'

There is no escaping the legacy Patrick Quirke has left the Ryan family. They accept that their lives will never be the same again, but they also acknowledge that many other lives have been destroyed. Generations have been engulfed by what happened to Bobby Ryan: Mary Lowry's three boys, Imelda's two sons, Bobby's grandchildren – all are irrevocably scarred by Pat's actions. While there is no public sympathy for Pat, there is great sympathy for the families so cruelly affected by what he did.

In many ways, it is the enduring love, togetherness and determination of the Ryan family that will serve to keep Mr Moonlight's memory alive. One of Michelle's last cherished memories of her father is the last time she saw him DJing, at Fox's pub. He pressed Play on 'Proud Mary', by Tina Turner, just as she walked through the door.

'Here, Shelly, sing a song,' he roared to her, ushering her up to sing.

'We were in hysterics that night,' Michelle Ryan said in an

interview after her father's disappearance. 'You'd swear it was foretold that it would be the last time I would ever see him. That night we had down there. The laughing, and everything else, was like all the years rolled into one night.'

As the night drew to a close, Bobby put his hand out to his daughter and she grabbed it tight. He put on the Collin Raye song 'Love, Me' and that was the last song they ever danced to.

That's where Mr Moonlight was at his happiest, on the dancefloor, his feet and heart racing. For those who knew him best and loved him most, that's the way they will always remember Bobby Ryan.

Daddy would be back. Now, finally, he's back where he belongs . . . God didn't take Daddy from us, someone else playing God did that and we're asking God today to give us some . . . justice that Daddy deserves.'

Michelle thanked God 'for giving him back to us, so we can lay him to rest'. She recalled how often they were in contact before he went missing: 'Dad should be ringing us now from his truck on his tea break or lunch break, spending twenty minutes talking about nothing . . . I'm not going to say goodbye to Daddy, because that's too final. And I know wherever we go, he's going to be mooching in, thinking he would miss something, so I'm just going to say that I'll see you later.'

Gifts were brought to the altar to represent his life: a guitar for his love of music, two CDs to represent his work as a disc jockey under the name Mr Moonlight, and a banner from his lorry in the Tipperary colours. The chief celebrant, Fr Bernie Moloney, said Bobby's family and friends had known 'the bitter taste of lamentation' over the last two years. He reflected on Bobby's life as a family man, friend and entertainer.

'Bobby had music in his heart and soul,' the celebrant said. 'Mr Moonlight touched the hearts of many, set the lips laughing and the feet dancing.'

Michelle had made it clear that she did not want Mary Lowry at the funeral. Although it hurt Mary not to be there, she respected Michelle's wishes and stayed away. Relations between the two women in Bobby's life were at an all-time low.

The day after Bobby's funeral, Pat was again making his way back to Tipperary town garda station to give a voluntary cautioned statement. He arrived at 2 p.m. and was taken into a

Garda Walsh placed the note in an evidence bag and handed it to Detective Sergeant Keane. He did the same with a brown envelope containing a document relating to Pat's leasing of Mary's land at Fawnagowan, which he had also found in the office during the three and a half hours he spent combing it.

Later, at around 3 p.m., a computer hard drive was discovered in the office. Along with a computer, an iPad, two mobile phones, two memory keys and a Vodafone phone bill, it was shown to Pat before they were all taken to Tipperary town garda station to be examined for evidence.

A pair of mudstained green work overalls hanging in the boiler house, a trailer and a damaged crew cab door were also seized. Swabs taken from all three would later prove to yield nothing of evidential value.

The team finished up at about 4.45 p.m. Detective Sergeant Keane called in to Pat before he left to let him know the operation was complete. The officers piled back into the patrol cars and pulled out of the yard and drove away. The farm at Breansha fell silent once again.

The Ryan family were slowly coming to terms with all that had happened. Several days after the search of Pat Quirke's farm, Bobby's body had been returned to his loved ones so they could finally prepare for his burial. His funeral took place on 20 May 2013, at the Church of St John the Baptist in Cashel, yards from the house where he had spent his childhood years. In an emotional eulogy to her father, Michelle told mourners that a cloud had been hanging over the family since her father had disappeared.

They had waited two years to find him and prayed every single day during that time 'that we would find Daddy, that

The Murder of Mr Moonlight

Acknowledgements

First and foremost, this is an opportunity to acknowledge Bobby Ryan, the innocent victim at the centre of this story. He was a much loved father, brother and friend to many who is sorely missed. His family have suffered immensely at the hands of his killer, but continue to honour his memory with dignity.

It is also important to acknowledge the meticulous work of the gardaí involved in the murder investigation that led to the conviction of Patrick Quirke. The case against him took years to build, during a time of limited resources in the force, and many members went above and beyond the call of duty to ensure that the Ryan family got justice.

I would like to sincerely thank the people who agreed to share their information and insights during the course of my writing this book. They wanted to remain anonymous and that was the deal I made before the tape recorder was switched on. There are two people in particular who committed to helping me from the beginning, probably not realizing how much of their time I would need, but still stuck with me until the end. Their input was invaluable and I will always be grateful for their trust and guidance.

Thank you to all those in Tipperary, people from the farming community in particular, who opened their doors and took my many calls.

Thank you to Catherine Costello, Searching for the Missing, Joe Blake, Trace Missing Persons Ireland, and Christy Kelleher, Abbeyfeale and District Search and Rescue, for their help when I was researching the missing-persons probe.

To Sebastian Hamilton, Editor-in-Chief at the *Irish Daily Mail*, sincere thanks for allowing me the time and space to complete this book. I feel incredibly lucky to have had the benefit of his professional guidance throughout my writing career at the *Mail*.

Thank you also to Linda Maher, features editor at the *Mail*, for her patience and goodwill while I took time away from writing duties at work.

My heartfelt thanks and appreciation to Michael McLoughlin, MD of Penguin Ireland, for taking a chance on me with such an incredible story. Thank you also to Patricia Deevy at Penguin for her enthusiasm and guidance every step of the way.

ACKNOWLEDGEMENTS

I am immensely grateful to Kieran Kelly of Fanning Kelly and Company for the legal read of the book.

Thanks are due to the talented and ever helpful Rachel Pierce, who made sure the manuscript was edited and delivered on time.

I would like to acknowledge my colleagues on the press bench, Eoin Reynolds, Ireland International News Agency, Vivienne Traynor, RTÉ, Deborah Naylor, Virgin Media News, Frank Greaney, Newstalk, Nicola Byrne, the *Irish Mail on Sunday*, and Maeve Sheehan, the *Sunday Independent*, for their professionalism and kinship while covering the trial of Patrick Quirke.

A special and sincere word of thanks must go to Nicola Anderson, of the *Irish Independent*, for her invaluable assistance and guidance during the research stages of the book. Nicola has been a great friend and colleague and I will always be indebted to her.

I am very grateful to my friends, both personal and professional, for all the words of encouragement and for remaining supportive even when I neglected you all for so long while writing.

My thanks to the two amazing women in my life, my mum, Patricia, and my mother-in-law, Noleen, for their help looking after my two boys while I worked on this book. I am also grateful to my father-in-law, Nick, for his help.

I would like to mention my siblings, Orla, Sinéad and Conor, for their camaraderie, help and encouragement.

Thank you to my wonderful dad, Maurice, for always having faith in me and encouraging me to write this book. I would not have crossed the finishing line without him.

My love to Brian, for his unwavering support and patience while I took some time away from our little family to do this. Finally, much love to my two boys, Seán and Conor.

Picture credits

The publisher and author would like to thank James Meehan at the *Irish Daily Mail* picture desk for his assistance in compiling the images for the photo section. Credits are as follows: Joe Dunne (pictures 1, 2, 3 and 4) and Tom Honan (14 and 15), *Irish Daily Mail*; Press 22 Photographic Agency (8 and 9); Collins Photo Agency (10, 11, 12, 13, 16, 17, 18, 19, 20 and 22); and the Garda Press Office (21). All other pictures supplied by the author.